Quest

Teacher's Edition

3

Reading and Writing

Student Book Authors
Pamela Hartmann
Laurie Blass

Teacher's Edition Writer
Kristin Sherman

McGraw-Hill

Quest 3 Reading and Writing Teacher's Edition

Published by McGraw-Hill ESL/ELT, a business unit of The McGraw-Hill Companies, Inc., 1221 Avenue of the Americas, New York, NY 10020.

ISBN 13: 978-0-07-326583-4
ISBN 10: 0-07-326583-7
2 3 4 5 6 7 8 9 QPD/QPD 12 11 10 09 08 07

Editorial director: Erik Gundersen
Series editor: Linda O'Roke
Development editor: Robyn L. Brinks
Production manager: Juanita Thompson
Production coordinator: Lakshmi Balasubramanian
Cover designer: David Averbach, Anthology
Interior designer: Karolyn Wehner

McGraw-Hill

www.esl-elt.mcgraw-hill.com

The *McGraw-Hill* Companies

TABLE OF CONTENTS

●●●●● WELCOME to the Teacher's Edition

The *Quest* Teacher's Edition provides support and flexibility to teachers using the *Quest* Student Book. Each chapter of the Teacher's Edition begins with a chapter overview which includes a brief summary of the Student Book chapter, a list of the vocabulary words found in the chapter, a list of the reading, critical thinking, and writing strategies highlighted throughout the chapter, as well as a list of the mechanics presented and practiced in that chapter. In addition, the Teacher's Edition provides step-by-step teaching procedures; tips for the TOEFL® iBT; notes on culture, grammar, vocabulary, and pronunciation; expansion activities; photocopiable masters of select expansion activities; website research ideas; answer keys; and end-of-chapter tests.

Procedures

❍ Experienced teachers can use the step-by-step procedural notes as a quick guide and refresher before class, while newer or substitute teachers can use the notes as a more extensive guide in the classroom. These notes also help teachers provide context for the activities and assess comprehension of the material covered.

Answer Keys

❍ Answer keys are provided for all activities that have definite answers. In cases where multiple answers could be correct, possible answers are included. Answer keys are also provided for the Vocabulary Workshop after each unit.

Notes

❍ Where appropriate, culture, grammar, vocabulary, and pronunciation notes provide background information, answers to questions students might raise, or points teachers might want to review or introduce. For example, in *Quest Level 3 Reading Writing* Chapter 1, a reading refers to San Francisco, so a cultural note provides some background information on this city. These notes are provided at the logical point of use, but teachers can decide if and when to use the information in class.

TOEFL® iBT Tips

❍ In each chapter, six tips for the TOEFL® iBT are given with corresponding notes on how strategies and activities from the student book chapter can help students practice and prepare for the exam. Examples of TOEFL® iBT question format are also given in these tips.

Expansion Activities

❍ Optional expansion activities are included in each chapter. These activities offer teachers creative ideas for reinforcing the chapter content while appealing to different learning styles. Activities include games, conversation practice, and working with manipulatives such as sentence strips, projects, and presentations. These expansion activities often allow students to practice all four language skills, not just the two skills that the student book focuses on.

Photocopiable Masters

○ Up to three Black Line Masters that teachers can photocopy are included after each chapter. These worksheets are optional and are described in expansion activities located within the chapter. One chapter worksheet is often additional editing practice, while the others might be a graphic organizer or a set of sentence strips.

Internet Research

○ At the end of Part 3 in each chapter of the Teacher's Edition, a list of suggested website resources provides additional information on the topics presented in the chapter. Teachers may use this optional resource to gather more background or to direct students to these sites to research the topics for an expansion activity.

End-of-Chapter Tests

○ The end-of-chapter tests assess students on reading comprehension, one or more of the reading or critical thinking strategies highlighted in the chapter, vocabulary, mechanics and editing. Item types include multiple choice, fill-in-the-blank, and true/false, for a total of 35 items per test. Answer keys are provided.

●●●●● Scope and Sequence

Chapter	Reading Strategies	Writing and Writing Strategies
UNIT 1 ANTHROPOLOGY		
Chapter 1 **Cultural Anthropology** • Introduction: Feng Shui *in California* • General Interest: *Symbolic Systems and Meanings* • Academic: *The Anthropological View of Religion*	• Understanding Italics • Using a Graphic Organizer to Show Cause and Effect • Guessing the Meaning from Context • Outlining Main Ideas, Important Details, and Examples • Marking a Book • Understanding Collocations • Understanding the Organization of a Research Paper	• Focus: Defining a Term • Strategy: Writing a Paragraph of Definition • Strategy: Using Material from a Source
Chapter 2 **Physical Anthropology** • Introduction: *Orangutans* • General Interest: *Humans and Other Primates* • Academic: *Modern Stone Age Humans*	• Understanding Pronoun References • Previewing: Using Headings • Previewing: Using Pictures and Captions • Having Questions in Mind • Understanding Quotation Marks	• Focus: Paragraph of Comparison • Strategy: Getting Started by Brainstorming • Strategy: Paraphrasing • Strategy: Writing a Paragraph of Comparison

The Mechanics of Writing	Critical Thinking Strategies	Test-Taking Strategies
UNIT 1 ANTHROPOLOGY		
• Adjective Clauses • Coordinating Conjunctions • Adjective Clauses with Prepositions • Adverbial Conjunctions • Avoiding Sentence Fragments	• Making Inferences • Keeping a Word Journal • Making Connections • Outlining • Summarizing	• Taking an Essay Exam • Underlining
• Review: Adverbial Conjunctions to Show Similarities and Differences • Complex Sentences: Subordinating Conjunctions • Subordinating Conjunctions to Show Differences	• Making Comparisons • Comparing	• Taking a Closed-Book Essay Exam • Defining

Scope and Sequence

Chapter	Reading Strategies	Writing and Writing Strategies
UNIT 2 ECONOMICS		
Chapter 3 **Developing Nations** • Introduction: *What Can One Person Do about Poverty?* • General Interest: *A Bank for the Down and Out* • Academic: *Developing Countries*	• Finding the Meaning of Words with Multiple Definitions • Dealing with Too Much Material: Divide and Conquer • Using Tables to Find Information	• Focus: Paragraph of Argument • Strategy: Writing a Paragraph of Argument: Cause/Effect • Strategy: Organizing a Cause/Effect Paragraph: Idea Mapping
Chapter 4 **The Global Economy** • Introduction: *The Global Marketplace* • General Interest: *Skills for the Global Marketplace* • Academic: *International Trade*	• Providing Definitions and Examples to Check Understanding • Summarizing Your Reading	• Focus: Paragraph about Free Trade • Strategy: Writing a Paragraph of Argument: Inductive Reasoning • Strategy: Providing Evidence
UNIT 3 LITERATURE		
Chapter 5 **The Nature of Poetry** • Introduction: *Poetry Lessons* • General Interest: *Appreciating Poetry* • Academic: *Three More Poems*	• Choosing the Correct Dictionary Definition: Using Parts of Speech • Analyzing Poems • Stating the Theme of a Poem: the Topic and Main Idea	• Focus: Analysis of a Poem • Strategy: Planning a Paragraph of Analysis: Idea Mapping • Strategy: Writing a Paragraph of Analysis

The Mechanics of Writing	Critical Thinking Strategies	Test-Taking Strategies
UNIT 2 ECONOMICS		
• Using Source Material • Finding Supporting Information • Introducing Citations • Knowing When to Quote and When to Paraphrase • Choosing the Right Reporting Verb • Weaving in Quotations	• Synthesizing • Summarizing	• Summarizing • Circling the Best Choice
• Transitions Followed by Phrases • Present Unreal Conditional • Conditionals with *Without* • Transition Expressions of Cause and Effect: Review of Coordinating, Adverbial, and Subordinating Conjunctions	• Evaluating Sources • Making Connections	• Taking a Side • Circling the Best Choice • Finding Errors
UNIT 3 LITERATURE		
• Expressing Possibility and Probability • Using Phrases for Symbols • Using Similes with *as . . . as* • Avoiding and Repairing Problems with Sentence Structure	• Discovering the Meaning of a Poem • Making Inferences	• Hedging • Avoiding Overstatement

Chapter	Reading Strategies	Writing and Writing Strategies
Chapter 6 **Heroes in Literature** • Introduction: *Old Country Advice to the American Traveler* • General Interest: *The Hero's Journey* • Academic: *Ta-Na-E-Ka*	• Understanding Italics for Foreign Words • Finding the Theme of a Story • Recognizing Euphemisms	• Focus: A Persuasive Essay • Strategy: Understanding the Organization of an Essay • Strategy: Writing a Thesis Statement • Strategy: Writing Topic Sentences in an Essay
UNIT 4 ECOLOGY		
Chapter 7 **Endangered Species** • Introduction: *A Dutch Scientist Teaches Indians to Hunt* • General Interest: *The Human Factor* • Academic: *The Edge of Extinction*	• Knowing Which New Words to Focus On • Understanding the Passive Voice • Formal Outlining	• Focus: Reference Lists in APA Format • Strategy: Writing a Research Paper • Strategy: Evaluating Online Sources • Strategy: Doing Library Research • Strategy: Writing a Reference List
Chapter 8 **Human Ecology** • Introduction: *Simple Solutions* • General Interest: *Are Pesticides Safe?* • Academic: *The Effects of E-Waste*	• Organizing Ideas	• Focus: A Research Paper • Strategy: Planning an Essay by Using a Formal Outline • Strategy: Writing Introductions • Strategy: Writing Conclusions

The Mechanics of Writing	Critical Thinking Strategies	Test-Taking Strategies
• Parallelism • Making a Strong Argument: *Should, Ought to,* and *Must* • Using Synonyms • Review: Paraphrasing	• Interpreting • Making Connections • Summarizing	• Writing Supporting Material in an Essay • Circling the Best Choice
UNIT 4 ECOLOGY		
• Understanding Punctuation: Ellipses and Brackets • Review: Using Source Material	• Understanding Irony • Outlining	• Finding Errors
• Reducing Adjective Clauses to Participial Phrases • Using Participial Phrases at the End of a Sentence • Using Participial Phrases at the Beginning of a Sentence • Using Internal Citations • Varying Citation Forms • Citing Sources that Cite Sources • Including Long Quotes	• Seeing Both Sides of an Argument	• Practicing Fill-in-the-Blank Questions • Finding Errors

UNIT 1 ●●● ANTHROPOLOGY

❍ Direct students' attention to the photo on page 1. Ask questions: *What do you see? Where can you find this? What does it tell you about the people who painted it?*
❍ Write *anthropology* on the board and help students brainstorm words related to it. Ask: *What topics do you think will be in this unit?* Circle the words they suggest.

CHAPTER 1 CULTURAL ANTHROPOLOGY

In this chapter, students will learn about cultural anthropology. In Part 1, students will read about a California legislator's proposal to implement *feng shui* in buildings in San Francisco. In Part 2, students will read about symbolic systems and meanings. In Part 3, students will read a research paper on the anthropological view of religion and an excerpt from a book describing a Native-American vision quest. Part 4 focuses on the mechanics of writing, including adjective clauses, adjective clauses with prepositions, coordinating conjunctions, adverbial conjunctions, and avoiding sentence fragments. In Part 5, students will write a paragraph of definition.

VOCABULARY

acquaintances	caste	dyeing	material	polytheistic
anthropomorphic	CEOs	foragers	metonym	principles
array	clan	foreign objects	monarch	realm
artificial	clutter	gap	monotheism	spells
authority	consumption	hazardous	Mount Olympus	stamina
bound up with	craze	hearth	notion	tidbits
budget cuts	deflect	hierarchy	nuclear family	urged

READING STRATEGIES
Understanding Italics
Using a Graphic Organizer to Show Cause and Effect
Guessing the Meaning from Context
Outlining Main Ideas, Important Details, and Examples
Marking a Book
Understanding Collocations
Understanding the Organization of a Research Paper

CRITICAL THINKING STRATEGIES
Making Inferences
Keeping a Word Journal
Making Connections
Note: The strategies in bold are highlighted in the Student Book.

MECHANICS
Adjective Clauses
Adjective Clauses with Prepositions
Coordinating Conjunctions
Adverbial Conjunctions
Avoiding Sentence Fragments

WRITING STRATEGIES
Writing a Paragraph of Definition
Using Material from a Source

TEST-TAKING STRATEGIES
Taking an Essay Exam
Underlining

CHAPTER 1 Cultural Anthropology

Chapter 1 Opener, page 3

○ Direct students' attention to the photo. Ask them what is happening in the photo.
○ Have students discuss the questions. This can be done in pairs, in small groups, or as a class.
○ Check students' predictions of the chapter topic.

EXPANSION ACTIVITY: Writing Prompt

○ Direct students' attention to the photo.
○ Ask students to write for five minutes, using the photo as a prompt. You may want to suggest questions to generate ideas: *Who is the man in the photo? Where does he live? What has his life been like? What is he feeling? Why?*
○ Put students in pairs to read or talk about their writing.
○ Call on students to tell the class one thing they thought about the photo.

PART ① INTRODUCTION
FENG SHUI IN CALIFORNIA, PAGES 4–8

EXPANSION ACTIVITY: Sort by Category

○ Explain the activity. Tell students that you will give them a question to ask classmates. Then they will move around the classroom, asking the question and standing with people who have the same or similar answers to the question.
○ Ask: *What's your favorite part of the house, apartment, or studio to study in?* Remind students to move around and talk to each other, so that they can group themselves according to response. When students are grouped, ask each group what they represent (e.g., *bedroom, living room, den, kitchen*). Ask students to explain why they like the room.

○ Ask additional questions related to the topics in the chapter. Create your own or use the ones below. This activity is meant to warm students up to the topics and help them anticipate content.
What is most important to you in a workspace? What animal do you think symbolizes your personal qualities?

Before Reading

CRITICAL THINKING STRATEGY: Thinking Ahead

Thinking ahead is an important critical thinking strategy used throughout the text. By looking at and discussing photos, students can anticipate the content of the reading. Predicting and anticipating content helps students understand new material.

A. Thinking Ahead

○ Have students look at the photos and read the questions.
○ Put students in pairs to discuss the questions.
○ Call on students to share their ideas with the class.

ANSWER KEY

Answers will vary.
1. the one with the windows
2. The top photo shows light from the outside; the bottom photo shows artificial light (from a ceiling light or lamp).
3. 1 and 13; 1 because it is the ground floor (G), and 13 because some consider it an unlucky number
4. The number 7 is sometimes considered lucky in the United States. Chinese culture considers 8 a lucky number. In Hong Kong, 38 is lucky. In the United States, 13 is unlucky. Some Asian countries consider 4 unlucky. Many Italians consider 17 unlucky.

5. People sometimes choose to do or not to do certain things on certain dates.
6. Answers will vary.

Reading

❍ Have students look at the reading.
❍ Go over the directions and the question.
❍ Have students read silently or have students follow along silently as you play the audio program.

ANSWER KEY

California State Assemblyman Leland Yee has proposed that California adopt building standards to promote *feng shui* principles.

Culture Notes

❍ The Golden State is a nickname for California. It comes from the 1800s and the discovery of gold.
❍ It was in 1848 that the first gold was discovered in Coloma, California by a man who was building a sawmill and noticed flakes of gold in the water.
❍ Before the discovery, Coloma had been a remote town, but its population swelled by thousands searching for gold.
❍ The crux of California's gold rush lasted from 1850–1857.

EXPANSION ACTIVITY: Research on *Feng Shui*

❍ Have students do Internet research to find out some of the specific principles or history of *feng shui* or *feng shui* in modern times.
❍ Put students in pairs to share what they found out.
❍ Call on students to share what they found out with the class.

After Reading

A. Comprehension Check

❍ Go over the directions.
❍ Have students answer the questions.
❍ Put students in pairs to compare answers.
❍ Go over the answers with the class.

ANSWER KEY

1. Mr. Yee wants them to adopt building standards that promote *feng shui,* to increase the positive energy available to residents.
2. *Feng shui* is a collection of Chinese traditions. It improves life through the design of buildings and the objects within them.
3. *Chi* is energy. Good *chi* is influenced by natural lighting and materials, electronic equipment, and good airflow. Bad *chi* is influenced by artificial lighting and materials, unlucky or unbalanced building shape, clutter, and items that remind people of bad experiences.
4. The principles originated four to five thousand years ago. *Feng shui* has become a worldwide fad in recent years.

CRITICAL THINKING STRATEGY: Making Inferences

❍ Go over the information in the box.
❍ Ask: *What is another word for* infer? *When do we need to infer, or make inferences?*

B. Making Inferences

❍ Go over the directions.
❍ Put students in pairs to discuss the questions.
❍ Call on students to share their ideas with the class.

ANSWER KEY

Answers may vary, but should include:
The author likes eliminating clutter to reduce stress and painting in certain colors to encourage a good mood (he calls them *common-sense techniques*). He doesn't like avoiding unlucky numbers, keeping toilet lids down, or placing mirrors to deflect energy (he calls them *old superstitions*).

Culture Note
❍ One of the most extensive lists of old superstitions on the Internet is available at www.oldsuperstitions.com.

TOEFL® iBT Tip

TOEFL iBT Tip 1: The TOEFL iBT tests the examinee's ability to read a text and make inferences based on information presented in the text. For this type of skill, examinees may be required to form generalizations and draw conclusions based on what is implied in a text.

❍ Point out to students that the *Critical Thinking Strategy* for *Making Inferences* will help them to determine what an author means when information is not stated directly.

❍ By using key words and phrases from the text, students will be able to make assumptions and apply this skill to the reading section of the TOEFL iBT. This will help students recognize the implied meaning or purpose of a text.

READING STRATEGY: Understanding Italics
❍ Go over the information in the box.
❍ Ask: *What are some reasons we use italics when we write? What word on page 4 is in italics? (feng shui) Why? (It's a foreign word.)*

C. Vocabulary Check
❍ Go over the directions.
❍ Answer the first one as a class.
❍ Have students write the words that match the definitions and then compare answers with a partner.
❍ Go over the answers with the class.

Academic Note
❍ When students are reading at this level, they need to learn that defining every word is not necessary to understand the reading. Since students are being prepared for academic work, they should be encouraged to define new words and phrases from context. This will allow them to be better prepared for the unfamiliar vocabulary they will encounter in academic coursework.

ANSWER KEY
1. urged; 2. artificial; 3. clutter; 4. deflect; 5. craze; 6. CEOs; 7. budget cuts

READING STRATEGY: Using a Graphic Organizer to Show Cause and Effect
❍ Go over the information in the box.
❍ Ask comprehension questions: *What is a graphic organizer? How can it help you? What is one type of graphic organizer? Can you name other types of graphic organizers?*

D. Using a Graphic Organizer
❍ Go over the directions.
❍ Have students complete the graphic organizer.
❍ Go over the answers with the class. You may want to reproduce the organizer on the board or with an overhead projector.

ANSWER KEY
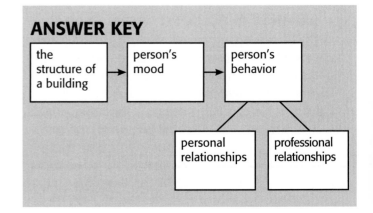

E. Taking a Survey

❍ Direct students' attention to the chart. Give students a few minutes to think about their answers to the questions.
❍ Model how to do the activity by asking a few students a question and filling in the chart.
❍ Have students stand and move around the classroom to take turns asking and answering the questions. Remind students to talk to three classmates and write their answers on the chart.

PART ② GENERAL INTEREST READING
SYMBOLIC SYSTEMS AND MEANINGS, PAGES 9–19

Before Reading
A. Thinking Ahead
❍ Go over the directions and the questions.
❍ Put students in small groups to discuss the questions.
❍ Call on students to share their ideas with the class.

ANSWER KEY

Answers may vary. Possible answers include:
1. Some popular sports are football (called *soccer* in America), American football, and basketball. Expressions: *slam dunk* (from basketball, meaning a great success), *to punt* (from American football, meaning to give up a responsibility), *kick-off* (from soccer, meaning the beginning of an event)
2. In the U.S., a family meal usually includes a meat, starch, and vegetables. A sweet dessert might be served after the meal. A business dinner might be more formal and is likely to include an appetizer, an entrée, and a dessert. Small amounts of alcohol may be served in the U.S., but drinking a lot of alcohol is inappropriate. At a party, alcohol is commonly served, and is an appropriate gift on most occasions. Food at a party is usually only *hors d'oeuvres*, or "finger food."
3. In the U.S., an owl symbolizes wisdom, a rat symbolizes a traitor or dishonest person, and a bull represents stubbornness. Many animals symbolize more than one thing. For example, a "fox" can be either a good-looking person or a cunning planner.

4. In the U.S., traditional houses have separate kitchens, dining rooms, and living rooms. People use each room for one purpose—cooking, eating, or relaxing. In modern houses, these three rooms are combined into an open area divided by low partitions. This arrangement is a return to the more communal style of early immigrants to America. However, bedrooms are still separate and closed off.
5. Symbols of traditional authority include crowns, scepters, and keys. But in the U.S., these symbols are not used for the government. Symbols of the U.S. government include the bald eagle, the White House, or other official buildings.

📖 EXPANSION ACTIVITY: Research on Sports Idioms

❍ Have students do an Internet search using the phrase *sports idioms.* You may want to assign students different sports such as basketball, soccer, boxing, horse racing, and baseball.
❍ Have students write down five sports idioms in English and how they are used.
❍ Put students in small groups to share the idioms they researched.

READING STRATEGY: Guessing the Meaning from Context

❍ Go over the information in the box.
❍ Ask questions: *What punctuation marks may indicate a definition? What expressions often introduce a definition? What verbs might be used before definitions?*

B. Guessing the Meaning from Context

❍ Go over the directions.
❍ Answer the first one as a class.
❍ Have students write their definitions on the lines and then compare ideas with a partner.
❍ Go over the definitions with the class.
❍ Direct students' attention to the photo. Ask questions: *What are the people in the photo doing? Is this a nuclear family? What are they eating?*

ANSWER KEY

Answers may vary.
1. mother, father, and children; 2. endurance; 3. people you know a little; 4. eating; 5. finger foods, snacks; 6. variety, group

READING STRATEGY: Outlining Main Ideas, Important Details, and Examples

○ Go over the information in the box.
○ Ask questions: *What is a main idea? Where can it usually be found? Where can we often find the main ideas about a subtopic? Why do we include examples?*

TOEFL® iBT Tip

TOEFL iBT Tip 2: The TOEFL iBT tests the ability to understand key facts and the important information contained within a text. Locating details and key words in a text will help students build vocabulary and improve their reading skills.

○ Point out that the reading section of the TOEFL iBT may require examinees to classify and organize information questions in a way that will help them to distinguish between major and minor points in a reading source.

○ The *Outlining Main Ideas, Important Details, and Examples* strategy can help students locate more than one fact presented in a reading. This will help to scaffold students' abilities upward toward mastering questions that require them to create paraphrases from information in a text or classify organization into a category chart and recognize major and minor ideas that belong or do not belong in the chart.

⌒ Reading

○ Have students look at the reading. Ask: *What do you think it will be about?*
○ Go over the directions and the questions. Have students underline the main ideas, important details, and examples as they read.
○ Have students read *Symbolic Systems and Meanings* silently or have them follow along silently as you play the audio program.

ANSWER KEY

Food symbolizes social relationships. For example, eating together may symbolize marriage or romance. Living space also symbolizes social relationships, especially family ties. For example, entering someone's bedroom may show that you are a close relative. Many special objects are used to represent authority, but for ordinary people, details of appearance such as long and short hair can symbolize their support or opposition to authority figures.

EXPANSION ACTIVITY: Marking the Pauses

○ Point out that correct intonation can increase comprehension. Explain that native American-English speakers often pause between different thought groups, or groups of words that express a single idea. Students may understand and remember more if they notice thought groups.
○ Have students mark the pauses they hear with a slash (/) as you play the audio program or read the text aloud.
○ Ask students what kind of words often form thought groups, or the phrases that are said without pauses. They should notice that we often pause before and after clauses, prepositional phrases, long noun phrases, verb and object combinations, and appositives.

After Reading

A. Comprehension Check

○ Go over the directions.
○ Put students in small groups to discuss the questions.
○ Call on students to share their ideas with the class.

ANSWER KEY

1. Answers will vary.
2. The main idea of the reading is in the first section, Lines 1–23.
3. The main idea of the second section is "Cultural rules determine every aspect of food consumption." The main idea of the third section is "Arrangements of space also make important symbolic statements about social groupings and social relationships." The

main idea of the final section is "If authority is represented by a series of symbols, opposition to that authority is symbolically represented by an inversion of those symbols."

4. Important details include the symbolism of food, social space, and of politics and authority.

5. Examples in the second section include different kinds of meals, marriage in the Trobriand islands, totemic animals, and the Indian caste system. Examples in the third section include the floor plans of Nuchanulth and Thai houses, and the change from a communal to an individualistic use of space among early American immigrants. Examples in the final section include symbolic animals, objects as symbols of office, metonyms for authority, and hairstyles as a signs of authority or rebellion.

6. Answers will vary.

READING STRATEGY: Marking a Book

❍ Go over the information in the box.
❍ Ask: *Why should you mark your books? What are some ways you can mark books?*

Academic Note

❍ You may want to point out that most classes at American universities that teach reading or study skills suggest marking only 10–20 percent of a reading.
❍ Elicit ideas about how to mark what's important but not everything (only key terms, names, phrases).
❍ Encourage students to actually mark in their books. It is O.K. if they mark the wrong thing since the book is designed to be used as a learning tool.
❍ Tell students that buying used books already marked is not a good idea since the student who owned it before may not have marked it correctly.

B. Marking a Book

❍ Go over the directions.
❍ Have students go back over the reading and highlight it using three different colors.
❍ Have students compare what they marked with a partner.

C. Vocabulary Check

❍ Go over the directions.
❍ Have students write the words or phrases on the lines and then compare answers with a partner.
❍ Go over the answers with the class.

ANSWER KEY

1. metonym; 2. monarch; 3. clan; 4. totemic ancestor;
5. caste system; 6. hearth; 7. authority; 8. dyeing;
9. bound up with

D. In Your Own Words: Summarizing

❍ Go over the directions.
❍ Have students complete the sentences and then compare ideas with a partner.
❍ Call on students to share their answers with the class.

ANSWER KEY

Answers may vary. Possible answers for the first section include:
1. The section is about the symbolic meaning of food.
2. The author says that social units—such as marriages or the nuclear family—are defined by who eats together.

E. Organizing Information

❍ Go over the directions.
❍ Have students complete the chart.
❍ Have students compare their ideas in pairs.
❍ Call on students to share their ideas with the class.

ANSWER KEY

Types of Symbolism	Main Ideas	Important Details	Examples
Food	Cultural rules determine every aspect of food preparation	1. Who eats together defines social units	a. nuclear family b. England: reg. meals (fam.), Sun. meals (rels.), cocktail parties (acquaintances)

		2. Eating—metaphor for marriage	Trobriand Islands: eating together first time = marriage totemic animals
		3. Other cultural rule: taboo against eating certain things	
		4. Association between food prohibitions and rank	caste system in India
Space	Arrangements of space make symbolic statements about groupings and social relationships	1. highest ranking 2. rules about marriage 3. ethnic identity	Nuchanulth plank houses Thailand sleeping rooms Early immigrants—communal rooms
Politics and Authority	Nations and authority figures are represented by symbols	1. Nations 2. Office 3. Opposition	Eagle and bear (U.S. and Soviet Union) Objects – crown, staff of pharaoh, head of department, fly, whisk Hair—length and color different from authority indicates opposition

TOEFL® iBT Tip

TOEFL iBT Tip 3: The TOEFL iBT tests the ability to understand facts, examples, and explanations in a text; however, it does not directly test understanding of the main idea of a passage. Examinees may be required to recognize the organization and purpose of a text, categorize that information, and distinguish between the major and minor points presented in the text.

○ The *Organizing Information* activity requires students to visually connect information. This will help to scaffold students' abilities upward toward mastering the schematic table questions on the test.

○ Remind students that being able to skim and scan to locate information is a technique that will help them with organizing information into a schematic table or chart.

F. Discussion
○ Go over the directions.
○ Have students discuss the questions in small groups.
○ Call on students to share their ideas with the class.

ANSWER KEY
Answers will vary.

CRITICAL THINKING STRATEGY: Keeping a Word Journal
○ Go over the information in the box.
○ Ask questions: *What is a word journal? How can it help you? What should you write in a word journal?*

G. Word Journal
○ Go over the directions.
○ Have students write words in their Word Journals.

EXPANSION ACTIVITY: Use Your Words
○ Have students choose three words from their Word Journals and then write the words in original sentences.
○ Have students rewrite their sentences on slips of paper or index cards, leaving out the featured vocabulary word.
○ Put students in pairs or small groups to exchange and complete sentences.
○ Call on students to read their sentences to the class.

PART ACADEMIC READING
THE ANTHROPOLOGICAL VIEW OF RELIGION, PAGES 20–30

Before Reading
A. Thinking Ahead
○ Direct students' attention to the photos and ask: *What are these objects? What do they have in common?*
○ Go over the directions.
○ Put students in small groups to discuss the questions.
○ Call on students to share their ideas with the class.

ANSWER KEY

Answers will vary.

EXPANSION ACTIVITY: Tell a Story

❍ Model the activity. Choose an article of clothing or an object that you are wearing in class, and tell the class a true story about the object (*This is a vest that my daughter made me buy. She was very small. We saw it in a store, and she said I just had to buy it. She liked the flowers on it because they were pretty. Every time I wear it, I think of my daughter.*).

❍ Put students in groups of three or four. Have each student take an object from a pocket or bag, or a piece of clothing or jewelry and tell a story about the object.

❍ Go around the room and have students say one word that their object represents to them.

B. Vocabulary Preparation

❍ Go over the directions.

❍ Answer the first one as a class.

❍ Have students circle the part of speech and write their guesses.

❍ Put students in small groups to check their answers. Remind students to use a dictionary if they are really unsure of a word's definition.

❍ Go over the answers with the class.

ANSWER KEY

1. n, an area or world; 2. adj, relating to the physical world; 3. adj, in human form; 4. n, system of organization with higher and lower ranks; 5. n, idea; 6. adj, dangerous; 7. n, space

READING STRATEGY: Understanding Collocations

❍ Go over the information in the box.

❍ Ask questions: *What is a collocation? What are examples of common collocations? Why should we learn collocations?*

C. Understanding Collocations

❍ Go over the directions.

❍ Have students look at the collocations and answer the questions.

❍ Go over the answers with the class.

ANSWER KEY

Noun phrases: *an array of forms, perception of the universe, the extraordinary realm, supernatural beings*
Prepositional phrases: *In general, In 1966, among foragers*
Verb phrases: *focus on it, seem to ask, provide shape, identified four types, hunt and gather*

TOEFL® iBT Tip

TOEFL iBT Tip 4: The TOEFL iBT tests the ability to determine the meanings of words in context.

❍ Point out that the strategy and activity for *Understanding Collocations* will help students improve their vocabulary for the TOEFL iBT. By interpreting a sentence based on other information, and using the logic of grammar, students can figure out the meaning of new words presented in context.

❍ Learning words that naturally collocate is an excellent way for students to increase vocabulary. This helps students better comprehend words that are linked together to convey meaning or connotation rather than trying to determine the definition of individual words.

D. Hunting for Collocations

❍ Go over the directions.

❍ Have students highlight collocations.

❍ Call on students to give examples and tell what kind of collocation it is.

ANSWER KEY

Answers may vary. Possible answers include:
1. outside the real world (PP), the place of dreams (NP)

2. of the material world (PP)
3. in the form of animals (PP)
4. a strict hierarchy (NP), an organized system (NP)
5. is similar to (VP), the notion of luck (NP)
6. fishing in the ocean (NP), storms at sea (NP)
7. need to take (VP), a real gap (NP)

🎧 Reading

❍ Go over the directions before the reading. Read the question aloud.
❍ Have students read and mark the article silently or play the audio program and have students follow along silently.

ANSWER KEY

Three characteristics of all religions are magic, symbolism, and ritual.

GRAMMAR NOTE

❍ Authors always use punctuation in certain ways. You can elicit or explain that the writer uses ellipses (. . .) to indicate text has been left out. Dashes are used to indicate definitions (e.g., *magic words*), examples (e.g., *a stone or a feather*), or additional information (e.g., *in an array of forms*).

Pronunciation Note

❍ Before playing the audio program or reading the text aloud, you may want to explain to students the intonation pattern to indicate parentheses, commas, or dashes. We usually use rising-falling intonation before these forms of punctuation, to indicate that we are continuing, but perhaps adding information.

After Reading

A. Main Idea

❍ Go over the directions and the questions.
❍ Have students confirm the main idea.
❍ Go over the answers with the class.

ANSWER KEY

All four types of religion make use of three characteristics—magic, symbolism, and ritual—to fulfill people's psychological and social needs.

READING STRATEGY: Understanding the Organization of a Research Paper

❍ Go over the information in the box.
❍ Ask comprehension questions: *What is a research paper? Where do you list sources? What is a thesis statement? When do you need to give source information in the body of the research paper?*

B. Understanding the Organization of a Research Paper

❍ Go over the directions.
❍ Put students in small groups to discuss the questions.
❍ Call on students to share their ideas with the class.

ANSWER KEY

1. the first two paragraphs; the end of the second paragraph
2. the same as the main idea (Lines 26–28)
3. paragraph 3, line 29 (Lines 26–28 indicate that the three subtopics will be explored.); magic, symbolism, and ritual, in that order
4. the last paragraph; the third sentence restates thesis
5. name, year, page; some citations give name, year, paragraph number
6. quotation marks for exact words
7. 4; books: Kottak, Lessa, Rosman, website: O'Neil

C. Comprehension Check

❍ Go over the directions.
❍ Have students fill in the chart and then compare answers with a partner.
❍ Go over the answers with the class.

ANSWER KEY

Characteristic of Religion	Definitions	Functions	Examples
Symbols	signs that have no necessary or natural connection to the things they signify	help people to comprehend abstract ideas such as fear, hope, values, and goals	Venus (in ancient Roman relig.) = love bread & wine (in Christianity) = body & blood of Christ
Magic	supernatural techniques designed to accomplish specific aims	reduces anxiety and increases confidence	lucky charm, spells, Trobriand Island sailors use magic to stay safe, baseball players use magic rituals to do well in game
Rituals	formal, stylized, repetitive acts	translate messages, values, and sentiments into observable action	healing ritual – Siberia Amazon – hallucinogenic drink, removing foreign objects Plains Indians – vision quest as rite of passage

D. Collocations with Prepositions
○ Go over the directions.
○ Have students look at the reading and complete the phrases.
○ Go over the answers with the class.

ANSWER KEY
1. of; 2. on; 3. of; 4. after; 5. of; 6. on; 7. to; 8. from/to; 9. with

E. Vocabulary Check
○ Go over the directions.
○ Have students look at the reading and write the words or phrases on the lines.
○ Go over the answers with the class.

ANSWER KEY
1. foragers; 2. polytheistic; 3. Mount Olympus; 4. hierarchy; 5. monotheism; 6. spells; 7. foreign object

F. Application
○ Go over the directions.
○ Put students in small groups to discuss the questions.
○ Call on students to share their ideas with the class.

ANSWER KEY
Answers may vary. Possible answers include:
1. Olympian religions include the Japanese Shinto religion, ruled by Amaterasu, goddess of the sun, and the religion of the Aztecs from ancient Mexico, ruled by Quetzalcoatl, god of knowledge.
2. The reading emphasizes that magic gives people a psychological feeling of control in times of uncertainty. It does not emphasize the role of supernatural beings or powers.
3. Avoiding unlucky numbers, keeping toilet seats down, and using mirrors to deflect energy are examples of "magic" in *feng shui.* These are ways of using symbols to try to control uncertain events.
4. Answers will vary.
5. Rites of passage: the Catholic sacrament of Confirmation, *Fiesta de Quinceañera,* high school or college graduation, beginning military service, and getting a driver's license
6. In Part 2, *hierarchy* is used to refer only to the group of people in authority. In Part 3, the word is defined as the "system of higher and lower ranks" including both the authorities and those beneath them.

⦿⦿⦿⦿⦿⦿⦿⦿⦿⦿⦿⦿⦿⦿⦿⦿⦿⦿⦿⦿⦿⦿⦿⦿⦿

CRITICAL THINKING STRATEGY: Making Connections

Making connections is an important critical thinking strategy. By connecting new information to something we know or have read, we are better able to understand, synthesize, and remember.

⦿⦿⦿⦿⦿⦿⦿⦿⦿⦿⦿⦿⦿⦿⦿⦿⦿⦿⦿⦿⦿⦿⦿⦿⦿

G. Making Connections
- Go over the directions.
- Have students read *Alone on a Hilltop* silently or follow along silently as you play the audio program.

Culture Note
- Some Native Americans believe boys become men after a psychological transformation. At the age of 16, the boys sit alone on a hilltop for four days and four nights. During this time, they have no food or water. Since Native American children are never left alone, this is their first experience alone and away from their families. While they are on the hilltop, the boys search for a sign that tells them what they should do with their future. They believe a vision will open their eyes and guide them into manhood.

H. Discussion
- Go over the directions.
- Put students in small groups to discuss the questions.
- Call on students to share their ideas with the class.

ANSWER KEY
Answers may vary.
1. to make the transition to manhood, get his man's name
2. There are specific objects one uses, the family is involved, certain steps are followed
3. and 4. blanket—cover his nakedness, the blanket he would use if he became a medicine man; peace pipe and tobacco—to help with visions; gourd with pieces of flesh and fossils—symbolize the pain his grandmother went through to give him something of herself, and power

EXPANSION ACTIVITY: What Objects Would You Take?
- Model the activity. Tell students what three objects you would take if you were going to be stranded on an island for a month, and why you would take each one.
- Have students write their three objects on a piece of paper or index card.

- Collect the cards.
- Read one aloud and elicit the reasons for each object. Ask the author if the reasons are correct.
- Continue with other cards.

I. Word Journal
- Go over the directions.
- Have students write words in their Word Journals.

J. Response Writing
- Go over the directions. Explain that this is a quick-writing activity and does not have to be perfect. Point out that response writing can be a warm-up to a more structured writing assignment, helping to generate ideas.
- Set a time limit of 15 minutes.
- Put students in pairs to read or talk about their writing.

 Internet Research
- For additional information on cultural anthropology go to:
  - www.isca.ox.ac.uk/
  - www2.lib.udel.edu/subj/anth/soccult/internet.htm
  - www.ualberta.ca/~slis/guides/canthro/anthro.htm
  - www.mnsu.edu/emuseum/cultural/anthropology/culturalanth.html

PART THE MECHANICS OF WRITING, PAGES 30–37

- Go over the information about Part 4.

Adjective Clauses
- Go over the information in the box about adjective clauses.
- Ask comprehension questions: *Where do adjective clauses appear in a sentence? What are some relative pronouns that introduce adjective clauses? What is the function of an adjective clause?*

A. Adjective Clauses
❍ Go over the directions and the first answer.
❍ Have students combine the sentences, making the second sentence an adjective clause.
❍ Go over the answers with the class.

ANSWER KEY
1. The bear is a symbol that is associated with Russia.
2. The Puritans were a group of people who fought against the Cavaliers in 17th-century England.
3. The temple was the place where people worshipped.
4. The Melanesians were people whose belief in *mana* affected everything in life.
5. A crown is a symbolic object that only royalty may wear.
6. Oliver Cromwell is the man whom we associate with opposition to King Charles I of England.

EXPANSION ACTIVITY: Describe Your Partner
❍ Explain the activity. Students will take turns interviewing a partner and then writing sentences with adjective clauses.
❍ Put students in pairs to interview each other for two minutes.
❍ Have students write sentences with adjective clauses about their partners.
❍ Call on students to share their sentences with the class.

Grammar Notes
❍ Point out that adjective clauses are often reduced to participial phrases (especially those with *be,* as in passive constructions and continuous tenses). For example, the first sentence in Activity A could be reduced to *The bear is a symbol associated with Russia.*
❍ Explain that participial phrases can often come at the beginning of a sentence (e.g., *Wearing the crown at last, the king fainted.*) but should not be confused with gerunds (*Wearing the crown was a heavy burden.*).

Adjective Clauses with Prepositions
❍ Go over the information in the box.
❍ Ask: *Where do we usually use formal structures for adjective clauses with prepositions? Where does the preposition come in an informal structure?*

B. Adjective Clauses with Prepositions
❍ Go over the directions.
❍ Read the first pair of sentences. Elicit ways to combine the sentences.
❍ Have students combine the sentences, using the second sentence as an adjective clause.
❍ Have students compare sentences in pairs.
❍ Call on students to read their sentences to the class.

ANSWER KEY
1. A funeral is a ritual at which Europeans wear black.
2. Informants are people with whom anthropologists discuss cultural material.
3. A rite of passage is a ritual during which people make a transition from one stage of life to another.
4. The Obi is a leader for whom people have great respect.
5. A cocktail party is an activity at which acquaintances make business contacts.
6. Shamanism is a religious belief about which I know nothing.

Coordinating Conjunctions
❍ Go over the information in the box.
❍ Ask questions: *What are some coordinating conjunctions? When do we use a comma?*

C. Coordinating Conjunctions
❍ Go over the directions and the example.
❍ Have students combine the sentences using coordinating conjunctions.
❍ Have students compare their answers in pairs.
❍ Go over the answers with the class. You may want to have students write the new sentences on the board.

ANSWER KEY

1. Anthropologists discuss cultural material with informants and examine actions in a cultural context.
2. Baseball is sometimes used as a metaphor for politics, for both are highly competitive.
3. In most societies, the family is the unit that regularly eats together, but/yet in some societies, men and women eat separately.
4. Women in New Guinea live in their own houses, prepare food there, and take their husbands' food to the men's house.
5. In India, members of a high-ranked caste are fearful of ritual pollution so will not eat with people from a low-ranked caste.
6. Brahmans will not share food with low-ranked individuals or accept food from them.
7. Political symbols may seem unimportant, but/yet people take them very seriously.

Grammar Note

○ The most often used coordinating conjunctions are *and, but, or,* and *so.* Students can be taught that *and* connects similar ideas, *but* connects contrasting ideas, *or* joins alternative ideas, and *so* shows the second idea is a result of the first. A well-known mnemonic for remembering all seven coordinating conjunctions is FAN BOYS:

For
And
Nor
But
Or
Yet
So

Adverbial Conjunctions

○ Go over the information in the box.
○ Ask comprehension questions: *What adverbial conjunctions are similar in meaning to* and? *Which ones are similar to* but? *What punctuation do we use before and after adverbial conjunctions?*

D. Adverbial Conjunctions

○ Go over the directions and the first answer.
○ Have students combine the sentences and then compare ideas with a partner.
○ Call on students to read their sentences to the class.

ANSWER KEY

Answers will vary.
1. Animals have always represented nations; for example the eagle and the bear were symbols of the conflict between the United States and the former USSR.
2. In American society, the color red means danger; therefore, stop signs and traffic signals are red.
3. In Western cultures, black is the color of mourning. In much of Asia, however, white is worn at times of death and mourning.
4. People who practice *feng shui* use many common-sense techniques such as eliminating clutter to reduce stress. In addition, they paint rooms in certain colors to encourage a good mood.
5. Fishing is seasonally hazardous because of violent storms at sea. In other words, it is dangerous in some seasons due to bad weather over the ocean.

Avoiding Sentence Fragments

○ Go over the information in the box.
○ Ask comprehension questions: *What is a common mistake people make in written English? What is a sentence fragment?*

E. Avoiding Sentence Fragments

○ Go over the directions.
○ Have students indicate if the sentence is a fragment or O.K., then correct the fragments.
○ Put students in pairs to compare answers.
○ Go over the answers with the class.

ANSWER KEY

1. F; 2. O.K.; 3. O.K.; 4. F; 5. F; 6. F; 7. O.K.; 8. F; 9. F; 10. F
Answers may vary. Possible answers include:
1. The unit that regularly eats together is a social unit, for example, the nuclear family.
4. Baseball or horse racing may represent politics.

5. Each caste is a ranked group which has an economic specialization.
6. Length of hair often symbolizes opposition to authority.
8. A metonym is a type of symbol. The head of a department in a university is an example of a metonym.
9. A totem pole is a pole with beings representing totemic ancestors.
10. For example, he may drink a hallucinogenic drink . . .

TOEFL® iBT Tip

TOEFL iBT Tip 5: Although the TOEFL iBT does not discretely test grammar skills, examinees' essay scores will be determined based on the range of grammar and vocabulary used in their essays.

○ Point out that the grammar activities in *The Mechanics of Writing* part of this chapter will help them improve their essay writing. The activity for *Avoiding Sentence Fragments* will make students more aware of their own writing errors.

○ The TOEFL iBT essays may be scored higher based on whether the examinee can use correct grammar and more sophisticated language. Students will need to express ideas in complete sentences and use correct punctuation.

F. Error Analysis/Editing
○ Go over the directions.
○ Direct students' attention to the first item and elicit the error (*in* is unnecessary).
○ Have students correct the errors and then compare answers with a partner.
○ Go over the answers with the class. Have students explain what the errors are and how to correct them. Students can write the corrected sentences on the board.

ANSWER KEY
Answers may vary. Possible answers include:
1. A temple is a building where people worship ~~in~~.
2. A funeral is a ritual ^at which Europeans wear black. ~~at a funeral.~~
3. Political symbols may seem unimportant, but people take them very seriously.
4. Sports involve competition and struggle. ; therefore, they are often used as metaphors for politics.
5. In anthropology, magic is not a performance. that we might see on a stage.
6. Magic functions to make people less anxious. . F for example, in the Trobriand Islands, cricket players recite magic spells when the ball is pitched to help it reach its intended target.
7. In India, members of high-ranked castes are fearful of ritual pollution, so ~~for~~ they will not eat with people of low-ranked castes.

EXPANSION ACTIVITY: Editing Practice
○ Photocopy and distribute Black Line Master *Editing Practice* on page BLM 1.
○ Go over the directions.
○ Have students correct the mistakes and then compare answers with a partner.
○ Go over the answers with the class.

ANSWER KEY
1. A vision quest is a solitary journey ~~who~~ that an adolescent takes in order to become a man or a woman and receive an adult name.
2. In Siberia, a shaman goes into a trance as part of a healing ritual ~~in~~ which fulfills a psychological need.
3. American baseball players practice certain rituals, ~~but~~ so they will do better in a game.

4. A christening is a ritual ^in which a baby often receives a name and is presented to God and the community ~~in~~.

5. During the 1960s, many young people felt rebellious towards those in authority. ~~However~~ ^Therefore, they grew their hair long in defiance of society's rules.

PART ⑤ ACADEMIC WRITING, PAGES 38–41

TEST-TAKING STRATEGY: Taking an Essay Exam

○ Go over the information in the box.
○ Ask comprehension questions: *What are three types of essay exams? How are open-book and take-home essay exams similar? What part of the essay question tells you what kind of paragraph you need to write? Should you include information you know from outside of class?*

EXPANSION ACTIVITY: What Type of Essay Do I Write?

○ Photocopy and distribute the Black Line Master *What Type of Essay Do I Write?* on page BLM 2.
○ Discuss the types of paragraphs and their explanations.
○ Have students determine which type of essay should be written for each of the questions.
○ Go over the answers.

ANSWER KEY

1. Definition; 2. Illustration (Example); 3. Description; 4. Analysis; 5. Comparison/Contrast; 6. Summary; 7. Process; 8. Cause and Effect; 9. Comparison/Contrast; 10. Definition; 11. Facts with explanation; 12. Analysis

Writing Assignment

○ Go over the description of the writing assignment in the box. Tell students which type of exam you want the students to practice.
○ Have students read the four steps.
○ Direct students' attention to Step A and have students choose to define either *metaphor* or *symbol*.
○ Direct students' attention to Step B. Have students review the reading in Part 2 and complete the outline on page 39.
○ You may want to have students compare ideas with a partner who chose the same word.
○ Direct students' attention to Step C. Have students find examples from Lame Deer's book.
○ Direct students' attention to Step D. Have students organize their information.

WRITING STRATEGY: Writing a Paragraph of Definition

○ Go over the information in the box.
○ Ask comprehension questions: *What types of definitions are there? What is a synonym? What verbs can we use to tell the function of a word? When do we use adjective clauses? When might we use negation? What is one way we almost always explain a new word or phrase?*
○ You may want to read the example paragraph aloud as students follow silently in their books.
○ Read the *Analysis* directions. Have students answer the questions.
○ Go over answers with the class.

ANSWER KEY

Types of definition: negation, classification, definition, function, example; the words in quotes are copied from the source; Kottak

TOEFL® iBT Tip

TOEFL iBT Tip 6: Both the integrated and independent essays of the TOEFL iBT will be scored based on how well the examinee completes the overall writing task. Many of the reading passages, as well as the writing tasks, involve expository essay format.

○ Point out that the *Writing a Paragraph of Definition* strategy will help students build skills for integrated writing tasks, where they may read a definition of a term or concept and then write about it. It will be important for students to recognize definitions and then interpret what the author presents or expresses and be able to mirror this in their own essays.

WRITING STRATEGY: Using Material From a Source

○ Go over the information in the box.
○ Ask comprehension questions: *What are some ways you can make sure you use your own words on an exam? How should you indicate that material is not in your own words? How much should you quote directly? How should you cite a source on an exam?*
○ Read the *Analysis* directions. Have students answer the questions.
○ Go over the answers with the class.

ANSWER KEY

Punctuation: italics, quotation marks, parentheses. The student's words are not in quotation marks, the source's words are. The source in the first example is Kottak, and in the second example, it is Gaeddert. The period is inside the quotation marks in the first sentence, but after the source in the second.

○ Direct students' attention to Step E. Have students write paragraphs, using the notes in Step D.
○ Direct students' attention to Step F. Go over the questions. Have students read and edit their paragraphs, using the questions as a guide.
○ For peer editing, have students exchange paragraphs with a partner, edit, and return to the writer.
○ Go over the directions for Step G. Have students carefully rewrite their paragraphs and hand them in to you.
○ After you have read and returned students' paragraphs, you may want to set aside time for students to read each others' writing or display the paragraphs in the classroom. Have students keep all of their final versions in a notebook or folder so that they can see their progress and improvement over time.

UNIT 1 ●●●● ANTHROPOLOGY

CHAPTER 2 PHYSICAL ANTHROPOLOGY

In this chapter, students will learn about physical anthropology. In Part 1, students will read about orangutans, the apes of Borneo in Southeast Asia. In Part 2, students will read about the similarities and differences between humans and other primates. In Part 3, students will learn about modern Stone Age humans, the people who lived in the Paleolithic Age. Part 4 focuses on the mechanics of writing, including a review of adverbial conjunctions to show similarities and differences, complex sentences, and subordinating conjunctions to show differences. In Part 5, students will practice taking a closed-book essay exam by writing a paragraph of comparison.

VOCABULARY

adolescence	descend	kin(ship) group	reenact
American Sign Language (AMESLAN)	dominate	macaque	rite of passage
	endangered	master	seclusion
analogous	ensure	microlith	solitary
art for art's sake	exogamy	obliterate	superimposed
auctioned off	exploiting	omnivorous	terrestrial
belonging to	fleshy	orangutan	tribal lore
ceremony of increase	foresight	outgoing	troop
cluster	initiation rite	peer	twig
curbing	instinctive	prey	

READING STRATEGIES

Understanding Quotation Marks
Previewing: Using Headings
Understanding Pronoun References
Previewing: Using Pictures and Captions
Having Questions in Mind

CRITICAL THINKING STRATEGIES

Making Comparisons
Comparing

MECHANICS

Review: Adverbial Conjunctions to Show Similarities and Differences
Complex Sentences: Subordinating Conjunctions
Subordinating Conjunctions to Show Differences

WRITING STRATEGIES

Getting Started by Brainstorming
Paraphrasing
Writing a Paragraph of Comparison

TEST-TAKING STRATEGIES

Taking a Closed-Book Essay Exam
Defining

CHAPTER 2 Physical Anthropology

Chapter 2 Opener, page 46
- ○ Direct students' attention to the photo. Ask them what is happening in the photo.
- ○ Have students discuss the questions. This can be done in pairs, in small groups, or as a class.
- ○ Check students' predictions of the chapter topic.

PART 1 INTRODUCTION
ORANGUTANS, PAGES 46–50

Before Reading
Thinking Ahead
- ○ Have students look at the photos.
- ○ Go over the directions and the questions on page 46.
- ○ Put students in pairs or small groups to discuss the questions.
- ○ Call on students to share their ideas with the class.

ANSWER KEY
Answers may vary.
1. Primates are a group of related animal species including apes, monkeys, prosimians (such as lemurs), and humans.
2. Wild orangutans live only in parts of Malaysia and Indonesia. They live in trees and eat bark and insects. They are seriously endangered because their forest habitat is reduced every year by logging, farming, and fires.

EXPANSION ACTIVITY: Yes or No?
- ○ Have a group of students come to the front of the room.
- ○ Write *yes* on one side of the board and *no* on the other.
- ○ Tell students you are going to read some questions and students should stand by the word that indicates their answers.

- ○ Read or ask a question about primates and remind students to move. Create your own questions or use the ones below.
  Are humans the only primates that can speak?
  Can any other primates use language?
  Do other primates use tools?
  Can apes think and solve problems?
  Do other animals, including primates, have the ability to express themselves through art?
  Do you think that primates have emotions like humans?
- ○ Call on students to explain their ideas.
- ○ Repeat with other questions and groups of students.
- ○ You may want to dictate the questions to the class and have students notice if the questions are answered in this chapter.
- ○ You could also have students choose a question to research either in the library or on the Internet.

🎧 Reading
- ○ Go over the directions and the question.
- ○ Have students read *Orangutans* silently or have students follow along silently as you play the audio program.

ANSWER KEY
Orangutans are solitary. They don't live in groups like other primates.

Vocabulary Notes
- ○ *Orangutan* is "man of the woods" or "forest man" in Malayan.
- ○ This description could have stemmed from Malayan inhabitants noting that the orangutan has similarities to a human. The differences from man are that they have darker skin, long, sparse, reddish hair, and very long arms.

Grammar Notes

○ You may want to point out that this reading contains a number of participial adjectives. Point out or elicit that participial adjectives are those formed from the present (*–ing*) or past participle (*–ed/–en*).

○ Elicit examples of participial adjectives in the reading (*hanging, varied, endangered, outgoing, undivided*).

Culture Note

○ According to Schonbrunner Tiegarten, "The Orangutans," appeared on Tourismindonesia.com (accessed 10/18/04 at www.zoovienna). The painting program for the orangutans started in the early 1990s as a behavioral enrichment program but is no longer in existence; in part because a new orangutan was born in 1998. Nonja always had to be separated for better concentration. Now, Nonja is at her "best age" and has more social interests in the male than in the painting programs. The enrichment program now consists of other things such as hiding food. The keepers from time to time offer chalk and paper to her and sometimes she makes lines and spots on the paper for herself.

After Reading

EXPANSION ACTIVITY: Main Idea

○ Explain that a main idea is a little like a one-sentence summary of a reading passage.

○ Have students write one-sentence summaries of the passage and then compare ideas with a partner.

○ Call on students to share their ideas with the class.

A. Comprehension Check

○ Go over the directions.

○ Have students highlight the answers and then compare ideas with a partner.

○ Go over the answers with the class.

ANSWER KEY

1. They live alone, not in groups.
2. Sumatra and Borneo
3. in the trees or canopy
4. bark, leaves, fruit, insects
5. Yes, there are only 15,000–24,000.
6. She splatters paint onto the paper by flicking her wrist.

CRITICAL THINKING STRATEGY: Making Comparisons

○ Go over the information in the box.

○ Ask questions: *What should you do when you read? Why?*

B. Making Comparisons

○ Go over the directions.

○ Have students write their answers in the chart and then compare ideas with a partner.

○ Go over the answers with the class.

ANSWER KEY

	Sumatran Orangutans	Kalimantan Orangutans
Similarities	Diet–fruit, bark, leaves, insects; Lives in canopy solitary	Diet–fruit, bark, leaves, insects; Lives in canopy solitary
Differences	Paler, ginger color	Reddish brown, coarser hair

TOEFL® iBT Tip

TOEFL iBT Tip 1: The TOEFL iBT tests the ability to understand important information contained within a reading. In preparation for the integrated writing or speaking tasks on the test, students may be asked to compare and contrast points of view presented in a text or conversation.

❍ Show students how the statements in the *Making Comparisons* strategy will help them differentiate between similarities and differences. Understanding how to organize notes and ideas into a chart by looking closely at similarities and differences will give learners the opportunity to improve their critical thinking skills.

❍ Comparing information in a reading will better help them prepare for content type questions where they will be required to identify relationships between what is stated and implied in a text.

🖥 EXPANSION ACTIVITY: Research
❍ Have students find a photo of Nonja's work and print it out. Refer students to www.anova.com/news/story/sm_1445427.
❍ Have students write three sentences describing the painting.
❍ Call on students to share their ideas with the class.

READING STRATEGY: Understanding Quotation Marks
❍ Go over the information in the box.
❍ Ask questions: *When do we use quotation marks? What is the reason for the quotation marks on page 47?* (translation, to give the meaning)

C. Vocabulary Check
❍ Go over the directions.
❍ Have students write the words or phrases that match the definitions.
❍ Go over the answers with the class.

ANSWER KEY
1. orangutan; 2. fleshy; 3. descend; 4. solitary; 5. belonging to [*this expression is on Line 24*]; 6. outgoing; 7. auctioned off

D. Discussion
❍ Go over the directions.
❍ Put students in small groups to discuss the questions.
❍ Call on students to share their ideas with the class.

ANSWER KEY
Answers will vary.

PART ② GENERAL INTEREST READING HUMANS AND OTHER PRIMATES, PAGES 51–61

Before Reading

A. Thinking Ahead
❍ Go over the directions and the questions.
❍ Put students in small groups to discuss the questions.
❍ Call on students to share their ideas with the class.

ANSWER KEY
Answers may vary. Possible answers include:
1. Humans and other primates are all animals that live together in social groups and nurture their young as families. All primates have hands that can grasp objects to use as tools.
2. Humans are much more intelligent than other primates, with more complicated use of tools and language and larger, more organized social groups.

B. Guessing the Meaning from Context
○ Go over the directions and the context clues.
○ Answer the first question as a class.
○ Have students write the definitions and type of context clues.
○ Go over the answers with the class.

ANSWER KEY
1. not learned, opposites; 2. a kind of monkey, definitions; 3. specific purpose in mind, expressions; 4. small branches, information in another part of the sentence and own life experience; 5. learn well, information in another part of the sentence; 6. a diet of both plants and animals, definition; 7. others of the same age, definitions; 8. monkeys that live on the ground, definitions

EXPANSION ACTIVITY: Original Sentences
○ Have students choose five new words or phrases from Activity B to use in original sentences.
○ Call on volunteers to write their original sentences on the board, substituting a blank line for the new vocabulary word.
○ Have the class complete the sentences.

READING STRATEGY: Previewing: Using Headings
○ Go over the information in the box.
○ Ask: *What is one way you can preview a reading?*

C. Previewing: Using Headings
○ Go over the directions.
○ Have students preview the reading and answer the questions.
○ Put students in pairs to compare ideas.
○ Call on students to share their ideas with the class.

ANSWER KEY
1. yes; 2. no; 3. learning, tools, communications systems, sharing and cooperation, mating and kinship

EXPANSION ACTIVITY: Use Photos
○ Ask students to bring in one of their favorite photos.
○ Have students look at the photos and write a sentence about each. Point out that the sentence could describe the photo or tell how they feel about it.
○ Put students in pairs to share their sentences.
○ Call on students to read their sentences to the class.

Reading
○ Go over the directions and the questions.
○ Have students read the excerpt from *Comparing Humans with Other Primates* silently or follow along silently as you play the audio program.
○ Remind students to highlight main ideas, important details, important vocabulary, and new vocabulary as they read.

ANSWER KEY
Researchers talk about degrees of difference between humans and other primates. *Degrees of difference* (or *differences in degree*) means that two things are basically similar (not *different in kind*) but one is greater than the other. For example, learning, tool use, and language in apes and monkeys are the same *kinds* of behavior as in humans, but much less complex and sophisticated.

Culture Notes
○ Harry Harlow was the director of a primate research lab at the University of Wisconsin. Unlike some other psychologists, he did not believe that animals lived in organized societies simply to regulate sexual contact. He believed that animals might show love. He studied the bonds between baby monkeys and their mothers, and between young monkeys and their playmates. In one famous experiment, he showed that rhesus monkeys preferred soft cloth "mothers" over wire "mothers," that affection might be more important than food in establishing a parent-child bond.
○ Jane Goodall was an English naturalist who went to Africa to study wild chimps. She received a Ph.D. from Cambridge University in 1965.

Academic Note

❍ You may want to point out or elicit how and where glossed words appear. In this reading, the glossed words are defined in footnotes. In other readings or books, glossed words may appear in a separate glossary at the end of the chapter or book, or in the margins. Sometimes glossed words are in bold print.

EXPANSION ACTIVITY: Word Work

❍ Have students write guesses next to unfamiliar words and highlight words they think are important and can't figure out.
❍ Put students in small groups to compare and share answers.

After Reading

A. Comprehension Check

❍ Go over the directions.
❍ Put students in small groups to discuss the questions.
❍ Call on students to share their ideas with the class.

ANSWER KEY

1. They talk about the degrees of difference, as in the first paragraph (*Many of the differences between humans and other primates are differences in degree rather than in kind.*). Examples include learning, using tools, and communicating.

2.

Areas	More Similarities or Differences?	Examples
Learning	☑ Similarities ☐ Differences	• From captivity: Harlow's macaques • From the wild: Japanese macaques (washing sweet potatoes and eating wheat)
Tools	☑ Similarities ☐ Differences	• In the wild: Goodall's chimps used "sponges" and termiting

Communication Systems	☑ Similarities ☐ Differences	Only humans speak, but chimps: • Use 25 distinct calls • Use facial expressions, noises, and body movements • Can learn and use American Sign Language
Sharing and Cooperation	☐ Similarities ☑ Differences	Humans are more cooperative, less aggressive. Chimps share meat, but other foraging is done individually. Information sharing from elder to younger humans
Mating and Kinship	☐ Similarities ☑ Differences	• For monkeys and apes, mating occurs during estrus, when females ovulate • Human ovulation is concealed, mating occurs throughout year • Human pair-bonds more exclusive and longer-lasting • Humans practice exogamy, which leads to having ties to two groups; when chimps and gorillas leave one group, they join another

B. Noticing Phrases

❍ Go over the directions and the first answer.
❍ Have students write the phrases and their types.
❍ Have students compare their answers with a partner.
❍ Go over the answers with the class.

ANSWER KEY

Answers may vary. Possible answers include:
1. raised in isolation (AP); 2. from the top down (PP);
3. from the bottom up (PP); 4. in the wild (PP);
5. in captivity (PP); 6. into the modern world (PP);
7. an omnivorous diet (NP); 8. reproductive success (NP); 9. the key point (NP); 10. leave home (VP)

EXPANSION ACTIVITY: Beanbag Toss

○ Give students five minutes to study the phrases in Activity B.
○ Ask students to close their books. Call on a student, toss a beanbag or ball and say part of one of the phrases (e.g., *raised*). Elicit an appropriate completion (e.g., *in isolation, in captivity, in the wild*).
○ Have the student call on a classmate, toss the beanbag or ball and begin a phrase.
○ Continue until everyone has had a chance to participate.

C. Vocabulary Check

○ Go over the directions.
○ Have students write the answers and then compare ideas with a partner.
○ Go over the answers with the class.

ANSWER KEY

1. form dominance relationships; 2. troop; 3. American Sign Language or Ameslan; 4. curbing; 5. exogamy;
6. kin groups; 7. adolescence

D. Making Inferences

○ Go over the directions.
○ Have students discuss the questions with a partner.
○ Call on students to share their ideas with the class.

ANSWER KEY

1. One troop learned to wash sweet potatoes, the other to eat wheat. It was quicker when the learning happened from the top down (males to others in troop). Note: Students must infer that males are the "top" of the social group.
2. Baboons dominate and threaten each other; humans, even in simple societies, share and avoid fighting.
3. Exogamy is marriage outside the group. Humans practice exogamy, but maintain ties with parents after marriage. Other primates tend to leave the group, and do not maintain ties.
4. Quotation marks indicate direct quotes and words used in special ways ("terminiting," "Tickle Washoe," "Washoe tickle," "You, me, go, out, hurry," "sponges"). Italics are used for words from another language (*Homo*) and for emphasis (*most humans maintain lifelong ties with sons and daughters*).

EXPANSION ACTIVITY: Venn Diagram

○ Photocopy and distribute Black Line Master *Comparing Humans and Chimpanzees* on page BLM 3.
○ Have students complete the Venn diagrams to compare humans and chimpanzees. You may want to have students do this as an out-of-class assignment and research other similarities and differences.
○ Put students in pairs to compare ideas.
○ Call on students to share their ideas with the class.

READING STRATEGY: Understanding Pronoun References

○ Go over the information in the box.
○ Ask questions: *Why do we use pronouns? What is a referent? What is one strategy you can use to figure out the referent?*

E. Understanding Pronoun References

○ Go over the directions and the first answer.
○ Have students check either singular or plural and highlight the referent and then compare answers with a partner.
○ Go over the answers with the class.

ANSWER KEY

1. singular, a three-year-old female monkey; 2. singular, that only humans manufacture tools with foresight; 3. plural, leaves; 4. plural, apes; 5. plural, elders

TOEFL® iBT Tip

TOEFL iBT Tip 2: The TOEFL iBT measures the ability to identify the relationships between pronouns and their antecedents or postcedents (words that follow them) in a reading.

○ Point out that the strategy and activity for *Understanding Pronoun References* will help students improve their ability to correctly identify and link pronouns and nouns on the TOEFL iBT.

F. In Your Own Words: Summarizing
○ Go over the directions.
○ Have students complete the sentences.
○ Call on students to read their sentences to the class.

ANSWER KEY

Answers may vary. Possible answers for the first section include:
1. The section is about learning in non-human primates.
2. The author says that many macaque behaviors are not instinctive, but must be learned from experience or another macaque.

G. Word Journal
○ Go over the directions.
○ Have students add new words to their Word Journals.
○ Put students in pairs to talk about the words they selected.

EXPANSION ACTIVITY: Make It Visual
○ Remind students that there are different learning styles and representing words visually may help some students remember words better.
○ For each word that students wrote in their Word Journals, have students draw a picture, icon, or doodle to remind them of the word's meaning.
○ Put students in pairs to share their ideas.

Academic Note
○ There are three main learning styles: visual, auditory, and kinesthetic/tactile. Each student will have one learning style that tends to be his or her strongest. Simple, easy-to-use charts for determining learning styles can be found on the Internet.

PART ❸ ACADEMIC READING
MODERN STONE AGE HUMANS, PAGES 62–72

Before Reading
A. Thinking Ahead
○ Go over the directions. Read the questions aloud.
○ Put students in small groups to discuss the questions.
○ Call on students to share their ideas with the class.

ANSWER KEY

Answers may vary. Possible answers include:
1. Paleolithic people were hunters and gatherers. They didn't farm, but they created art about the animals they hunted.
2. Evidence about Paleolithic people includes their skeletons, their footprints, and especially their art (cave paintings).

B. Vocabulary Preparation

○ Go over the directions.
○ Have students write the part of speech of each word in orange on the line and highlight the meaning in the second sentence.
○ Go over the answers with the class.

ANSWER KEY

1. v, to make a result certain; 2. adj, similar; 3. n, groups; 4. v, acting out again; 5. v, paint over, destroy; 6. n, being away from other people; 7. adj, drawn over; 8. n, [*there is no dictionary definition*], expression of individual artistic temperament

EXPANSION ACTIVITY: Word Families

○ Point out that students will practice paraphrasing later in the chapter (Part 5). One way to paraphrase is to use different parts of speech for words in the same word families.
○ Have students generate word families for the words in Activity B (or previous vocabulary activities in the chapter). Suggest students use a dictionary if they have difficulty.

ANSWER KEY

1. sure; 2. analogy, analog; 3. cluster (v); 4. reenactment; 5. obliteration; 6. seclude, secluded; 7. impose, imposition, superimpose; 8. NA

READING STRATEGY: Previewing: Using Pictures and Captions

○ Go over the information in the box.
○ Ask: *How can you use pictures and captions to preview a reading?*

C. Previewing: Using Pictures and Captions

○ Go over the directions.
○ Have students discuss the questions with a partner.
○ Call on students to share their ideas with the class.

ANSWER KEY

Answers will vary.
In their cave paintings, Paleolithic humans showed men hunting animals. The Mesolithic people used harpoons.

D. Previewing: Using Headings

○ Go over the directions.
○ Elicit the two main topics (Upper Paleolithic and Mesolithic).

READING STRATEGY: Having Questions in Mind

○ Go over the information in the box.
○ Ask: *What do some readers and writers do to make the reading more engaging?*

E. Having Questions in Mind

○ Go over the directions.
○ Have students write three questions on the lines.
○ Call on students to share their ideas with the class.

ANSWER KEY

Answers may vary. Possible answers include:
1. What do the words *Paloeolithic* and *Mesolithic* mean? (Old Stone Age and Middle Stone Age)
2. What are some differences between life in the Paleolithic and Mesolithic ages?
3. What are some differences between Stone Age humans and modern humans?

🎧 Reading

○ Go over the directions before the reading. Read the questions aloud. Point out that students could mark the answers as they read.
○ Have students read *Modern Stone Age Humans* silently or play the audio program and have students follow along silently.

ANSWER KEY

Cave paintings tell us what animals Paleolithic people hunted and that art was an important part of their lives. The paintings also suggest possible magical and religious beliefs of the culture.

In the Mesolithic, a generalized, broad-spectrum economy emerged. Economic roles of men and women became more equal because big-game hunting (which men did), became less important, and gathering (which women did), became more important.

Grammar/Pronunciation Note

❍ Point out that this reading includes rhetorical questions. These are questions that are asked for a purpose other than obtaining information. The author is not really asking these questions of the reader. Rather, the author is asking the question in order to provide the answer himself. Often rhetorical questions used to encourage thought have greater variations in stress and intonation.

Pronunciation Note

❍ Before listening to the audio or reading the passage aloud, you may want to teach students that there are content words and function words. Content words contain meaning and are usually nouns, verbs, adjectives, and adverbs. Function words help the structure of the sentence and include prepositions, articles, and demonstratives. Content words receive the stress in sentences. Point out that we do not stress the function words.

EXPANSION ACTIVITY: Stress Patterns

❍ Point out that only certain words receive stress in each sentence (often nouns and verbs but sometimes adjectives and adverbs).
❍ Play any section of the audio program and have students circle the stressed words in each sentence.
❍ Have students compare answers with a partner.
❍ Photocopy and distribute Black Line Master *Activity for Stressed Words* on page BLM 4.
❍ Have students attempt to fill in the missing content words.
❍ Go over the answers (in bold).

ANSWER KEY

Chimpanzees have a lot in common with **humans**. Like **humans,** chimps can use **tools.** For example, they use twigs to get **termites** to eat. **Chimps** also **use** leaves as **"sponges"** to soak up **water** to drink. Chimps don't **speak,** but they do use other communication systems. They make **facial** expressions and **body** movements to communicate. They also can be **taught** to use Ameslan.

After Reading

A. Comprehension Check

❍ Go over the directions.
❍ Put students in pairs to answer the questions.
❍ Call on students to share their ideas with the class.

ANSWER KEY

1. Cave paintings might tell us how humans attempted to control animals, either to ensure success in hunting, or to control animal reproduction. They may also be a kind of pictorial history or part of an initiation rite.
2. hunting and gathering/broad-spectrum

B. Comprehension Check

❍ Go over the directions and the questions.
❍ Have students complete the two graphic organizers.
❍ Put students in pairs to compare ideas.
❍ Go over the answers with the class. You may want to have students reproduce the graphic organizers on the board.

CHAPTER 2 • Physical Anthropology • **27**

ANSWER KEY

1.

Motives	Examples
To ensure success in hunting	Animals are depicted with spears in their bodies.
To control animal reproduction	Part of ceremonies of increase, some animals are pregnant and some are copulating
To record history in pictures	Reenacting a hunt, calendar of phases of the moon
Part of initiation rite, bush schools	Several small heel prints fossilized in European cave, humans shown dancing (perhaps shamans)

2.

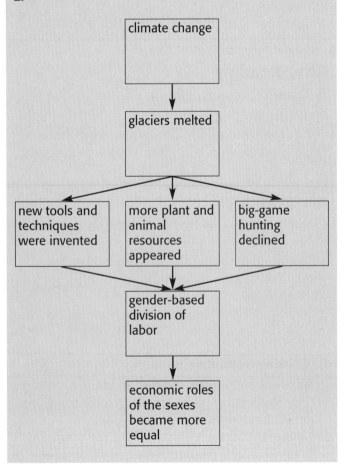

C. Verb Phrases with Prepositions
- ○ Go over the directions.
- ○ Have students write the prepositions on the lines.
- ○ Go over the answers with the class.

ANSWER KEY
1. with; 2. over; 3. on; 4. over; 5. from; 6. on; 7. with; 8. by; 9. to; 10. to

D. Vocabulary Check
- ○ Go over the directions.
- ○ Have students write the words or phrases on the lines and then compare answers with a partner.
- ○ Go over the answers with the class.

ANSWER KEY
1. prey; 2. ceremonies of increase; 3. superimposed; 4. initiation rite/rite of passage; 5. tribal lore; 6. microlith; 7. exploiting

E. Word Journal
- ○ Go over the directions.
- ○ Have students write words in their Word Journals.

F. Making Connections
- ○ Go over the directions.
- ○ Have students complete the chart and then compare answers with a partner.
- ○ Call on students to share their ideas with the class.

ANSWER KEY

Paleolithic Economy	Mesolithic Economy
✓ big game hunting	✓ hunting • roe deer • wild ox • wild pig
✓ no need for techniques to preserve meat	✓ preserving meat • smoking • salting
	✓ tools for hunting and fishing • microliths used as fishhooks and harpoons • dugout canoes • bow and arrow • axes, chisels, gouges
	✓ gathering • wild plants • small animals • insects • shellfish

G. Response Writing

○ Go over the directions.
○ Explain that this is a quick-writing activity and does not have to be perfect. Point out that response writing can be a warm-up to a more structured writing assignment, helping to generate ideas.
○ Set a time limit of 15 minutes.
○ Put students in pairs to read or talk about their writing.

TOEFL® iBT Tip

TOEFL iBT Tip 3: The TOEFL iBT requires examinees to synthesize information from spoken and written texts and respond in a speaking task or a writing task. Journal writing is a good way to help students express themselves openly in preparation for these types of tasks.

○ Point out that being able to read and explain or interpret a passage will be helpful in building up to the integrated speaking task. The *Response Writing* activity will help students get their ideas down on paper and clearly articulate an opinion or describe a situation. They will be able to focus on the grammar, organization, and punctuation of their writing later on.

 Internet Research

○ For additional information on cave paintings, see
  • www.culture.gouv.fr/culture/arcnat/lascaux/en/
  • www.culture.gouv.fr/culture/arcnat/chauvet/en/
  • vm.kemsu.ru/en/palaeolith/cavepaint.html
  • www.deutsches-museum.de/ausstell/dauer/ altamira/e_alta.htm

PART ④ THE MECHANICS OF WRITING, PAGES 73–76

Review: Adverbial Conjunctions to Show Similarities and Differences

○ Go over the information about Part 4.
○ Go over the information in the box about adverbial conjunctions to show similarities and differences.
○ Ask comprehension questions: *What conjunctions show similarities? Which ones show differences?*

A. Adverbial Conjunctions to Show Similarities and Differences

○ Go over the directions.
○ Answer the first one as a class.
○ Have students combine the sentences.
○ Go over the answers with the class.

ANSWER KEY

Answers may vary.
1. Human behavior depends extensively on learning. In a similar way, monkeys and apes profit from experience.
2. Tool use appears among several nonhuman species; however, Homo employs tools more often than any other animal does.
3. People communicate nonlinguistically (without words). Similarly, chimps communicate through expressions, noises, and body movements.
4. Monkeys fend for themselves in the quest for food. In contrast, people bring resources back to camp and share them.
5. Baboons and chimpanzees mate only when females go into heat. However, among humans, sexual activity occurs throughout the year.

Human females, by contrast, lack . . . ; Line 173: However, most humans maintain . . .

Part 3: Line 28: For example, because animals . . . ; Line 36: Similarly, cave paintings . . .

TOEFL® iBT Tip

TOEFL iBT Tip 4: Although the TOEFL iBT does not discretely test grammar skills, examinees' essay scores will be determined based on the range of grammar and vocabulary used in their essays.

❍ Point out that the activity for *Adverbial Conjunctions to Show Similarities and Differences* will help them improve their use of adverbial conjunctions and transitions for essay writing. In order to express similarities and differences, or write a comparison essay, students will need to demonstrate the use of appropriate transition words.

❍ The TOEFL iBT essays may be scored higher based on whether the examinee can use grammar and punctuation correctly in their essays. Using more advanced grammatical structures as well as more sophisticated phrases will help students improve their overall essay writing.

EXPANSION ACTIVITY: Find Examples

❍ Put students in three groups and give each group a reading from the chapter.
❍ Have students find and underline examples of adverbial conjunctions in their assigned readings. Elicit the examples and write them on the board.

ANSWER KEY

Part 1: Line 14: Females, however, virtually never leave the trees; Line 27: As a result, Nonja is very outgoing with humans; Line 31: For example, if she detects little stains . . .

Part 2: Line 3: However, studies of primates have revealed . . . ; Line 11: For example, monkeys learn from experiences . . . ; Line 23: However, macaques that had been allowed just twenty minutes . . . ; Line 47: However, tool use also appears . . . ; Line 72: Finally, they pull out the twigs . . . ; Line 79: Furthermore, once the twig is in the hill . . . ; Line 89: However, evidence is accumulating . . . ; Line 96: Africa vervet monkeys, for example . . . ; Line 116: However, work with other chimps . . . ; Line 119: However, a unique concentration . . . ; Line 146:

Complex Sentences: Subordinating Conjunctions

❍ Go over the information in the box.
❍ Ask questions: *What are some subordinating conjunctions that show relationships in time? What are some that show cause and effect relationships? When do we use a comma?*

B. Subordinating Conjunctions

❍ Go over the directions.
❍ Have students combine the sentences and then compare ideas with a partner.
❍ Have volunteers write the sentences on the board.

ANSWER KEY

Answers may vary in the order of the clauses.
1. Apes' artwork is never representational since apes are not able to draw forms and figures.
2. After the dominant male first tried the new kind of food, the whole troop soon began to eat it.
3. When a low-ranking macaque began to wash sweet potatoes, it took the rest of the troop a long time to learn from her.
4. If Paleolithic artists created art simply for the sake of beauty, it seems strange that it was hidden in such remote caves.
5. Humans needed to develop new methods of hunting because their environment was changing.

Subordinating Conjunctions to Show Differences

❍ Go over the information in the box.
❍ Ask questions: *Which subordinating conjunctions show difference? When is a comma used?*

C. Subordinating Conjunctions to Show Differences

○ Go over the directions and the example.
○ Have students combine the sentences and then compare sentences in pairs.
○ Call on students to read their sentences aloud.

ANSWER KEY

Answers may vary. Possible answers include:
1. Although male orangutans travel on the ground to search for food, females never leave the trees.
2. Orangutans have a solitary lifestyle whereas other primates live in groups.
3. While orangutans forage for food primarily by moving about in the canopy, males sometimes descend to the ground to travel long distances in search of food.

EXPANSION ACTIVITY: First Sentences

○ Model the activity. Say a sentence about the information in the chapter (e.g., *For a long time, people thought only humans used tools.*), and then give an adverbial conjunction (e.g., *however*). Elicit sentences from the class that complete the thought (e.g., *However, we have learned that chimps make "sponges" and catch termites with twigs.*).
○ Have students write a first sentence about something related to the topics in the chapter and choose an appropriate adverbial conjunction.
○ Call on a student to read the sentence and adverbial conjunction. Then have that student call on a classmate.
○ Continue until everyone has had a chance to participate.

Grammar Note

○ Adverbial conjunctions are followed by a comma when they begin a new sentence. Sometimes, an adverbial conjunction is used to connect two complete sentences. In such cases, the adverbial conjunction is preceded by a semicolon and followed by a comma. Example: *For a long time, people thought only humans used tools; however, we have learned that chimps make "sponges" and catch termites with twigs.* If the adverbial conjunction does not connect two complete sentences but rather one complete and one incomplete thought, it is preceded and followed by commas.

D. Error Analysis/Editing

○ Go over the directions.
○ Have students find and correct the errors and then compare answers in pairs.
○ Go over the answers with the class.

ANSWER KEY

1. Some nonhuman primates can learn to communicate/ ; ∧ however, only humans can speak.
2. Humans learn from experience. ~~In contrast~~, ∧ *Similarly, or in a similar way,* chimps can learn new behavior by watching other chimps.
3. Most primates live in groups/ , ∧ *whereas* ~~Whereas~~ orangutans tend to have a solitary lifestyle.
4. While humans use tools ∧ tool use is also common among nonhuman primates.
5. Men played the most important role in getting food in the Paleolithic period/ ∧ ; however, men and women shared that role more equally in the Mesolithic period.
6. The artist Jeff Koons creates art in order to earn money/ ∧ ; in contrast, Paleolithic artists painted because they believed it was necessary for their survival.

PART ⑤ ACADEMIC WRITING, PAGES 77–81

TEST-TAKING STRATEGY: Taking a Closed-Book Essay Exam
○ Go over the information in the box.
○ Ask questions: *What are the three types of essay exams? Why do you need to be able to anticipate closed-book questions? What are some things you should memorize?*

Taking a Closed-Book Essay Exam
○ Go over the information.
○ Challenge students to think of pros and cons to a closed-book exam.
○ Put students in pairs to do a comparison of open- and closed-book exams.

A. Anticipating the Question
○ Go over the directions.
○ Have students write questions on the lines.
○ Put students in pairs to share their questions.
○ Call on students to share their ideas with the class.

ANSWER KEY
Answers may vary. Possible answers include:
Part 2: How did anthropologists learn that some primate behaviors are not instinctive? What is exogamy and how does it create the structure of primate social groups? Which are more important—the similarities between humans and other primates, or the differences? Why?
Part 3: What were the major changes in human life between the Paleolithic and the Mesolithic? How did the climate help to create these changes? The reading gives many possible purposes for cave paintings; do you think that magic, history, art, or initiation was the most important purpose? Why?

Academic Notes
○ You may want to elicit types of questions that could be on an essay exam. Brainstorm a list of verbs that tell what type of question it is (*describe, explain, compare and contrast, define, list, analyze*). Refer to the list of types and definitions on page BLM 2.
○ You may also want to remind students that essay questions often have multiple parts (e.g., compare and contrast, define and give an example).

B. What to Study
○ Go over the directions.
○ Have students complete the chart.
○ Put students in pairs to compare ideas.
○ Call on students to share their ideas with the class.

ANSWER KEY
Answers will vary.

Writing Assignment
○ Go over the directions.
○ Have the students read the six steps.
○ Direct students' attention to Step A and have students choose a topic.

WRITING STRATEGY: Getting Started by Brainstorming
○ Go over the information in the box.
○ Ask: *How can brainstorming be helpful?*

Brainstorming
○ Go over the directions.
○ Put students in small groups to list points of comparison.
○ Have students write their ideas on the lines.
○ Call on students to share their ideas with the class.

WRITING STRATEGY: Paraphrasing
○ Go over the information in the box.
○ Ask questions: *What is paraphrasing? What are some strategies you can use to paraphrase?*

TOEFL® iBT Tip

TOEFL iBT Tip 5: The TOEFL iBT tests the ability to read a passage, listen to a lecture related to that passage, and then write in response to a question based on the two stimuli. This integrated writing skill requires students to think critically about material that they have read, interpret that information and relate it to a lecture, and then present ideas in essay format.

○ Remind students that the strategy for *Paraphrasing* will help them develop an important skill for academic writing and essay writing on the TOEFL iBT. When listening to a lecture and taking notes, or reading a passage and taking notes, students must be able to then paraphrase and cite the information they wish to analyze. Students will encounter paraphrasing activities in the reading section of the TOEFL iBT as well, which they can in turn, use as writing strategies.

○ Excellent notetaking and paraphrasing of spoken and written information will help students improve their overall writing skills for the test.

○ Direct students' attention to Step B and have students paraphrase the information in the reading.
○ Put students in pairs to share their paraphrasing.

WRITING STRATEGY: Writing a Paragraph of Comparison
○ Go over the information in the box.
○ Ask comprehension questions: *What do we do in a paragraph of comparison? What should you say in your topic sentence? How many examples should you include?*
○ You may want to read the example paragraph aloud as students follow silently in their books.
○ Read the *Analysis* directions. Ask students to identify the subordinating conjunction and the three adverbial conjunctions.
○ Go over the answers with the class.

ANSWER KEY
Subordinating conjunction: while
Adverbial conjunctions: on the other hand, however, for example

TOEFL® iBT Tip

TOEFL iBT Tip 6: Both the integrated and independent essays of the TOEFL iBT are scored based on how well the examinee completes the overall writing task. Examinees may be required to compare and contrast points of view in a text and lecture and draw information from each source to show that contrast.

○ Point out that the strategy for *Writing a Paragraph of Comparison* in this chapter will help students improve their coherence and the flow of ideas in their essays by focusing on the paragraph level. The "process writing" approach will help students organize their thoughts and take meaningful steps toward developing their essays.

○ Remind students that working slowly with sentence-by-sentence combinations will help them develop their paragraphs more concisely, improve the organization of the essay, and likely improve their overall essay scores.

○ Direct students' attention to Step C. Have students write topic sentences and then choose supporting information.
○ Direct students' attention to Step D. Have students write paragraphs, using the notes in Step C. Remind students that they will edit and revise in the next step.
○ Direct students' attention to Step E. Have students read and edit their paragraphs, using the questions as a guide. You may wish to have students circle or underline the elements in their paragraphs.
○ To encourage peer editing, have students exchange paragraphs with a partner, edit, and return to the writer. Remind students that peer editing will help them improve editing skills.
○ Direct students' attention to Step F. Go over the directions. Have students rewrite the paragraphs and hand them in to you.

○ After you have read and returned students' paragraphs, you may want to set aside time for students to read each other's writing or display the paragraphs in the classroom. Have students keep all of their final versions in a notebook or folder so that they can see their progress and improvement over time.

EXPANSION ACTIVITY: Editing Practice
○ Photocopy and distribute the Black Line Master *Editing Practice* on page BLM 5.
○ Go over the directions.
○ Have students correct the mistakes and then compare answers with a partner.
○ Go over the answers with the class.

ANSWER KEY

Answers may vary.

1. Sumatran orangutans have fine hair/ ^while ~~While~~ Kalimantan orangutans have coarser hair.

2. Some primates show artistic ability, like Nonja. ~~In contrast~~ ^In a similar way or Similarly , some other animals such as elephants seem to like to paint and draw.

3. Humans share food, ^while ~~when~~ monkeys fend for themselves.

4. While humans can speak ^, the vocal tract of apes doesn't permit them to use language in the same way.

5. Washoe, the chimp, learned to use American Sign Language. Similar ^ly or In a similar way , Koko the gorilla acquired a vocabulary of 2,000 signs in Ameslan.

6. ~~Although~~ ^Since winter lasted nine months, people had fewer problems preserving food in this subarctic environment.

Grammar Note
○ Sometimes *while* and *although* are synonyms. Other times they can't be used interchangeably. *Whereas* means *in contrast.* It is not a correct answer for #3 in the Expansion Activity above.

Unit 1 Vocabulary Workshop

A. Matching
○ Read the directions.
○ Have students match the definitions to the words.
○ Go over the answers.

ANSWER KEY
1. g; 2. h; 3. f; 4. j; 5. a; 6. b; 7. e; 8. i; 9. c; 10. d

B. Collocations
○ Review prepositions as a class.
○ Have students write the correct preposition on the line.
○ Go over the answers.

ANSWER KEY
1. of; 2. on; 3. of; 4. on; 5. from/to; 6. in; 7. from; 8. in; 9. from; 10. with

C. Stems and Affixes
○ Go over the information in the box.
○ Read the directions.
○ Put students in pairs to guess the meanings of the words.
○ Go over the answers as a class.

ANSWER KEY
1. same time; 2. believer in many gods; 3. in animal form; 4. not industrial; 5. in human form; 6. married to many; 7. send across; 8. look at; 9. above or beyond the natural; 10. from a date before; 11. study of ancient time; 12. Old Stone Age; 13. put above or on top of; 14. from the earth; 15. say before; 16. marriage out; 17. Middle Stone Age; 18. eating all things

D. The Academic Word List
○ Read the directions. Remind students the Academic Word List consists of some of the most commonly used words in English.
○ Have students write the correct words on the lines.
○ Go over the answers.

ANSWER KEY
1. cultural; 2. aspect; 3. consumption; 4. nuclear; 5. links; 6. cooperative; 7. individually; 8. resources; 9. adults; 10. cooperation; 11. intrinsic

UNIT 2 ECONOMICS

Unit Opener, page 85

○ Direct students' attention to the photo on page 85. Ask questions: *Who do you see in the picture? What can you see in the background? Where do you think the woman is?*

○ Write *economics* on the board and help students brainstorm words related to business. Ask: *What topics do you think will be in this unit?* Circle the words they suggest.

CHAPTER 3 DEVELOPING NATIONS

In this chapter, students will learn about economic issues related to developing nations. In Part 1, students will read about two activists, Bono and Anita Roddick, who are working in different ways to help battle poverty. In Part 2, students will read about a unique bank in Bangladesh that works on a small scale to help the very poor. In Part 3, students will learn about the economics of developing countries. Part 4 focuses on the mechanics of writing, including using source material, finding supporting material, introducing citations, knowing when to quote and when to paraphrase, choosing the right reporting verb, and weaving in quotations. In Part 5, students will write one paragraph of argument (cause and effect) on the eradication of poverty.

VOCABULARY

allocation	capital	external debt	illiterates	population density
assets	capital flight	extinguish	ills	predicament
barriers	crude birthrate	fluctuations	incentive	stumbling block
beg	default	free enterprise	landlocked	tightly knit
bona fide	destitute	fronts	launch	trade barriers
bribes	developing countries	frugality	life expectancy	unmatched toll
brink	eliminated	headway	macroeconomic policies	vow
burden	eradication	hinder	plight	zero population growth

READING STRATEGIES

Finding the Meaning of Words with Multiple Definitions
Dealing with Too Much Material: Divide and Conquer
Using a Table to Find Information

CRITICAL THINKING STRATEGIES

Synthesizing
Summarizing

MECHANICS

Using Source Material
Finding Supporting Information
Introducing Citations
Knowing When to Quote and When to Paraphrase
Choosing the Right Reporting Verb
Weaving in Quotations

WRITING STRATEGIES

Writing a Paragraph of Argument: Cause/Effect
Organizing a Cause/Effect Paragraph: Idea Mapping

CHAPTER 3 — Developing Nations

Chapter 3 Opening Photo, page 87

○ Direct students' attention to the photo. Ask them what is happening in the photo.

○ Have students discuss the questions. This can be done in pairs, in small groups, or as a class.

○ Check students' predictions of the chapter topic.

EXPANSION ACTIVITY: Writing Prompt

○ Direct students' attention to the photo on page 87.

○ Ask students to write for five minutes, using the photo as a prompt. You may want to suggest questions to generate ideas: *What do you think this child is feeling and why? What is it like to be this age? What is this child thinking about? What is your best memory of this time?*

○ Put students in pairs to read or talk about their writing.

○ Call on students to tell the class one thing they thought about the photo.

PART ① INTRODUCTION
WHAT CAN ONE PERSON DO ABOUT POVERTY?, PAGES 88–93

EXPANSION ACTIVITY: Pair Interview

○ Explain that the first reading is about two people who are activists in the fight against poverty.

○ Put students in pairs. Have each person talk about someone they know personally or just know about who is doing something to improve a situation in the world. Set a time limit of five minutes for each partner.

○ Call on students to tell the class about the person their partner talked about.

CRITICAL THINKING STRATEGY: Thinking Ahead

Thinking ahead is an important critical thinking strategy used throughout the text. By looking at and discussing photos, students can anticipate the content of the reading. Predicting and anticipating content helps students understand new material.

Thinking Ahead

○ Have students look at the photos and read the questions.

○ Have students discuss the questions in small groups.

○ Call on students to share their ideas with the class.

ANSWER KEY

Answers may vary. Possible answers include:

1. Bono, the singer for U2, comes from Ireland, and his parents were from opposite sides of Ireland's religious war. He has been married since 1982 to his high school sweetheart. Bono supports many charities, especially for debt relief in Africa. His famous songs include *Sunday Bloody Sunday* and *Where the Streets Have No Name*.

2. The Body Shop sells soaps, cosmetics, and grooming products for both men and women. (The term *body shop* usually means a car mechanic in the U.S., but that is not the meaning here.)

Culture Notes

○ George Bernard Shaw was an Irish playwright and literary critic. He lived from 1856 to 1950. His plays include *Major Barbara, Pygmalion,* and *Arms and the Man.*

○ Samuel Johnson was an English writer, born in 1709. He is best known for his essays and a dictionary of the English language, published in 1755. He is widely known for his quotes, 1,700 of which can be found at www.samueljohnson.com/popular.html.

○ Maimonides was a Jewish rabbi and philosopher who lived between 1135 and 1204 C.E. He wrote books on medicine and a code of Jewish law.
○ John F. Kennedy was the 35th president of the United States, from 1961 until his assassination in 1963.
○ Woodrow Wilson was the 28th president of the United States, serving from 1913 to 1921.

💻 EXPANSION ACTIVITY: Famous Quotes Online

○ To familiarize students with sayings or proverbs about poverty, have them do research on the Internet using key words to search for *famous quotes about poverty* or *proverbs about poverty*.
○ Put students in small groups to share what they found out.

🎧 Reading

○ Have students look at the reading. Read the title and the two subheadings within the reading. Ask questions: *What issue is Bono concerned about? What did Anita Roddick do to fight poverty?*
○ Go over the directions and the question.
○ Have students read silently or have students follow along silently as you play the audio program.

ANSWER KEY

Answers will vary.

Academic Note

○ You may want to point out that this reading includes two sidebars. Sidebars are smaller readings related to the topic in the main reading. They often explain, give examples, or provide timelines for ideas in the main reading.

Grammar Note

○ You may want to direct students' attention to the bulleted items in the first section. Point out that these are written in the imperative. Bullets are used to show that all items in the list are equal. They reflect the different approaches that the fight on poverty is taking.

After Reading

A. Comprehension Check

○ Go over the directions.
○ Have students discuss the question in small groups.
○ Go over the answers with the class.

ANSWER KEY

1. Bono makes his money as a singer of a very popular group. Roddick makes makeup and other products for the body.
2. They both want to help developing nations and poor people.
3. Because so many people have died/are dying of the disease, children don't have parents, households don't have income earners, and nations don't have able-bodied workforces.
4. It pays fair prices; it helps producers support their families; it allows money to go back to communities.

B. Vocabulary Check

○ Go over the directions.
○ Have students write the words and phrases that match the definitions.
○ Go over the answers with the class.

ANSWER KEY

1. launch; 2. ills; 3. fronts; 4. unmatched toll; 5. assets; 6. vowed; 7. frugality

EXPANSION ACTIVITY: Beanbag Toss

○ Give students five minutes to study the words and phrases in Activity B on page 91.
○ Ask students to close their books. Call on a student, toss a beanbag or ball and read one of the words or

a word from one of the phrases (e.g., *begin*). Elicit an appropriate completion (e.g., *launch*).
○ Have the student call on a classmate, toss the beanbag or ball, and say a definition.
○ Continue until everyone has had a chance to participate.

READING STRATEGY: Finding the Meaning of Words with Multiple Definitions
○ Go over the information in the box.
○ Ask questions: *If a word has multiple definitions, what should you do first? What should you do next?*

C. Finding the Meaning of Words with Multiple Definitions
○ Go over the directions.
○ Have students write the number of the appropriate definition on the line, and then compare answers with a partner.
○ Go over the answers with the class.

ANSWER KEY
1. 6b; 2. 1; 3. 4b; 4. 7a; 5. 2b; 6. 4a

EXPANSION ACTIVITY: Multiple Definitions
○ Write the following words from the chapter on the board: *capital, front, ill, launch, vow*
○ Point out that each of these words has multiple definitions: *capital: net worth, advantage or gain, a city that is the head of the government;
front: a line of battle, the surface or first part, the part of a building that contains the entrance;
ill: unfriendly, sick or unhealthy, difficult or hard;
launch: to throw forward, to introduce
vow: to promise, to swear, to bind two things together.*
○ Have students choose a word and write sentences using the word in two different ways.
○ Put students in pairs to exchange sentences and explain the meanings of the words.

D. In Your Own Words: Summarizing
○ Go over the directions.
○ Have students complete the sentences, using a noun phrase in the first sentence and an independent clause in the second.
○ Call on students to share their ideas with the class.

ANSWER KEY
Answers may vary. Possible answers for the first section include:
1. The section is about the ONE Campaign.
2. The author says that rock singer Bono started the ONE Campaign to combat AIDS and poverty in Africa.

TOEFL® iBT Tip

TOEFL iBT Tip 1: The TOEFL iBT writing section requires examinees to summarize major points and important details from sources. This is more evident in integrated tasks, but this skill can also be applied to independent writing tasks.

○ Point out to students that the strategies throughout this chapter (vocabulary, reference, main idea, details, inference, and paraphrasing skills) will help them to interpret what they hear and read and then write about the topic *in their own words.*

○ Students should be able to summarize the major and minor points from a lecture or reading clearly and concisely and be able to convey the original meaning of the author or speaker.

PART ② GENERAL INTEREST READING
A BANK FOR THE DOWN AND OUT, PAGES 94–97

Before Reading
A. Thinking Ahead

○ Go over the directions and the questions.
○ Have students work in small groups to discuss the questions.
○ Call on students to share their ideas with the class.

ANSWER KEY

Answers may vary.
1. Bangladesh (or India or Pakistan). Women have heads covered, wear saris, and look Asian or Middle Eastern.
2. hard, poor, struggling
3. car, house, boat, property, land, stocks, jewelry

Vocabulary Note

○ *Collateral* and other banking terms may likely be new to students. An excellent source of information detailing borrowing and lending information is the Small Business Administration's website at www.sba.gov/test/wbc/docs/finance/loanqual.html.

Culture Note

○ Natives to Bangladesh are Bengalis. Although Bangla or Bengali is their official language, English is often spoken. Bangladesh is one of the most densely populated countries in the world having over 133 million people on only 133 thousand square kilometers of land. The country has suffered many catastrophes in its short existence; it became a country in 1971. The country suffers famine, disease, frequent flooding, and hurricanes. The capital city is Dhaka, and its government is a parliamentary democracy. There are two major religions: Islam (83%) and Hinduism (16%).

🎧 Reading

○ Go over the directions and the question.
○ Have students read *A Bank for the Down and Out* silently or follow along silently as you play the audio program.

ANSWER KEY

Answers may vary.
Grameen bank issues micro-credit. Loans can be for as little as $30. The bank caters to the extremely poor and destitute.

EXPANSION ACTIVITY: Graphic Organizer

○ Photocopy and distribute the Black Line Master *Graphic Organizer for A Bank for the Down and Out* on page BLM 6.
○ Teach students what a process diagram is and why it is useful.
○ Have students complete the chart and then compare ideas with a partner.
○ Call on students to share their ideas with the class.

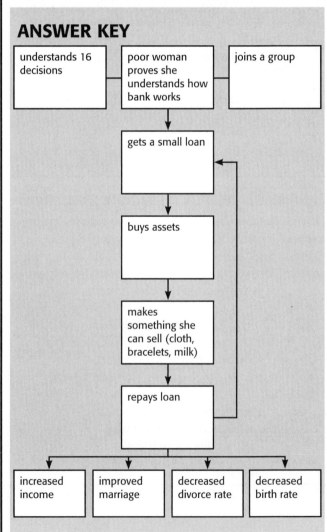

ANSWER KEY

| understands 16 decisions | poor woman proves she understands how bank works | joins a group |

gets a small loan

buys assets

makes something she can sell (cloth, bracelets, milk)

repays loan

| increased income | improved marriage | decreased divorce rate | decreased birth rate |

After Reading

A. Comprehension Check

❍ Go over the directions and the questions.
❍ Put students in pairs to highlight the answers to the questions.
❍ Go over the answers with the class.

ANSWER KEY

1. micro-credit (line 18)—his bank gives loans of as little as $30
2. It actively seeks out the most deprived, yet claims a loan repayment rate of 99 percent.
3. the destitute and women; doesn't require collateral
4. abide by the 16 decisions (join a group of 4)
5. 99 percent

EXPANSION ACTIVITY: Business Plan

❍ Put students in pairs or small groups to create a business plan using micro-credit.
❍ Set a loan limit of $100. Tell students they must use the money to buy something that they can use to begin producing a product. Explain that students must detail how they will spend the money, what they will produce, and their timeline.
❍ Have students present their business plans to the class.
❍ Have the class vote on three plans that should receive the loans.

B. Vocabulary Check

❍ Go over the directions.
❍ Have students match the words and phrases to their definitions and then check the answers with a partner.
❍ Go over the answers with the class.

ANSWER KEY

1. a; 2. g; 3. h; 4. d; 5. k; 6. b; 7. i; 8. f; 9. c; 10. j; 11. e

TOEFL® iBT Tip

TOEFL iBT Tip 2: The TOEFL iBT tests the ability to understand key words and vocabulary contained within a text.

❍ Point out that being able to understand vocabulary in context and make good guesses about the meaning of the words will help students improve their overall vocabulary. The TOEFL iBT readings (and lectures) will incorporate words that may be derived from words that students are familiar with, but forms that may not be as common.

❍ A vocabulary activity that requires students to refer back to the reading and look for a definition that would make sense in the context is a good way to build skills for this type of task on the test.

C. Expansion

❍ Go over the directions and the questions with students.
❍ Have students discuss the "16 decisions" and their answers to the questions in small groups.

ANSWER KEY

Answers will vary.

PART ❸ ACADEMIC READING
DEVELOPING COUNTRIES, PAGES 98–109

Before Reading

A. Thinking Ahead

❍ Go over the directions. Read the questions aloud. Make sure students understand the meanings of the words *obstacle (something that stops progress)* and *inflation (an increase in money that results in goods and services costing more)*.
❍ Direct students' attention to the cartoon. Ask questions: *What do you see? What's in the window? What are the men talking about?*
❍ Put students in small groups to discuss the questions.
❍ Call on students to share their ideas with the class.

ANSWER KEY
Answers will vary.

Academic Note
❍ Point out that in some subject areas, cartoons are often included in student texts (e.g., political science). Explain that cartoons usually use humor to convey the artist's opinion or point of view on a topic. To analyze a cartoon thoroughly, students should be able to comment on the images they see, the words or captions, and how the two work together to express a larger meaning.

EXPANSION ACTIVITY: Cartoon Analysis
❍ Supply cartoons from a news magazine, the Internet, or the opinion-editorial page of a newspaper, or have students bring them in.
❍ Put students in pairs to analyze the message of the cartoon.
❍ Put two pairs together and each pair takes a turn presenting the cartoon and their analysis.

B. Vocabulary Preparation
❍ Go over the directions.
❍ Have students circle the part of speech of the words in orange and write their guesses. Remind students to use a dictionary if necessary.
❍ Go over the answers with the class.

ANSWER KEY
1. n, bad or serious situation; 2. v, make difficult; 3. adj, surrounded by land; 4. v, put out; 5. n, edge; 6. n, money in exchange for political favors; 7. n, something that prevents you from doing something else; v, get rid of completely; 8. n, variations, changes; 9. n, amount given; 10. n, something to encourage you

TOEFL® iBT Tip

TOEFL iBT Tip 3: TOEFL iBT tests the ability to determine the meaning of words in context.

❍ Point out that the activity for *Vocabulary Preparation* will help students improve their vocabulary for the TOEFL iBT. Remind students that in the reading section of the test, scientific or specialty terms and academic vocabulary may be defined in the passage.

❍ Definitions of key words and terms will provide useful clues for questions that may be asked on the test, and should be given careful attention. Students will need to make educated guesses about words they don't know but that seem to be appropriate to the text.

EXPANSION ACTIVITY: Original Sentences
❍ Have students write their own sentences using the new words in Activity B on page 99.
❍ Put students in pairs to read their sentences.
❍ Call on students to read their sentences to the class.

READING STRATEGY: Dealing with Too Much Material: Divide and Conquer
❍ Go over the information in the box.
❍ Ask questions: *What are two strategies you have already learned and practiced to help you deal with extensive reading? What does* reading in depth *mean?*

C. Dealing with Too Much Material
❍ Go over the directions and the steps.
❍ Have students reread the introduction to *Developing Countries* on page 101.
❍ Divide the class into two groups, A and B. Have Group A read Section 1 in depth and Group B read Section 2 in depth. Remind students to follow the steps for reading in depth from the strategy box.

꩜ Reading

○ Have the students read *Developing Countries* or follow along silently as you play the audio program.

Culture Notes

○ Make sure students understand what is meant by the term *developing country.* Elicit examples. You may want to point out examples of more developed countries (e.g., *the United States, Europe, Japan, Korea*) to contrast with the developing countries (e.g., *El Salvador, Nigeria, Bangladesh, Bhutan, Afghanistan*). Some other examples of developing countries are listed in lines 50 and 51.

○ Ferdinand Marcos was the 10th president of the Philippines, serving from 1965 to 1986. In his first term, Marcos opened up markets to free trade, but in his second term, he instituted an authoritarian government. His later years in office were troubled, marked by corruption and increasing dissent.

After Reading

A. Vocabulary Check

○ Go over the directions.
○ Have students write the correct words on the lines for the section their group was responsible for in Activity C on page 42 of the Teacher's Edition.
○ Tell students to share their vocabulary with a member from the other group.
○ Go over the answers with the class.

ANSWER KEY

Section 1: 1. crude birthrate; 2. life expectancy; 3. zero population growth; 4. external debt; 5. capital flight
Section 2: 1. priorities; 2. trade barriers; 3. macroeconomic policies; 4. free enterprise; 5. population density

B. Comprehension Check

○ Go over the directions.
○ Have students complete the appropriate chart for their group and then share ideas with a partner from the other group.
○ Go over the answers with the class.

ANSWER KEY

Ideas from Section 1 (Group A)

	Obstacles	Examples
1.	Population growth	China – lowered birth rate
2.	Natural resources and geography	Japan – engaged in international trade
3.	Education and technology	
4.	Religion	Hindus and Buddhists believe in karma, less incentive to grow economically; Catholicism, Protestantism, and Judaism more compatible with economic growth
5.	External debt	Developing countries
6.	Capital flight	
7.	Corruption	Ferdinand Marcos in the Philippines

Ideas from Section 2 (Group B)

Priorities for Industrialized Nations
1. Reduce trade barriers
2. Reform macroeconomic policies
3. Increase financial support
4. Support policy reform

Priorities for Developing Countries
1. Invest in people
2. Improve climate for free enterprise
3. Open economies to international trade
4. Revise macroeconomic policies

READING STRATEGY: Using a Table to Find Information

○ Go over the information in the box.
○ Ask questions: *Why do textbooks often have tables? Why should you pay attention to tables?*

C. Using a Table to Find Information
❍ Go over the directions.
❍ Direct students' attention to the chart and read the first question. Elicit the answer (*12.21, 45.14*).
❍ Have students work in pairs to answer the questions.
❍ Go over the answers with the class.

ANSWER KEY
1. 12.21, 45.14; 2. $55,100, $1,900; 3. Europe and North America; 4. Africa and Afghanistan; 5. Austria, Niger; 6. Luxembourg, Somalia; 7. The GDP and the crude birthrate are inversely related, as one goes up the other goes down.

CRITICAL THINKING STRATEGY: Synthesizing
❍ Go over the information in the box.
❍ Ask questions: *What do you do when you synthesize? What should you do as you read?*

TOEFL® iBT Tip

TOEFL iBT Tip 4: The TOEFL iBT tests the ability to read a passage, listen to a lecture related to that passage, and then reply in response to a question based on the two stimuli. This integrated speaking skill requires students to think critically about material that they have read, interpret that information, and relate it to a lecture, then present ideas in spoken context. These reading and listening passages will often present a general principle and a counter example, or a problem and solution to which the examinee must formulate a response.

❍ Point out that the test-taking strategy for *Synthesizing* will help students organize their ideas regarding two sides of an issue. They should be able to make logical connections between what they have heard and what they've read and reply to questions about the two sources.

D. Synthesizing
❍ Go over the directions.
❍ Have students discuss the questions in small groups.
❍ Call on students to share their ideas with the class.

ANSWER KEY
Answers may vary.
1. South Korea opened its economy to international trade and revised its macroeconomic policies to decrease deficits.
2. Bono is trying to overcome a lack of education and technology, high crude birthrates (more children, but dying parents), high external debt, and corruption.
3. investing in people
4. investing in people (and free enterprise)

E. Phrases with Prepositions
❍ Go over the directions.
❍ Have students complete the phrases and compare answers with a partner.
❍ Go over the answers with the class.

ANSWER KEY
1. to; 2. to; 3. of; 4. of; 5. in/of; 6. with/of; 7. on/of; 8. in; 9. in

Grammar Notes
❍ A phrase is a group of words, but it does not contain a subject or a verb. Sometimes a phrase will contain neither. Prepositional phrases are comprised of a preposition, an article, and the object of the preposition. They add information about time, place, or direction.
❍ When a prepositional phrase begins a sentence, it should be followed by a comma. Example: During the winter, it snows in Colorado.
❍ When a prepositional phrase ends a sentence, no comma is required. Example: It snows in Colorado during the winter.
❍ When a prepositional phrase adds information in the middle of the sentence, no comma is required. Example: I went to the theater at the Galleria Mall.

F. Word Journal
❍ Go over the directions.
❍ Have students write words in their Word Journals.

G. Response Writing
❍ Go over the directions.
❍ Explain that this is a quick-writing activity and does not have to be perfect. Point out that journal writing can be a warm-up to a more structured writing assignment, helping to generate ideas.
❍ Set a time limit of 15 minutes.
❍ Put students in pairs to read or talk about their writing.

 ## Internet Research
❍ For additional information on poverty and related topics in this chapter, see:
  • www.worldbank.org/aids-econ/vacc/
    accelerateb.pdf
  • www.globalpolicy.org/socecon/bwi-wto/
    bankind.htm
  • www.avert.org/aidsinafrica.htm
  • www.globalissues.org/TradeRelated/Poverty.asp
  • usinfo.state.gov/journals/ites/0901/ijee/
    ijee0901.htm

PART  THE MECHANICS OF WRITING, PAGES 110–115

❍ Go over the information about Part 4.

Using Source Material
❍ Go over the information in the box.
❍ Ask comprehension questions: *When do you need to cite sources? What is plagiarizing? When do you need to use quotation marks?*

Finding Supporting Information
❍ Go over the information in the box.
❍ Ask questions: *When do we have to give support for opinions? What is the first step?*

A. Finding Supporting Information
❍ Go over the directions.
❍ Have students find and highlight the information in the readings that supports the statements.
❍ Call on students to share their ideas with the class.

ANSWER KEY
Answers may vary.
1. in the sidebar; 2. Lines 64–65; 3. Lines 55–56; 4. Lines 13–14; 5. Lines 36–42; 6. Line 65–68; 7. Lines 69–70; 8. Lines 93–95

Introducing Citations
❍ Go over the information in the box.
❍ Ask questions: *What expressions do we use to cite support? Which structures need a comma? When do we use the present tense in a citation? When do we use the past tense?*

B. Introducing Citations
❍ Go over the directions.
❍ Have students use expressions of citation and then copy the supporting sentences on the lines in Activity A (on pages 110–111 of the Student Book).
❍ Have students compare sentences in pairs.
❍ Call on students to share their ideas with the class.

ANSWER KEY:
1. Bono tells the story of a man who wants Bono to take his son so that the son will have a chance to live. Shriver thinks that Bono "is haunted by the unacceptable fact that any father should be faced with such a choice."
2. Jolis reports that "Studies of the Grameen method suggest that after a wife joins the bank, her husband is likely to show her more tenderness and respect."
3. According to Yunus, "The existing system made it certain that the poor could not save a penny."
4. Clayton points out that "Longer life expectancies, coupled with a high crude birthrate, make it difficult to increase per capita GNP."
5. Clayton says that Hindus and Buddhists are less motivated to improve their economic situations because of their belief in *karma*.

ANSWER KEY, continued

6. According to Clayton, Marcos stole at least $500 million from the Philippines as his people lived in poverty.
7. As Clayton says, "Assistance to developing countries helps assure the industrial nations of a stable supply of critical raw materials."
8. Clayton writes that "Governments in developing countries need to invest more in education, family planning, nutrition, and basic health care."

TOEFL® iBT Tip

TOEFL iBT Tip 5: The TOEFL iBT writing section requires examinees to incorporate major points and important details from sources into their writing. This is more evident in integrated tasks, but this skill can also be applied to independent writing tasks.

○ Point out to students that the *Knowing When to Quote and When to Paraphrase* activity will help them to interpret what they read and then write about the topic *in other words.* They can apply the vocabulary skills they learned in other parts of this chapter. They need to be able to cite the quoted material that they are going to incorporate into their writing.

○ Students will benefit from learning the phrases used to introduce a paraphrase and the most frequently used verbs that introduce an idea, such as *asserts that, explains that, offers, argues that, describes, notes, reports that.*

Knowing When to Quote and When to Paraphrase

○ Go over the information in the box.
○ Ask questions: *What is the difference between quoting and paraphrasing? When is it a good time to quote? When is it better to paraphrase?*

C. Noticing Quoted Material

○ Go over the directions.
○ Have students look at the reading to answer the questions about the use of quotes.
○ Call on students to share their ideas with the class.

ANSWER KEY

both, although usually it's because the language is distinctive

D. Using Synonyms

○ Go over the directions.
○ Have students think of other ways to say the phrases.
○ Have students share their ideas in pairs.
○ Call on students to read their sentences with substitutions to the class.

ANSWER KEY

Answers will vary.

E. Choosing Language to Quote

○ Go over the directions.
○ Have students highlight phrases they should quote (special language and technical terms).
○ Put students in small groups to compare ideas.
○ Call on students to share their ideas with the class.

ANSWER KEY

Answers may vary.

One obstacle to economic development is (population growth). The populations of most developing countries grow at a rate much faster than those of industrialized countries. One reason for this growth is the high (crude birthrate)—the number of live births per 1,000 people.

People in many developing countries are also experiencing an increasing (life expectancy)—the average remaining lifetime in years for persons who reach a certain age. Longer life expectancies, coupled with a high (crude birthrate), make it difficult to increase (per capita GNP).

ANSWER KEY, continued

Some countries, like China, have encouraged lower birth rates and smaller families. Some people even feel that societies should work for (zero population growth) (ZPG)—the condition in which the average number of births and deaths balance. Others feel efforts to (disrupt population growth) are wrong from both (moral and religious perspectives).

Choosing the Right Reporting Verb
○ Go over the information in the box.
○ Ask questions: *Which is stronger,* speculate *or* urge? *Which is weaker,* suggest *or* warn? *What expressions should you use when you're not sure?*

F. Choosing the Right Reporting Verb
○ Go over the directions.
○ Have students match the situation with the reporting verb.
○ Have students check their answers with a partner.
○ Go over the answers with the class.

ANSWER KEY
1. d; 2. b; 3. g; 4. e; 5. c; 6. f; 7. a

G. Choosing the Right Reporting Verb
○ Go over the directions.
○ Have students circle the answers and then check their answers with a partner.
○ Go over the answers with the class.

ANSWER KEY
1. B, C, D; 2. C; 3. C, D (The verbs are in the past tense because the quote is famous.); 4. B, D; 5. A, B, D

Weaving in Quotations
○ Go over the information in the box.
○ Ask questions: *What does* weave *mean? How can you "weave in" quotations? How can you make sure your grammar and style are good? What is an exception to the suggestion to weave in quotes?*

H. Error Analysis/Editing
○ Go over the directions and the questions.
○ Have students find and correct the errors and then compare answers with a partner.
○ Go over the answers with the class.

ANSWER KEY
Answers may vary.
1. Correct.
2. *Jolis says that* ∧ Grameen Bank is trying to address the problem of poverty by using a system of micro-credit, which "is both terribly simple and, in the field of development and aid, completely revolutionary." *[no citation]*
3. A woman who borrows from Grameen Bank pays the loan back in small installments. ~~Jolis says, "She repays the loan in tiny installments.~~" *[doesn't support previous sentence, just repeats it]*
4. Grameen Bank borrowers are not able to put up collateral for their loans. Jolis ~~expresses~~ *says* ∧ that "peer pressure and peer support effectively replace collateral." *[inappropriate reporting verb]*
5. When people feel hopeless, the consequences can be serious. ~~As~~ Clayton argues that "the result can be revolution, social upheaval, and even war." *[incorrect use of as]*

EXPANSION ACTIVITY: Editing Practice
○ Photocopy and distribute the Black Line Master *Editing Practice* on page BLM 7.
○ Have students correct the paragraph and then compare ideas with a partner.
○ Go over the answers with the class.

ANSWER KEY
According to Jolis ∧ Mohammud Yunus is a visionary, his dream "the total eradication of poverty from the world.∧" Yunus is attempting to do this

through micro-credit, the lending of very small amounts of money to the destitute. Jolis ~~mentions~~ ^says^ that this idea ^"^is both terribly simple and, in the field of development and aid, completely revolutionary^."^ In order to receive the loan, the borrower must join a group, which Jolis says ~~that~~ "provides a borrower with self-discipline and courage."

A typical borrower from his bank would be a Bangladeshi women/who has never touched money before. Yunus lends her money and doesn't regret it. She uses the loan to buy an asset that can immediately start paying income $\overline{\wedge}$ such as cotton to weave/ or raw materials for bangles to sell/or a cow she can milk. She repays the loan in tiny installments until she becomes self-sufficient. Then if she wants/ she can take out a new, larger loan. Either way, she is no longer poor.

PART ⑤ ACADEMIC WRITING, PAGES 116–120

TEST-TAKING STRATEGY: Summarizing
○ Go over the information in the box.
○ Ask questions: *How is summarizing similar to paraphrasing? What is the difference? What should you do first? What should you leave out?*

Summarizing
○ Go over the directions.
○ Have students follow the steps to write summaries of each passage.
○ Put students in pairs to compare summaries.
○ Call on students to read their summaries to the class.

ANSWER KEY
Answers will vary.

1. Mohammud Yunus is a visionary banker who wants to end poverty, so he invented micro-credit. Yunus loans very poor people, especially women, small amounts of money that they use to buy assets like cotton or a cow. She can earn income immediately and start repaying the loan in small installments.
2. Population growth can discourage economic development. Population growth is a combination of a high crude birthrate (number of live births per 1,000 people) and longer life expectancy (the average remaining years for people who reach a certain age). Some people advocate for zero population growth, while others believe that is wrong both morally and according to their religious beliefs.
3. Belief in certain religions can also discourage economic growth. Buddhists and Hindus are less motivated to improve their financial standing because they believe a simple lifestyle is better for spiritual growth. Catholics, Protestants, and Jews are more likely to support economic development, while Muslims are somewhere in the middle.

WRITING STRATEGY: Writing a Paragraph of Argument: Cause/Effect
○ Go over the information in the box.
○ Ask comprehension questions: *What expressions often tell you that you need to write a cause/effect paragraph? What do you do in the topic sentence? What do you do with source information?*
○ You may want to read the example paragraph aloud as students follow silently in their books.
○ Read the *Analysis* directions. Discuss the questions with the class.

ANSWER KEY
Quotes: extinguish desire and reject the temptations of the material world"; "some cultures may not be as interested in the Western concept of material growth as we imagine."
Paraphrase: the second paragraph of the section on religion is paraphrased, but information on Buddhism is omitted.
The source of the quotes is Clayton.
The evidence is not summarized because the paragraph expresses an opinion without giving any evidence for it.

TOEFL® iBT Tip

TOEFL iBT Tip 6: The integrated writing skill on the TOEFL iBT requires students to think critically about material that they have read, interpret that information and relate it to a lecture, then present ideas in essay format.

○ Point out that the *Writing a Paragraph of Argument: Cause and Effect* activity corresponds to a strategy they will need to use when writing their independent or integrated essays. They will often be given two ideas and asked to argue for or against one of those ideas or show a relationship between the ideas presented.

○ The "process writing" approach will help students organize their thoughts and take meaningful steps toward developing their essays. Students should also be able to apply the grammar skills that they practiced in the *Mechanics of Writing* part of this chapter to writing the cause/effect essay.

○ Go over the list of editing questions in Step E. Have students read and edit their paragraphs, using the questions as a guide. You may wish to have students circle or underline the elements in their paragraphs.

○ For peer editing, have students exchange paragraphs with a partner, edit, and return to the writer. Some students may find peer editing challenging at first. Explain that it is a good way to improve editing skills. It is also easier to see errors in someone else's writing, so it is helpful to have someone else check your writing. With practice, students will become more comfortable with checking a classmate's paragraph.

○ Go over the directions for Step F. Have students carefully rewrite their paragraphs and hand them in to you.

○ After you have read and returned students' paragraphs, you may want to set aside time for students to read each other's writing or display the paragraphs in the classroom. Have students keep all of their final versions in a notebook or folder so that they can see their progress and improvement over time.

Writing Assignment

○ Go over the directions.
○ Have students read the six steps aloud.
○ Direct students' attention to Step A and have students choose one question and country to write about.
○ Focus students' attention on Step B. Go over the directions and the questions. Have students gather support from the readings and their own experience. Then have students interview two classmates to complete the chart.

WRITING STRATEGY: Organizing a Cause/Effect Paragraph: Idea Mapping

○ Go over the information in the box.
○ Ask questions: *What is an idea map? How can you use it to plan your paragraph?*
○ Direct students' attention to Step C. Have students create idea maps for their paragraphs.
○ Direct students' attention to Step D. Have students write paragraphs, using the notes in Step C. Point out that in this step, the most important thing is to write out their ideas. They will edit and revise in the next step.

UNIT 2 ●●●●●● ECONOMICS

CHAPTER 4 THE GLOBAL ECONOMY

In this chapter, students will learn more about the global economy. In Part 1, students will read about the global marketplace and the importance of taking language and cultural differences into account. In Part 2, students will read a newspaper article about language skills necessary in the global marketplace. In Part 3, students will read a section of a textbook on international trade. Part 4 focuses on the mechanics of writing, including present unreal conditionals, conditionals with *without*, transition expressions of cause and effect, and transitions followed by phrases. In Part 5, students will write a paragraph of argument using inductive reasoning.

VOCABULARY

absolute advantage	displace	infant industries argument	nuance	sectors
armament	diversify	interact	opium	slogan
attribute	dumping	jingle	potential	staffing
balance of payments	essential raw materials	levy	print advertisement	sweat
bilingual	exotic	logo	protectionists	take into consideration
campaign	exports	managerial candidates	protective tariff	tariff
comparative advantage	free trader	merchandise	quota	technical support professionals
consumers	goods	most favored nation clause	recruit	turn on and off
country of origin	image	multilingual	retention	undersold
crucial	imports		revenue	volume
deal with	impose		revenue tariff	

READING STRATEGIES

Providing Definitions and Examples to Check
  Understanding
Summarizing Your Reading

CRITICAL THINKING STRATEGIES

Evaluating Sources
Making Connections

MECHANICS

Present Unreal Conditional
Conditionals with *Without*
Transition Expressions of Cause and Effect: Review of
  Coordinating, Adverbial, and Subordinating
  Conjunctions

WRITING STRATEGIES

Writing a Paragraph of Argument: Inductive Reasoning
Providing Evidence

TEST-TAKING STRATEGY

Taking a Side

CHAPTER 4 The Global Economy

Chapter 4 Opening Photo, page 121

❍ Direct students' attention to the photo. Ask them what is happening in the photo.
❍ Have students discuss the questions. This can be done in pairs, in small groups, or as a class.
❍ Check students' predictions of the chapter topic.

ANSWER KEY
Answers will vary.

PART ① INTRODUCTION THE GLOBAL MARKETPLACE, PAGES 122–126

EXPANSION ACTIVITY: Sort by Category

❍ Explain the activity. Tell students that you will give them a question to ask classmates. Then they will move around the classroom, asking the question and standing with people who have the same or similar answers to the question.
❍ Ask: *What's your favorite fast-food restaurant?* Remind students to move around and talk to each other, so that they can group themselves according to response. When students are grouped, ask each group what they represent. Ask students to explain why they like the restaurant.
❍ Ask additional questions related to the topics in the chapter. Create your own or use the ones below. This activity is meant to warm students up to the topics and help them anticipate content.
What's your favorite soft drink?
What's your favorite car?
What skill do you think is most important in the global marketplace?

Before Reading

Thinking Ahead

❍ Have students look at the photos on page 122.
❍ Go over the directions and questions.
❍ Have students discuss the questions in small groups.
❍ Call on students to share their ideas with the class.

ANSWER KEY
Answers may vary.
McDonald's
Coca-Cola
Nokia
Toyota

B. Discussion

❍ Go over the directions.
❍ Put students in small groups to complete the chart.
❍ Call on students to share their ideas with the class.

ANSWER KEY

Answers may vary. Suggested answers for the Slogan column and the Coca-Cola row are listed below.

Companies/ Products	Slogans	Jingles or Other Music	Famous People	Differences in Another Country or Language
McDonald's/ fast food	"I'm lovin' it."	Yes: hip-hop version of "I'm lovin' it."	Serena Williams	Yao Ming appears in ad in China
Coca-Cola/soft drinks	"Coca-Cola Enjoy" "Life Tastes Good" "All the world loves a Coke"	"I'd like to teach the world to sing"	Bill Cosby Whitney Houston Michael Jordan	In 2003, Coca-Cola launched a new graphic in Chinese script.
Toyota/cars and trucks	Toyota. Moving Forward Get the Feeling. Toyota. Drive Your Dreams. The car in front is a Toyota. I love what you do for me— Toyota! Your new experience of motoring			
Nokia/cell phones	Life goes mobile Connecting people			

Culture Note

○ Coca-Cola frequently changes and updates its slogans. Students might also be familiar with these slogans in the U.S.:

1963 "Things Go Better with Coke"
1970 "It's the Real Thing"
1971 "I'd Like to Buy The World a Coke"
1975 "Look Up America"
1976 "Coke Adds Life"
1979 "Have a Coke and a Smile"
1982 "Coke Is It!"
1985 "We've Got a Taste for You"
1986 "Catch The Wave - Red White, & You"
1989 "Can't Beat the Feeling"
1990 "Can't Beat the Real Thing"
1993 "Always Coca-Cola"
1993 "Taste It All"

 EXPANSION ACTIVITY: Internet Research

○ Put students in small groups. Have each group choose a product type (e.g., car) and each group member choose a company (e.g., Volkswagen).
○ Have students use a search engine and enter the name of their company and the word *slogans*. Tell students to write down at least two slogans for that company.
○ Have students meet with their small groups and compare slogans. Ask the groups to decide on the one or two best slogans for their product type.
○ Call on representatives of each group to share their ideas with the class.

 Reading

○ Have students look at the reading.
○ Go over the directions and the question.
○ Have students read *Lost in Translation* silently or have students follow along silently as you play the audio program.

ANSWER KEY

They must take into consideration the languages and the cultures in which they want to do business.

After Reading

A. Comprehension Check
- ○ Go over the directions.
- ○ Have students highlight the sentences in the reading that answer the questions.
- ○ Go over the answers with the class.

ANSWER KEY
1. consider language and culture so they don't make mistakes
2. Language: Electrolux, T-shirt, Parker Pen, Schweppes, Pocari Sweat; Culture: Opium
3. Customers could be offended (Opium).
4. Answers will vary.

B. Vocabulary Check
- ○ Go over the directions.
- ○ Have students write the words or phrases on the lines.
- ○ Put students in pairs to check their answers.
- ○ Go over the answers with the class.

ANSWER KEY
1. take into consideration; 2. potential; 3. image; 4. goods; 5. campaign; 6. sweat; 7. opium

C. Understanding Details
- ○ Go over the directions.
- ○ Have students complete the graphic organizer and then compare answers in small groups.
- ○ Go over the answers with the class.

ANSWER KEY

Slogans/Products	→	Problems
Nothing sucks like an Electrolux.		"Sucks" is American slang for "to be very bad."
T-shirt "I saw the potato."		Mistranslated "pope" to "potato" in Spanish
Parker Pen "It won't leak in your pocket and make you pregnant."		Translated "embarass" into Spanish as "embarazar" which is to be pregnant
Schwepps toilet water		Italian translation of "tonic" to "toilet"
Pocari Sweat		"Sweat" in English isn't something you want to drink.

TOEFL® iBT Tip

TOEFL iBT Tip 1: The TOEFL iBT tests the ability to understand key facts and the important information contained within a text. Locating details and key words in a text will help students build vocabulary and improve their reading skills.

- ○ Point out that the reading section of the TOEFL iBT may require examinees to identify information that is NOT included in the reading.

- ○ The *Understanding Details* activity helps students locate more than one fact presented in a passage. This will help to scaffold students' abilities upward toward mastering the *negative fact question* on the test.

D. Discussion

○ Go over the directions.
○ Put students in small groups to discuss the questions.
○ Call on students to share their ideas with the class.

EXPANSION ACTIVITY: Marketing Mistakes

○ Have students do Internet research by searching for *marketing mistakes*.
○ Put students in small groups to share examples of marketing mistakes that were made because of a lack of knowledge about language or culture.
○ Call on students to share what they found out with the class.
○ Challenge students to write a new advertisement that would correct the marketing mistake.
○ Have students present their new marketing to the class.

PART   GENERAL INTEREST READING
SKILLS FOR THE GLOBAL MARKETPLACE, PAGES 127–132

Before Reading
A. Thinking Ahead

○ Go over the directions and the questions.
○ Have students work in small groups to discuss the questions.
○ Call on students to share their ideas with the class.

ANSWER KEY
Answers will vary.

EXPANSION ACTIVITY: Write Your Ad

○ Have students work individually to list skills or qualities that they have that might be useful in the global marketplace.
○ Put students in pairs to talk about their ideas.
○ Have students write classified ads to describe themselves and their skills and qualities.
○ Call on students to read their ads to the class.
○ Elicit ideas for appropriate jobs for that skill set.

EXPANSION ACTIVITY: Previewing Using Pictures and Captions

○ Remind students that they learned and practiced previewing using pictures and captions in Chapter 2 on page 63 of the Student Book.
○ Have students read the title of the passage and preview the pictures and captions.
○ Have students write three predictions about the content of the reading.
○ Write predictions on the board and compare the predictions to the facts after students read the passage.

Reading

○ Go over the directions and the questions.
○ Have students read *Skills for the Global Marketplace* silently or follow along silently as you play the audio program.

ANSWER KEY

There is a growing immigrant population in America that is not fluent in English. American companies are becoming more global—expanding their operations overseas and that requires employees speak another language.

Culture Note

❍ Many U.S. businesses outsource their call centers to countries such as India. Employees in India are often well-trained in the English language and technically literate with computers. Workers are often highly-skilled and well educated and an increasing number of call-center employees are college graduates. Because so many companies are using centers in India, the number of employers based in India is growing, and India could easily become the largest hub of call centers worldwide. Call centers often provide contact and business services and handle customer relations and technology problems.

After Reading

A. Comprehension Check

❍ Go over the directions.
❍ Put students in pairs to discuss the questions.
❍ Go over the answers with the class.

ANSWER KEY

1. There is a growing immigrant population in the U.S. that is not fluent in English, and American companies are becoming more global.
2. pharmaceutical, life sciences, technology, and financial services
3. consumer services—banking, retailing, telecommunications
4. Spanish
5. NPR, documentaries, action movies, sitcoms
6. They have an accent. A typical caller is someone in middle America who has never spoken to someone with an accent before.

Grammar Note

❍ You may want to point out that simplified grammatical structures in the headlines and subheads of newspaper articles are common to save space.

EXPANSION ACTIVITY: Call Centers

❍ Remind students that T-charts are a good way to organize information about advantages and disadvantages.
❍ Have students create T-charts to record their ideas.
❍ Put students in pairs to list advantages and disadvantages for outsourcing call centers to other countries.
❍ Call on students to share their ideas with the class.

B. Vocabulary Check

❍ Go over the directions.
❍ Have students match the definitions to the words and phrases and then check their answers in pairs.
❍ Call on students to share their ideas with the class.

ANSWER KEY

1. e; 2. g; 3. l; 4. a; 5. c; 6. k; 7. i; 8. j; 9. h; 10. f; 11. d; 12. b

C. Words with Multiple Definitions

❍ Go over the directions.
❍ Have students write the number of the definition on each line.
❍ Go over the answers with the class.

ANSWER KEY

1. 5b; 2. 1; 3. 5a; 4. 6a

CRITICAL THINKING STRATEGY: Evaluating Sources

❍ Go over the information in the box.
❍ Ask questions: *What are sources? How do you know who or what is a good source? What information about a source is often included in an article?*

D. Evaluating Sources

❍ Go over the directions.
❍ Have students answer the questions.
❍ Go over the answers with the class.

ANSWER KEY

1. She is a vice president of recruiting and retention at a staffing firm.
   Companies are becoming more global.
2. president of global marketing at Korn Ferry International
   The demand for bilingual managerial candidates in pharmaceutical, life sciences, technology, and financial services is increasing.
3. She's a regional director of an employment services firm.
   To give a statistic about the percentage of staff who are bilingual

E. Citing Sources

○ Go over the directions and the questions.
○ Elicit examples of direct quotes, paraphrasing, and reporting verbs.

ANSWER KEY

Direct quote: "It comes out more even, so somebody in North America is able to easily understand them," she said. "In the language group, our goal customer is the person in middle America that's never really spoken to anyone with an accent before. As long as they can understand them and deal with them without having any problem, we're O.K."
Paraphrasing: Koehler said the workers' Indian accent never goes away, but she does hear echoes of NPR in their language sometimes.
Reporting verb: said

EXPANSION ACTIVITY: Correct or Incorrect Inferences?

○ Model the activity. Say a statement about the information in the article on pages 127–129 (e.g., *Koehler wants students to listen to more information programs than entertainment*) and elicit if the inference is correct or incorrect and why (*correct – She likes workers to listen to NPR and watch Ken Burns documentaries*).
○ Have students write three inferences based on the article. Remind students to make some true and some false.

○ Put students in pairs to challenge their partners to guess which statements are true and which are false.
○ Call on students to read their statements to the class, and elicit if the inference is correct or incorrect.

F. In Your Own Words: Summarizing

○ Go over the directions.
○ Have students complete the sentences.
○ Call on students to share their ideas with the class.

ANSWER KEY

Answers may vary. Possible answers for the first section include:

1. The article is about bilingual employees in the U.S.
2. The author says that American companies have an increasing need for bilingual employees because companies are becoming more global.

G. Application

○ Go over the directions.
○ Put students in small groups to brainstorm things Indian call-center employees should know about their cultures and ways to acquire this knowledge.
○ Call on students to share their ideas with the class.

H. Making Connections

○ Go over the directions.
○ Have students discuss the questions in small groups.
○ Call on students to share their ideas with the class.

TOEFL® iBT Tip

TOEFL iBT Tip 2: The TOEFL iBT tests the ability to understand key facts and the important information contained within a text. Locating key words in a text will help students build vocabulary and improve their reading skills.

❍ Point out that students will benefit from doing the *Making Connections* activity that focuses on making connections between ideas in order to prepare for the classification/matching details question type.

❍ This activity requires students to connect and organize information. It will help to scaffold students' abilities upward toward mastering the schematic table questions on the test.

PART ③ ACADEMIC READING
INTERNATIONAL TRADE, PAGES 133–145

Before Reading
A. Thinking Ahead
❍ Go over the directions.
❍ Have students discuss the questions in small groups.
❍ Call on students to share their ideas with the class.

ANSWER KEY
1. Answers will vary.
2. Possible answers include: The middle eastern countries of OPEC specialize in oil production because of their access to this rare resource. Having few natural resources, Japan specializes in technological innovation. The Bahamas and many other small island nations specialize in tourism.
3. Possible answers include: Many people object to international trade because they feel that it harms local workers and traditional values.
4. Answers will vary.
5. Answers will vary.

EXPANSION ACTIVITY: Where Is It From?
❍ For an in-class activity, have students look at the labels of 10 items in the classroom to find "Made in _____" information. For an out-of-class assignment, have students check the labels on 10 items at a store.
❍ Put students in pairs or small groups to share what they found out.
❍ Call on students to tell the class what they found out. Ask questions: *Where were most items made? What does that tell you about international trade?*

B. Vocabulary Preparation
❍ Go over the directions.
❍ Have students circle the part of speech and then write the definitions for the words or phrases.
❍ Go over the answers with the class.

ANSWER KEY
1. adj, unusual, foreign; 2. n, necessary natural things; 3. noun used as an adjective, income; 4. v, sold for less; 5. v, make someone pay; 6. noun used as an adjective, weaponry; 7. adj, very important; 8. v, make leave, take the place of; 9. n, amount; 10. v, were put on

C. Previewing: Using Headings
❍ Go over the directions.
❍ Have students answer the questions and then compare ideas with a partner.
❍ Go over the answers with the class.

ANSWER KEY
1. Absolute and Comparative Advantage, Barriers to International Trade
2. The U.S. and International Trade, The Basis for Trade
3. three
4. Restricting International Trade, Arguments for Protection
5. seven smaller-sized
5. Answers will vary.

🎧 Reading

○ Go over the directions before the reading. Read the questions aloud.
○ Have students read *International Trade* silently or play the audio program and have students follow along silently.
○ Elicit answers to the questions from the class.

ANSWER KEY

International trade is necessary because without it, many products would not be available on the world market.
Pros of international trade: Trade increases total world output by promoting specialization where relative advantages exist. Competition puts pressure on industries to modernize.
Cons of international trade: Trade may harm national defense and infant industries, reduce domestic jobs, and harm the balance of payments.
The reading was written for students in the U.S. You can tell because most of the examples are about America.

Pronunciation Note

○ You may want to point out we can indicate headings when we read aloud. Usually we pause before and after a heading to set it apart from the text that precedes and follows it.

EXPANSION ACTIVITY: Heading Dictation

○ Play the audio program for *International Trade*.
○ Have students listen with books closed and write the headings they hear.
○ Go over the answers with the class.

After Reading

A. Comprehension Check

○ Go over the directions.
○ Put students in pairs to discuss the questions.
○ Call on students to share their ideas with the class.

ANSWER KEY

1. International trade is necessary because of specialization–some products, including necessities, are available only in certain parts of the world.
2. Pros–may be cheaper to import than manufacture, may be able to get something otherwise unavailable, increases total world output
Cons–can displace industries and workers

Academic Note

○ You may want to direct students' attention to the figures in the reading and make sure they know how to interpret the information in the figures. Figures often provide a visual representation of information in the text, but like tables, often present information that is somewhat different from that in the text. In this reading, the text gives a summary of Figure 1 and a more complete analysis of Figure 2.

EXPANSION ACTIVITY: Text to Figure Comparison

○ Photocopy and distribute the Black Line Master *Comparing Information from Text and Illustrations* on page BLM 8.
○ Have students complete the graphic organizer as they look at *International Trade* and then compare ideas with a partner.
○ Call on students to share their ideas with the class.

ANSWER KEY

Topic	Information in Text	Information in Illustrations
U.S. imports from other countries	$1,590 billion in 2003 $5,460 for every person; Counting services and merchandise would make numbers bigger Import minerals, metals, and raw materials	$131 billion from Japan, $201 bil. from Canada, $215 bil. from Europe, $42 bil. from OPEC, $10 billion from Australia

U.S. exports to other countries	Biggest trade imbalance with Japan, then Western Europe and Canada	$56 bil. to Japan, $167bil. to Canada, $163 bil. to Europe, $264 bil. to rest of world, $19 bil. to OPEC
Oil producing countries	NA	Algeria, Indonesia, Iran, Iraq, Kuwait, Libya, Nigeria, Qatar, Saudi Arabia, UAE, Venezuela
Absolute advantage	Definition Ex.: Alpha and Beta are same size; climate and soil differ Coffee—Alpha can produce 40 mil, Beta 6 mil; Cashews—Alpha can produce 8, Beta 6 Alpha has absolute for both	Before specialization graph
Comparative advantage	Definition Alpha comparative advantage in coffee; Beta comparative advantage in cashews	Opportunity costs Effect of specialization Alpha: 1 cashew = 5 coffee Beta: 1 cashew = 1 coffee

B. Vocabulary Check
○ Go over the directions.
○ Have students write the correct words or phrases on the lines and then check their answers with a partner.
○ Go over the answers with the class.

ANSWER KEY
1. absolute advantage; 2. comparative advantage; 3. tariff; 4. quota; 5. protective tariff; 6. revenue tariff; 7. dumping; 8. protectionists; 9. free traders; 10. infant industries argument; 11. balance of payments

READING STRATEGY: Providing Definitions and Examples to Check Understanding
○ Go over the information in the box.
○ Ask questions: *What is a good way to check your understanding of new concepts? What is one way you can record definitions and examples?*

C. Providing Definitions and Examples to Check Understanding
○ Go over the directions.
○ Put students in pairs to fill in the graphic organizers.
○ Go over the answers with the class.

ANSWER KEY

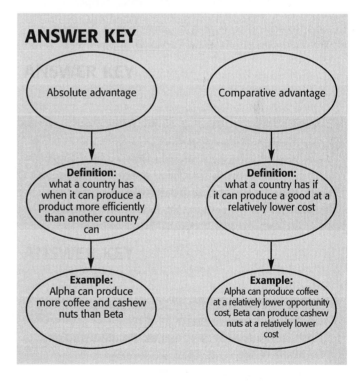

D. Discussion
○ Go over the directions.
○ Have students answer the questions in small groups.
○ Go over the answers with the class.

ANSWER KEY

Answers may vary. Possible answers include:

1. The U.S. is very involved in international trade. It depends on oil imports from Canada, South America, and the Middle East. It imports most of its manufactured goods from Asia. It sells entertainment and media around the world.
2. Answers will vary.
3. A large country may be able to produce all goods more efficiently than a small country. However, it will specialize in those goods for which its advantage is the *greatest,* creating a need to import other products. A smaller country can then export those products to the larger one, even though it produces them less efficiently.
4. revenue tariffs, protective tariffs, and quotas
5. National defense: Imports make countries too dependent on foreign countries for resources they might need in a war. Infant industries: New industries need time to grow before competing with larger foreign companies. Protecting domestic jobs: Barriers to trade protect workers from losing their jobs to foreigners. Keeping the money at home: restricting imports will keep money from moving to other countries. Balance of payments: Restricting imports means countries will receive more money from abroad than they spend abroad.

READING STRATEGY: Summarizing Your Reading

○ Go over the information in the box.
○ Ask questions: *When do you need to write summaries of your reading? How can summarizing be helpful?*

E. Summarizing Your Reading

○ Go over the directions.
○ Have students write summaries. Remind students to refer to page 116 of the Student Book for a guideline on how to summarize.
○ Put students in pairs to compare their summaries.

F. Application

○ Go over the directions.
○ Have students discuss the questions in small groups.
○ Call on students to share their ideas with the class.

ANSWER KEY

Answers will vary.

G. Phrases with Prepositions

○ Go over the directions.
○ Have students complete the phrases with the correct prepositions and then compare their answers with the phrases in the reading.
○ Go over the answers with the class.

ANSWER KEY

1. in; 2. for; 3. to/of; 4. to; 5. to; 6. on/of; 7. out of; 8. on; 9. against; 10. on/for

---

TOEFL® iBT Tip

TOEFL iBT Tip 3: The TOEFL iBT tests the ability to determine the meaning of words in context. Examinees will also be expected to produce sophisticated language in their essays and in the speaking section of the test.

○ Point out that the activity *Phrases with Prepositions* will help students improve their overall vocabulary for the TOEFL iBT. Idioms and phrases with prepositions are an important component of language fluency. Understanding and using these expressions is important across all the skills areas of the test—particularly in the integrated tasks.

H. Word Journal

○ Go over the directions.
○ Have students write words in their Word Journals.

I. Response Writing

○ Go over the directions.
○ Explain that this is a quick-writing activity and does not have to be perfect. Point out that response writing can be a warm-up to a more structured writing assignment, helping to generate ideas.
○ Set a time limit of 15 minutes.
○ Put students in pairs to read or talk about their writing.

Internet Research

○ For additional information on international trade, see:
  • ita.doc.gov/td/industry/otea/
  • tse.export.gov/
  • trade.gov/index.asp
  • tse.export.gov/NTDHome.aspx?UniqueURL=2fs1d1 553e1eir454jm2u1jm-2006-4-8-12-49-48
  • www.usitc.gov/
  • www.intracen.org/tradstat/welcome.htm

EXPANSION ACTIVITY: Country Research

○ Have your students choose a country to do Internet research on.
○ Direct students to the preceding websites or have them find websites on their own. Ask students to find out about the trade balance between that country and the United States (or another country). They should get information about specific products traded, exports, imports, and any tariffs.
○ Put students in small groups to present what they found out.

PART ④ THE MECHANICS OF WRITING, PAGES 146–151

○ Go over the information about Part 4.

Present Unreal Conditional

○ Go over the information on the present unreal conditional.
○ Ask comprehension questions: *When do we use the present unreal conditional? What tense do we use in the if clause? What tense do we use in the result clause? When do we use a comma?*

A. Present Unreal Conditional

○ Go over the directions and the example.
○ Have students complete the sentences.
○ Have students compare sentences in pairs.
○ Call on students to share their ideas with the class.

ANSWER KEY

Answers will vary.

TOEFL® iBT Tip

TOEFL iBT Tip 4: Although the TOEFL iBT does not discretely test grammar skills, examinees' essay scores will be determined based on the range of grammar and vocabulary used in their essays.

○ Point out that the grammar activities in *The Mechanics of Writing* part of this chapter will help them improve their use of conditionals for essay writing. Practice and mastery of the conditional forms and the use of appropriate modals with this grammatical structure will help them express their ideas in argumentative or cause-effect essays.

○ The better students are able to use grammatical structures correctly and effectively in their essays, the better score they will receive on the integrated and independent writing tasks.

EXPANSION ACTIVITY: What Would Happen If?

○ Model the activity. Ask a question beginning with *What would happen if . . .* (*What would happen if you won the lottery?*) and elicit answers with infinitives of purpose (*I would buy a house for my parents*).
○ Have students write five questions to ask a classmate.
○ Put students in pairs to take turns asking and answering questions. Remind students to use the present unreal conditional in their answers.
○ Call on students to share their answers with the class.

Conditionals with *Without*

❍ Go over the information in the box.
❍ Ask: *What is another way to express a present unreal conditional? What is different grammatically between this structure and using an* if *clause?*

Grammar Note
❍ Make sure students understand that in this structure, there is only one clause, a main clause, and it is used with a phrase beginning with *without*. This is different from the usual way of expressing a present unreal conditional that has two clauses, an *if* clause expressing condition and a result clause.

B. Conditionals with *Without*

❍ Go over the directions.
❍ Have students transform the sentences into statements with *without*.
❍ Call on students to read their sentences to the class.

ANSWER KEY

1. Without trade barriers, a country could become too specialized and dependent on other countries.
2. Without a revenue tariff on imported tomatoes, we couldn't protect domestic producers from foreign competition.
3. Without quotas on steel imports, domestic steelworkers would lose their jobs.
4. Without intense competition, prices would be much higher.
5. Without multilingual employees, the agency wouldn't be able to produce ads that work in different countries.
6. Without protection, infant industries wouldn't be able to compete against foreign imports.

Transition Expressions of Cause and Effect: Review of Coordinating, Adverbial, and Subordinating Conjunctions

❍ Go over the information in the box.
❍ Ask questions: *What is a coordinating conjunction that means because? What is an adverbial conjunction that is similar to so? When do we use commas? What expressions are followed by phrases, not clauses?*

C. Transition Expressions of Cause and Effect

❍ Go over the directions.
❍ Have students complete the paragraphs with transition expressions of cause and effect.
❍ Have students compare their ideas in small groups.
❍ Call on students to share their ideas with the class.

ANSWER KEY

Answers may vary.
1. Because, Since, As; 2. Consequently, As a result; 3. as, because; 4. Because of, Due to; 5. Due to, Because of; 6. As a result, For this reason

D. Error Analysis/Editing

❍ Go over the directions.
❍ Have students find and correct the errors.
❍ Go over the answers with the class.

ANSWER KEY

1. If we ~~don't~~ *didn't* have intense competition, prices would be much higher.
2. Indian call-center employees could get a higher salary if they ~~study~~ *studied* American culture and conversation techniques.
3. Because ~~of~~ American TV programs such as *Friends* contain a lot of cultural information, some call-center employee-training courses in India use them.
4. Without international trade ~~did not exist~~, many products would not be available on the world market.
5. The manufacturers of *Opium* perfume did not adequately analyze American culture. As a result ~~of~~, they offended some American consumers.
6. James ~~can~~ *could* get a job with Electrolux if he spoke Swedish.

EXPANSION ACTIVITY: Editing Practice

❍ Photocopy and distribute the Black Line Master *Editing Practice* on page BLM 9.
❍ Have students correct the sentences and then compare ideas with a partner.
❍ Go over the answers with the class.

ANSWER KEY

Answers may vary.

1. If there ~~are~~ ^were^ no trade barriers, more domestic workers would be displaced.

2. If the company researched the language and culture^,^ it would know that the product name was inappropriate.

3. Without ~~I didn't have~~ a driver's license, I couldn't drive.

4. The United States ~~is~~ ^would be^ in better shape economically if it didn't have to import so much oil.

5. Call centers in India and other countries ~~will~~ ^would^ be more accepted by American customers if their employees spoke English with a less-pronounced accent.

6. Customer-service centers would be less effective without ~~they had more~~ bilingual workers.

7. ~~Due to~~ ^Because^ we import so much from Japan, we have a trade imbalance.

8. "Sucks" in American slang has a negative connotation^;^ therefore^,^ the Electrolux ad campaign was not successful.

PART ⑤ ACADEMIC WRITING, PAGES 152–155

WRITING STRATEGY: Writing a Paragraph of Argument: Inductive Reasoning

❍ Go over the information in the box.
❍ Ask comprehension questions: *What is inductive reasoning? What is one strategy you can use to begin the inductive reasoning process? How can you convince your readers? What should your topic sentence be?*
❍ Read the example paragraph aloud as students follow silently in their books.
❍ Read the *Analysis* directions.
❍ Elicit answers from the class.

ANSWER KEY

It moves from specific to general. The writer cites Bob Grabowski's report in *Staffing Magazine*. The topic sentence is the last sentence.

TOEFL® iBT Tip

TOEFL iBT Tip 5: Both the integrated and independent essays of the TOEFL iBT will be scored based on how well the examinee completes the overall writing task.

❍ Point out that the *Writing a Paragraph of Argument: Inductive Reasoning* strategy will help students improve their coherence and the flow of ideas in their independent and integrated essays by taking smaller steps in their essay development. Demonstrating the use of inductive reasoning in an essay is a challenge for students at this level, but they should be able to achieve this goal by using strategies to present and argue their opinions.

❍ Remind students that working at the paragraph level and demonstrating the ability to support their opinions more concisely will improve their overall essay scores.

Writing Assignment

○ Go over the information in the box.
○ Have students read the six steps.
○ Direct students' attention to Step A and have students choose one of the arguments to write about.

TEST-TAKING STRATEGY: Taking a Side

○ Go over the information in the box.
○ Ask: *What does it mean to take a side? What side should you choose to argue? Why?*

Taking a Side

○ Go over the directions.
○ Set a time limit of five minutes for students to read the statements and choose a position on each.
○ Put students in pairs to discuss their positions. You may wish to do the following Expansion Activity as a variation.
○ Call on students to share their ideas with the class.

TOEFL® iBT Tip

TOEFL iBT Tip 6: In the independent and integrated writing sections of the test, students may be required to demonstrate the ability to take a position and defend it, or express an opinion and support it.

○ The strategy for *Taking a Side* will help students learn the "chunks" of language that pertain to varying degrees of agreement/disagreement.

○ In the integrated task, students will be asked to compare and contrast points of view taken in a lecture or presented in the reading and draw information from each source to show that contrast. Learning whole phrases and how and when to use them will help students respond more concisely and completely to the writing task.

EXPANSION ACTIVITY: Vote with Your Feet

○ Write *Agree* on one side of the board and *Disagree* on the other.

○ Call a small group of students to the board. Tell students that you will read one of the statements from *Taking a Side*. They should move to the word that expresses the side they want to argue.
○ Read the first statement and have the students move. Call on a student from the *Agree* side to state one argument in favor of the position. Call on a student from the *Disagree* side to counter. Continue alternating positions until one side is out of arguments. Continue the activity with other students and statements.

○ Direct students' attention to Step B. Go over the directions and the chart. Put students in small groups to complete the chart.

ANSWER KEY

Answers will vary.

WRITING STRATEGY: Providing Evidence

○ Go over the information in the box.
○ Ask questions: *What can you use as evidence in an argument paragraph? What kind of evidence is reliable?*

○ Direct students' attention to Step C. Go over the directions and have students write notes on their evidence.
○ Direct students' attention to Step D. Have students write their paragraphs.
○ Direct students' attention to Step E. Go over the questions. Have students read and edit their paragraphs, using the questions as a guide.
○ For peer editing, have students exchange paragraphs with a partner, edit, and return to the writer.
○ Go over the directions for Step F. Have students carefully rewrite their paragraphs and hand them in to you.
○ After you have read and returned students' paragraphs, you may want to set aside time for students to read each other's writing or display the paragraphs in the classroom. Have students keep all of their final versions in a notebook or folder so that they can see their progress and improvement over time.

Unit 2 Vocabulary Workshop

A. Matching
○ Read the directions.
○ Have students match the definitions to the words.
○ Go over the answers.

ANSWER KEY
1. k; 2. f; 3. b; 4. c; 5. i; 6. j; 7. g; 8. e; 9. a; 10. h;
11. l; 12. d

B. Phrases Using Prepositions
○ Review prepositions as a class.
○ Have students write the correct preposition on the line.
○ Go over the answers.

ANSWER KEY
1. to; 2. of; 3. in/of; 4. with/of; 5. on/of; 6. in; 7. to;
8. to/of; 9. on; 10. on/for

C. The Academic Word List
○ Read the directions. Remind students the Academic
   Word List consists of some of the most commonly
   used words in English.
○ Have students write the correct words on the lines.
○ Go over the answers.

ANSWER KEY
1. Fluctuations; 2. quota; 3. displace; 4. volume;
5. imposed; 6. barriers; 7. crucial; 8. interact;
9. sectors; 10. attributed

D. Vocabulary Expansion
○ Read the directions.
○ Have students complete the chart with the proper
   parts of speech.
○ Go over the answers.

ANSWER KEY

	Verbs	Nouns	Adjectives
1.	eradicate	eradication	eradicated
2.	stabilize	stabilization stability	stable
3.	fluctuate	fluctuation	fluctuating
4.	displace	displacement	displaced
5.	recruit	recruit recruitment	recruited
6.	allocate	allocation	allocated
7.	impose	imposition	imposed
8.	purify	purity	pure

Unit Opener, page 159

○ Direct students' attention to the photo on page 159. Ask questions: *Who do you see in the picture? Where is she? How is she feeling? Why do you think so?*
○ Brainstorm ideas for what the unit will include and write student ideas on the board.

CHAPTER 5 THE NATURE OF POETRY

In this chapter, students will learn about poetry and how to analyze it. In Part 1, students will read an article about science and engineering professors who studied poetry for a week. In Part 2, students will read about how to appreciate poetry and analyze three poems. In Part 3, students will read and analyze three more poems. Part 4 focuses on the mechanics of writing, including expressing possibility and probability, using phrases for symbols, using similes with *as . . . as,* and avoiding and repairing problems with sentence structure. Finally, in Part 5, students will write a paragraph of analysis about the meaning of one poem.

VOCABULARY

analysis	end rhymes	layer	patterns	symbols
analyze	essay	lyric poem	put back	theme
bewildered	face	metaphors	quatrain	title
clear-cut	field	muss up	recite	tormented
closed form	figurative language	mythology	rhythm	total effect
couplet	formulas	narrative poem	similes	wood
course	free verse	open form	speaker	
deferred	imagery	outbreak	stanzas	
diverged	it doesn't make any sense	paper	surface	

READING STRATEGIES

Choosing the Correct Dictionary Definition: Using Parts
  of Speech
Analyzing Poems
Stating the Theme of a Poem: The Topic and Main Idea

CRITICAL THINKING STRATEGIES

Thinking Ahead
Discovering the Meaning of a Poem
Making Inferences
Note: The strategy in bold is highlighted in the Student
  Book.

MECHANICS

Expressing Possibility and Probability
Using Phrases for Symbols
Using Similes with *as . . . as*
Avoiding and Repairing Problems with Sentence
  Structure

WRITING STRATEGIES

Planning a Paragraph of Analysis: Idea Mapping
Writing a Paragraph of Analysis

TEST-TAKING STRATEGY

Hedging and Avoiding Overstatement

CHAPTER 5 The Nature of Poetry

Chapter 5 Opener, page 161
○ Direct students' attention to the photo. Ask them what is happening in the photo.
○ Have students discuss the questions. This can be done in pairs, in small groups, or as a class.
○ Check students' predictions of the chapter topic.

Culture Note
○ The photo is of Langston Hughes, a famous African-American poet (1902–1967). Among other works, he wrote 16 books of poems, two novels, and 20 plays. Students will read one of his poems in Part 3 of this chapter.

PART 1 INTRODUCTION
POETRY LESSONS, PAGES 162–166

EXPANSION ACTIVITY: Pair Interview
○ Write these questions on the board: *What type of classes do you like best? What class activities do you enjoy the most? Who was your favorite teacher and why?*
○ Model the activity. Describe a favorite teacher and why you liked him or her.
○ Put students in pairs to take turns describing their favorite classes, activities, and teachers.
○ Call on students to tell the class about their partner's ideas.

Before Reading

CRITICAL THINKING STRATEGY: Thinking Ahead
Thinking ahead is an important critical thinking strategy used throughout the text. By looking at and discussing photos, students can anticipate the content of the reading. Predicting and anticipating content helps students understand new material.

A. Thinking Ahead
○ Have students look at the photos on page 162.
○ Go over the directions and questions.
○ Have students discuss the questions in small groups.
○ Call on students to share their ideas with the class.

ANSWER KEY
Answers may vary. Possible answers include:
1. The slouching students on the left look bored; the smiling students on the right look interested.
2. In the second picture, students are seated close together at a table. They appear to be sharing their notes and discussing their work. In the first picture, students are at separate desks. The second picture shows an active, discussion-based teaching method, and the first picture shows a passive, lecture-based teaching method.
3. Answers will vary.
4. Answers will vary.
5. Science classes require students to remember exact answers, and a student's personal opinions about the subject don't matter.
6. Humanities classes often have no clear-cut answers and require students to connect information to their personal opinions.
7. Answers will vary.

READING STRATEGY: Choosing the Correct Dictionary Definition: Using Parts of Speech

❍ Go over the information in the box.
❍ Ask questions: *Can a word be more than one part of speech? What is one way you can figure out the correct definition?*

B. Choosing the Correct Dictionary Definition

❍ Go over the directions.
❍ Have students write the part of speech and then choose the best definition.
❍ Have students compare ideas with a partner.
❍ Go over the answers with the class.

ANSWER KEY

1. n, newspapers; 2. v, to cover the walls with wallpaper; 3. n, a report or long piece of writing done for school; 4. n, a set of lessons, a class; 5. v, to move quickly; 6. n, direction or movement; 7. n, the front of the head; 8. v, to meet something difficult; 9. v, to answer questions successfully; 10. n, a branch of knowledge or study

Reading

❍ Have students look at the reading.
❍ Go over the directions and the question.
❍ Have students read *Poetry Lessons* silently or have students follow along silently as you play the audio program.

ANSWER KEY

The professors learned that classes can be fun for students, and that humanities classes may help science students to see patterns and judge the importance of information.

Culture Notes

❍ Cornell University's Department of Engineering has 230 faculty members who are scholars, professors, and researchers. They are committed to advancing scientific discovery while teaching the future generations of engineers.
❍ Cornell engineering professors teach such courses as computer science, biomedical engineering, materials science, theoretical mechanics, and aerospace engineering.

EXPANSION ACTIVITY: Multiple Intelligences

❍ Explain that Howard Gardner developed a theory about multiple intelligences—basically suggesting that people have different kinds of intelligence. According to this theory, mathematical intelligence is different from linguistic intelligence, or the intelligence related to the use of language.
❍ Have students go online, searching for *"multiple intelligence test."* When students find a test, have them take it to find out what "intelligences" they have.
❍ Put students in small groups to talk about how this theory might explain the ways they like to learn and what subjects they are interested in.
❍ Call on students to share their ideas with the class.

After Reading

A. Comprehension Check

❍ Go over the directions and the questions.
❍ Put students in pairs to discuss the questions.
❍ Go over the answers with the class.

ANSWER KEY

1. the importance of spoken words; 2. that there could be a variety of responses to a poem; 3. both have layers of meaning; 4. to use more careful definitions and be more informative about social and linguistic history; 5. that humanities might help students see patterns, and that the poetry classes were fun

B. Guessing the Meaning from the Context

❍ Go over the directions.
❍ Put students in pairs or small groups to analyze the images.
❍ Call on students to share their ideas with the class.

ANSWER KEY

1. creaking, shuffling, scratching, crackling; 2. chairs, feet, pens, books; 3. Answers will vary.

TOEFL iBT Tip 1: The TOEFL iBT tests the ability to understand key words contained within a text.

○ Point out that the activity *Guessing the Meaning from Context* will help students improve their vocabulary for the TOEFL iBT. Locating key words in a sentence and linking them to meanings in another sentence will help students build vocabulary and improve their reading skills. They will benefit by observing the adjectives and trying to determine the meaning of those words as they are used in the text.

○ The test may also require students to determine how or why the author uses a particular phrase to define a term or describe something. Paying attention to context while reading will help students master this skill.

C. Vocabulary Check

○ Go over the directions.
○ Have students write the words and phrases on the lines and then check their answers with a partner.
○ Go over the answers with the class.

ANSWER KEY

1. formulas; 2. bewildered; 3. clear-cut; 4. essay;
5. layers; 6. surface; 7. analysis; 8. patterns

D. Pronoun Reference

○ Go over the directions.
○ Have students highlight the references.
○ Go over the answers with the class.

ANSWER KEY

1. The (students) in the poetry class listened to lectures and took notes. They had reading assignments and had to write three short papers.
2. You can look in various places for the essential statement a (poem) makes, or you can be persuaded that it doesn't make a statement at all or that it makes contradictory statements.

3. This (search) for different levels of meaning doesn't happen much in undergraduate classes [first four years of college], but it is important later, in graduate school. And it is always important in literature.

E. Making Inferences

○ Go over the directions.
○ Have students make an inference and discuss it with a partner.
○ Call on students to share their ideas with the class.

ANSWER KEY

1. Answers will vary. Poetry: shorter in length, rhyming words, organization; Prose: longer in length, complete sentences, organized in paragraphs
2. Answers will vary.

PART ② GENERAL INTEREST READING
APPRECIATING POETRY, PAGES 167–175

Before Reading
A. Thinking Ahead

○ Go over the directions and the questions.
○ Have students work in small groups to discuss the questions and write answers in the T-charts.
○ Call on students to share their ideas with the class.

ANSWER KEY

1. Answers may vary.
   Poetry: shorter, rhyming words, patterns
   Prose: longer, narrative, complete sentences
2. Answers will vary.

B. Previewing

○ Go over the directions.
○ Have students write the subtopics on the lines.
○ Go over the answers with the class.

ANSWER KEY

The Sound of Poetry, The Language of Poetry, The Form of Poetry, The Meaning of Poetry

---

EXPANSION ACTIVITY: Predicting Content

❍ Photocopy and distribute the Black Line Master *Predicting Content* on page BLM 10 and cut along the dotted lines. Mix up the order of the slips. Make enough copies so each pair of students has two slips.
❍ Put students in pairs.
❍ Give each pair a set of slips and have students put each slip in one of the four subtopic headings (*Sound, Language, Form,* and *Meaning*).
❍ Call on students to share their ideas with the class.

ANSWER KEY

Sound
Rhyme is when the stressed vowel sound and the consonants after them sound the same in two or more words.
End rhymes can fall into a repeating pattern called a rhyme scheme.
Rhythm is the order of stressed and unstressed syllables.

Language
Imagery helps us to see, hear, feel, taste, and smell the world.
Figurative language includes similes and metaphors.

Form
A poem often has several stanzas.
A poem with a closed form follows traditional rules of rhythm, rhyme, number of syllables, and number of lines.
Open form poems have no formal groupings.

Meaning
The title of a poem is a kind of introduction.
The theme is the meaning of the poem.
A narrative poem tells a story.
A lyric poem expresses personal thoughts and emotions.

🎧 Reading

❍ Go over the directions.
❍ Have students read *Appreciating Poetry* silently or follow along silently as you play the audio program.

❍ Remind students to highlight the elements of poetry as they read.

Culture Notes

❍ Edgar Allen Poe (1809–1849) was an American poet and short story writer.
❍ Robert Frost (1874–1963) was an American professor and poet. He won the Pulitzer Prize for poetry four times. He also read his poetry at President Kennedy's inauguration in 1961.
❍ E.V. Rieu was a translator of classics, including Homer and the Bible. He also wrote poetry.

EXPANSION ACTIVITY: Stress with Manipulatives

❍ Bring manipulatives of two different sizes to class. For example, you could bring M&Ms and Red Hots or other candies that are two different sizes or colors.
❍ Give a handful of each to students.
❍ Model the activity. Read the line of Robert Frost's poem: *My little horse must think it queer.* Write it on the board and draw a larger circle over each stressed syllable (lit-, horse, think, queer) and a smaller one over each unstressed syllable (My, -tle, must, it). Read the line again and point to the circles as you read with stress. Tell students to write the sentence and mark the stressed syllables with the larger candies and the unstressed syllables with the smaller candies.
❍ Play the section of the audio program with the poem *Annabel Lee* by Edgar Allen Poe (Lines 22–27 on page 168). Have students recreate the stress pattern using their manipulatives. They can look at the lines of the poem in the book as they work. Walk around to monitor the activity and provide help as needed.
❍ Have students compare ideas with a partner.

ANSWER KEY

Answers may vary.
Ĭt wăs măný ănd măný ă yéar ăgó,
Ĭn ă kíṅgdŏm bў thĕ séa.
Thăt ă máidĕn thĕre líved whŏm yŏu máy knów
Bў thĕ náme ŏf Ánnăbél Lée;
Ănd thĭs maidĕn shé líved wĭth nó óthĕr thóught
Thăn tŏ lóve ănd bĕ lóved bў mé.

After Reading

A. Preparing to Analyze Poems
○ Go over the directions.
○ Put students in pairs or small groups to brainstorm themes.
○ Call on students to share their ideas with the class.

ANSWER KEY
Answers may vary. Possible themes include: nature, romance, memories and nostalgia, childhood, growing older, loneliness, and personal beliefs and values.

READING STRATEGY: Analyzing Poems
○ Go over the information in the box.
○ Ask questions: *Can you think of a poem that has an important central theme? When is the title unnecessary?*

B. Analyzing Poems: Themes
○ Go over the directions.
○ Have students read the three poems silently or follow along silently as you play the audio program.
○ Ask: *What are these poems about?* Elicit ideas about the themes of the poems.

Culture Notes
○ Charles Harper Webb is a professor of English at California State University (CSU, Long Beach). Other poems by Webb are *Blind, Enthusiasm,* and *The Wife of the Mind.* His poetry topics are varied. Sometimes he writes about playful, happy things; other times sad and serious ideas.
○ Between 1825 and 1925, hundreds of thousands of Norwegians emigrated to the United States. Only Ireland, a country similar in size, has more American emigrants.
○ Edwin Arlington Robinson (1869–1935) was a poet now known for his narrative poetry and mastery of conventional forms. Robinson lived most of his life as an unknown and poor poet. The failure theme is suffered by several other of Robinson's characters such as Luke Havergal, Aaron Stark, and John Evereldown.

C. Finding Topics
○ Go over the directions.
○ Have students match the title with the topic.
○ Go over the answers with the class.

ANSWER KEY
"Marrying" = b; "Going to Norway" = a; "Richard Cory" = c

D. Recognizing Other Elements
○ Go over the directions.
○ Have students check their answers and then compare ideas with a partner.
○ Call on students to share their ideas with the class.

ANSWER KEY

Which poem . . .	Marrying	Going to Norway	Richard Cory
has end rhymes?			✔
has a rhyme scheme?			✔
has regular, predictable rhythm?			✔
has closed form?	✔		✔
can you *not* understand without its title?	✔		
has a speaker who is probably the poet?	✔	✔	
is a narrative?		✔	✔

E. Figurative Language
○ Go over the directions.
○ Put students in pairs to discuss the questions.
○ Call on students to share their ideas with the class.

ANSWER KEY

Answers may vary.
1. haberdasher; possible mates
2. heaven, the end to their suffering

ANSWER KEY

Answers may vary.
1. In "Marrying," the poet compares getting married with buying a hat.
2. "Going to Norway" tells the story of an older couple who dreams of going to Norway but puts the trip off for too long.
3. In "Richard Cory," the poet explores the difference between how someone is seen and envied by others and the way he truly is.

TOEFL® iBT Tip

TOEFL iBT Tip 2: On the TOEFL iBT, students are required to recognize and convey a speaker's attitude and intent and identify and summarize the major points from both written and aural sources in an integrated writing task.

○ Point out that the activity for *Figurative Language* will help students identify words or terms that are new or unfamiliar. Figurative and literal meanings will be the key to identifying an author's attitude toward the subject or his or her intention of expressing a certain idea.

○ Understanding how speakers use language figuratively or literally will help students to express themselves more clearly in the integrated writing tasks.

READING STRATEGY: Stating the Theme of a Poem: The Topic and Main Idea
○ Go over the information in the box.
○ Ask questions: *What is a theme? How are topic and main idea different? What are some ways you can state the theme?*

F. Stating the Theme
○ Go over the directions.
○ Have students state the main idea of each poem and then compare ideas with a partner.
○ Call on students to share their ideas with the class.

PART ③ ACADEMIC READING
THREE MORE POEMS, PAGES 176–183

Before Reading
A. Thinking Ahead
○ Go over the directions.
○ Direct students' attention to the chart and ask questions: *When was the Boer War? What was the Spanish Inquisition?*
○ Have students discuss the two periods in small groups and complete the chart.
○ Call on students to share their ideas with the class.

ANSWER KEY
Answers may vary.

Periods and Events	Years	Explanation
Ice Age	The most recent ended 10,000 years ago.	a period when Earth's temperatures stay cold for a long period of time causing ice sheets to cover large portions of the Earth's surface
Stone Age	Upper Paleolithic – 30,000 B.C.E. Mesolithic – 12,000 B.C.E.	people were still living in caves, hunting and gathering, transition to tool use

Culture Note

○ Over the past 750,000 years of Earth's history, the planet has endured several Ice Ages. Ice Ages occur at regular intervals, approximately 100,000 years each. The most recent is known as the Wisconsin Glaciation and ended only 10,000 years ago.

B. Discussion

○ Go over the directions.
○ Have students discuss the questions in small groups.
○ Call on students to share their ideas with the class.

ANSWER KEY

Answers will vary.

C. Vocabulary Preparation

○ Go over the directions.
○ Have students write their guesses on the lines and then compare their answers with a partner.
○ Go over the answers with the class.

ANSWER KEY

Answers may vary.
1. sudden appearance; 2. to make suffer; 3. made messy; 4. put in a lower grade; 5. it's not reasonable; 6. put off, delayed; 7. came together, met; 8. forest, group of trees

EXPANSION ACTIVITY: Beanbag Toss

○ Give students five minutes to review the phrases in Activity C on page 177.
○ Ask students to close their books. Call on a student, toss a beanbag or ball and say part of one of the phrases (e.g. *mussed*). Elicit an appropriate completion (e.g. *up*).
○ Have the student call on a classmate, toss the beanbag or ball, and begin a new phrase.
○ Continue until everyone has had a chance to participate.

🎧 Reading

○ Go over the directions before the reading. Read the questions aloud.
○ Have students read the poems silently, or play the audio program and have students follow along silently.
○ Elicit answers to the questions from the class.

ANSWER KEY

"The History Teacher" is about the way a teacher tries to hide the violence of history from his students, even though the students know about violence from playground bullying. Collins implies that the teacher is really more naïve than his students.
"Deferred" is about the way many different speakers dream of a better future that never comes. The poem does not mention the race of the speakers, but Langston Hughes usually wrote about the struggle for equality of African Americans.
"The Road Not Taken" is about choosing between two paths that look similar, but may have different destinations. Frost suggests that even small choices may have great consequences in our future lives.

Culture Notes

○ Billy Collins served as Poet Laureate for the United States in 2001. He lives in New York where he is a professor of English at Lehman College, City University of New York.
○ Langston Hughes was born in Missouri but spent most of his adult years in Harlem, a neighborhood in New York City. His works offered insights to African-American life in America. His residence was named a landmark by the New York City Preservation Commission.
○ Robert Frost was born in San Francisco, California, but moved to New England. Frost spent most of his life in New England. As a result, many of his works are about the life and landscape of this region of the United States.

Pronunciation Note

○ You may want to point out that poetry is sometimes read with a different intonation pattern than we use in regular speech. Sometimes the end of the line, or line break, is read with rising intonation. This can be done to let the listener know how the poem looks on the page.

EXPANSION ACTIVITY: Marking Intonation Patterns

○ Play the audio program or read the first poem and have students note the ending intonation (rising, falling, rising-falling) with a curved line.
○ Have students mark their books for the rest of the poems.
○ Put students in pairs to compare ideas.

After Reading

A. Sound and Form

○ Go over the directions.
○ Put students in pairs to answer the questions.
○ Go over the answers with the class.

ANSWER KEY

Answers may vary.
1. 1, 14, 4; 2. "The Road Not Taken", A, B, A, A, B;
3. "The Road Not Taken," also "Deferred" to some extent; 4. "The History Teacher" and "Deferred";
5. "Deferred," uses actual speech

CRITICAL THINKING STRATEGY: Discovering the Meaning of a Poem

○ Go over the information in the box.
○ Ask questions: *What is symbolism? What does ambiguity mean? What is an example of a poem where the speaker is different from the poet?*

B. Language and Meaning

○ Go over the directions.
○ Have students answer the questions.
○ Put students in small groups to discuss their answers.
○ Go over the answers with the class.

ANSWER KEY

1. The Ice Age was really just the Chilly Age, a period of a million years when everyone had to wear sweaters. The Stone Age became the Gravel Age, named after the long driveways of the time. The Spanish Inquisition was nothing more than an outbreak of questions. The War of the Roses took place in a garden. The Enola Gay dropped one tiny atom on Japan.
2. that soldiers told long boring stories
3. to protect their innocence
4. fought and tormented each other
5. The teacher believes the students are innocent, but when they leave the room, some children are mean to the weaker or smarter children.
6. Answers may vary.
   • You know, as old as I am (Stanza 11)
   • This year, maybe (Stanza 1)
   • Someday/ all I want (Stanzas 4 and 5)
   • Maybe now I can have that stove (Stanza 2)
   • I'd like to take up Bach (Stanza 12)
7. Answers will vary.
8. It has a closed form, rhyme, subject is religious—maybe a pastor, someone religious.
9. And my boy's most grown, there ain't no stove, It don't make sense, I ain't never; dialect, maybe African-American speech
10. Answers may vary. stove—dreams of her younger self; French and Bach—cultural self-improvement; bottle of gin—despair
11. no, there dreams were deferred
12. that he couldn't follow both paths
13. two choices; life; too far in the future to see where that path would lead; the choice that fewer people made; one action leading to another; the choice to do something different; the choice he did not make
14. Answers will vary.

EXPANSION ACTIVITY: Venn Diagram for Two Poems

○ Write these questions on the board: *How are "Deferred" and "The Road Not Taken" different in form? How are their themes similar?*
○ Have students create Venn diagrams comparing the two poems, using the questions as prompts.
○ Put students in pairs to compare answers.
○ Elicit ideas from the class.

"Going to Norway"	"Deferred"	Both poems are about what happens to our dreams when we put them off too long.
"Richard Cory"	"The History Teacher"	Both "Richard Cory" and "The History Teacher" are about how different people are from our impressions.

C. In Your Own Words: Summarizing

○ Go over the directions.
○ Have students write sentences about the topics and the main ideas and then compare sentences with a partner.
○ Call on students to share their ideas with the class.

ANSWER KEY

Answers may vary.

"Deferred" is about dreams that people have and don't act on. Hughes is saying that if we wait too long to act on our dreams, they may never be realized.

"The Road Not Taken" is about the choices we make in life. Frost is saying that the speaker has made choices in his life that are not common and those choices have determined the path his life has taken.

D. Making Connections: Comparing Themes

○ Go over the directions.
○ Have students write their answers in the chart and then compare ideas with a partner.
○ Call on students to share their ideas with the class.

ANSWER KEY

Poems from Part 2	Poems from Part 3	Theme: What are both poems about? Write one sentence that is general enough to cover both poems.
"Marrying"	"The Road Not Taken"	Both poems are about the choices we make and how they affect our futures.

TOEFL® iBT Tip

TOEFL iBT Tip 3: The TOEFL iBT tests the ability to read a passage, listen to a lecture related to that passage, and then reply in response to a question based on the two stimuli. This integrated writing skill requires students to think critically about material that they have read, interpret that information and relate it to a lecture, then present ideas in an essay. Examinees should be able to compare and contrast ideas that are presented in both a listening and reading passage and make connections between those sources.

○ Remind students that the activity for *Making Connections: Comparing Themes* can help them to be more effective note-takers and facilitate their ability to find information quickly. This activity requires students to put details into a chart. This skill, and the ability to recognize advantages and disadvantages, can help learners make connections between the major and minor points in a lecture or conversation.

EXPANSION ACTIVITY: Illustrations

○ Remind students that imagery can be an important key to understanding a poem.
○ Have students choose one poem from the chapter to illustrate. Suggest they illustrate one or more of the images in the poem or create their own images to convey similar ideas.
○ Have students post their illustrations around the room.
○ Have students circulate through the gallery, taking notes on the illustrations and guessing which poem each depicts.

E. Word Journal
○ Go over the directions.
○ Have students write words in their Word Journals.

F. Response Writing
○ Go over the directions.
○ Explain that this is a quick-writing activity and does not have to be perfect. Point out that journal writing can be a warm-up to a more structured writing assignment, helping to generate ideas.
○ Set a time limit of 15 minutes.
○ Put students in pairs to read or talk about their writing.

 Internet Research
○ For additional information on poetry and its analysis, see:
  • www.poems.com/
  • poetry.eserver.org/
  • www.loc.gov/poetry/180/
  • rpo.library.utoronto.ca/display/index.cfm
  • www.poetrymagic.co.uk/critiquing.html

PART ④ THE MECHANICS OF WRITING, PAGES 184–188

○ Go over the information about Part 4.

Expressing Possibility and Probability
○ Go over the information in the box about expressing possibility and probability.
○ Ask comprehension questions: *What modals suggest possibility? Which modal is used to express strong probability?*

Grammar Note
○ These expressions present our guesses (possibility) and our conclusions (probability) about a topic.

A. Expressing Possibility and Probability
○ Go over the directions.
○ Have students write answers to each question using an expression of possibility or probability.
○ Have students compare sentences in pairs.
○ Go over the answers with the class.

ANSWER KEY
Answers may vary.
1. The speaker appears to be a cynical person, who sees the children as much more hardened than the teacher thinks they are.
2. The white enamel stove could symbolize the speaker's dream of a comfortable married life.
3. The speaker must have had a job with long hours.
4. The speaker probably learned the lines in church.
5. It appears that the poem takes place in the fall because the wood is yellow.
6. The road could have been grassy because no one had walked there and worn away the grass.

TOEFL® iBT Tip

TOEFL iBT Tip 4: Although the TOEFL iBT does not discretely test grammar skills, examinees' essay scores are determined based on the range of grammar and vocabulary used in their essays.

○ Point out that the grammar activities in *The Mechanics of Writing* part of this chapter will help them improve their use of verb tenses as well as transition words for cause and effect and analytical essay writing.

○ Recognizing the modals of possibility and probability will also help them identify information presented in a reading that was written in a cause and effect or analytical mode.

Using Phrases for Symbols
○ Go over the information in the box.
○ Ask: *What expressions can we use to talk about symbols? When do we need to talk about symbols?*

B. Using Phrases for Symbols
○ Go over the directions.
○ Have students finish the sentences and compare ideas with a partner.
○ Call on students to share their ideas with the class.

ANSWER KEY
Answers will vary.

EXPANSION ACTIVITY: Personal Symbols
○ Model the activity. Tell the class about some object you have that symbolizes something to you (e.g., *My Miata convertible symbolizes freedom to me. When my children were young, I drove a minivan, but after they went off to college, I wanted something more fun. Then unfortunately, I went through a divorce. I decided I needed a change, so I bought a sports car.*).
○ Give students a couple of minutes to think about something they have that is symbolic of their personality or place in life.
○ Have students write a brief description of the symbol and what it means. Tell students that the descriptions will be read to the class, and they should not include any names or identifying information.
○ Collect the descriptions.
○ Read a description to the class and elicit guesses as to the writer.
○ In a variation of this activity, you may want to have students draw or bring in their "symbols."

Using Similes with *as . . . as*
○ Go over the information in the box.
○ Ask questions: *What is one way we can compare two things? What is a common simile in English?*

C. Using Similes with *as . . . as*
○ Go over the directions.
○ Have students write their answers on the chart.
○ Have students stand and walk around the room asking classmates to complete the simile.
○ Call on students to share their ideas with the class.

ANSWER KEY
Answers will vary. Remind students to look at page 192 to see the similes in English.

Avoiding and Repairing Problems with Sentence Structure
○ Go over the information in the box.
○ Ask questions: *What is a run-on sentence? How can you correct it? What is a comma splice?*

D. Avoiding and Repairing Problems with Sentence Structure
○ Go over the directions.
○ Have students identify each sentence and then correct any errors.
○ Go over the answers with the class. Have students explain what the errors are and how to correct them.

ANSWER KEY
Answers may vary.

  R   1. Frost spent two years at Harvard ∧ ∧ $\overset{H}{\text{he}}$ didn't enjoy his time there.

 O.K.   2. Problems with health and business and grief over the death of two of his children caused Frost to turn more to poetry.

  F   3. As he says ∧ $\overset{\text{Cory was}}{\wedge}$ "imperially slim."

  CS   4. In 1912, Frost sold his farm /∧ his family went to England.

  F   5. Richard Cory appears to have a perfect life, but clearly this isn't the case /∧ $\overset{\text{as he}}{\wedge}$ "Went home and put a bullet through his head."

 O.K.   6. We don't know if the speaker is wistful for "the road not taken."

  R   7. The family had financial needs ∧ $\overset{so}{\wedge}$ Frost began to give public readings and lectures.

 O.K.   8. Hughes tells us that this has been a "montage of a dream deferred."

ANSWER KEY, continued

CS 9. Frost had weak lungs/⋀ therefore, his doctor
          ;
ordered him to spend winters in a warmer
climate.

R 10. Robert Frost suffered tragedy and sorrow⋀
          ;
however ⋀ he was also one of the most
          ,
beloved, greatly honored poets of the
United States.

EXPANSION ACTIVITY: Editing Practice

○ Photocopy and distribute the Black Line Master
  Editing Practice on page BLM 11.
○ Have students correct the paragraph and then
  compare ideas with a partner.
○ Go over the answers with the class.

ANSWER KEY

Answers may vary.

1. Robert Frost says in his poem/ ~~That~~ taking the
                              ⋀^that
road less traveled "has made all the difference."

2. The speaker in "Deferred" believes that he can
study French now that his job has changed/⋀
                                          ;
however ⋀ he may be fooling himself.
       ,

3. Billy Collins does not seem to share the attitude of
the history teacher/⋀ ^H ~~he~~ seems to be less naïve.
                   ⋀ ⋀

4. In "Marrying," Charles Webb compares/ ~~Marriage~~
                                    ⋀^marriage
to buying a hat.

5. Many people thought Richard Cory had all he
could want out of life ^but he didn't.
                        ⋀ ⋀

6. "The History Teacher" uses humor to make a point/
^as ~~As~~ in the line about the Boer War.

7. Langston Hughes was an important poet of the
   ⋀
20th century/⋀ ^H ~~he~~ was African American⋀ but
            /⋀ ⋀   ,
his themes are universal.

8. ^Although ^a ~~All~~ the poets in this chapter are
   ⋀   ⋀/
male, many important poets are women.

PART ⑤ ACADEMIC WRITING, PAGES 188–192

Writing Assignment

○ Go over the directions in the box.
○ Have students read the seven steps.
○ Direct students' attention to Step A and have
  students discuss the choices in small groups before
  choosing a topic.
○ Direct students' attention to Step B and have
  students write one sentence about their topic.
○ Direct students' attention to Step C and have
  students find support.

WRITING STRATEGY: Planning a Paragraph: Idea Mapping

○ Go over the information in the box.
○ Ask: *How can an idea map help you plan your
  paragraph? What should you begin with? How
  much evidence do you need to gather?*

○ Direct students' attention to Step D. Go over the
  directions. Have students put their information on an
  idea map. Put students with a partner who has
  chosen the same poem to talk about their idea maps.

TEST-TAKING STRATEGY: Hedging and Avoiding Overstatement

○ Go over the information in the box.
○ Ask: *What is hedging? When and why should you
  use hedging? When is it especially important to
  use hedging when analyzing a poem? What are
  some ways to express uncertainty?*

Hedging and Overstatement

○ Go over the directions.
○ Have students change the sentences to use hedging
  and then compare sentences in pairs.
○ Call on students to share their ideas with the class.

ANSWER KEY

Answers may vary.

1. The "people on the pavement" ∧(must have been) ~~were~~ poor in spirit, too, for they "waited for the light."

2. The history teacher ~~was absolutely~~ ∧(may have been) naïve.

3. The speaker in the second stanza in "Deferred" ~~associates~~ ∧(appears to associate) the "white enamel stove" with a comfortable, secure life.

4. The speaker in the eighth stanza ~~is~~ ∧(may be) an elderly person who learned these lines in a hymn in church.

5. ∧(It's possible that) ∧(t)The speaker in "The Road Not Taken" regrets his choice.

6. ∧(It seems likely that) ∧(t)The speaker in "The Road Not Taken" is content with his choice.

WRITING STRATEGY: Writing a Paragraph of Analysis

○ Go over the information in the box.

○ Ask comprehension questions: *What should you include in your topic sentence? How can you include quotes as support?*

○ You may want to read the example paragraph aloud as students follow silently in their books.

○ Read the *Analysis* directions. Ask students to answer the questions. Go over answers with the class.

ANSWER KEY

Answers may vary.
The writer begins with an interpretation and supports it with a quote in most cases.
Answers will vary.
Hedging: He seems to have been kind; However, they must have been poor in spirit; They must have been shocked; The reader probably can't either.

TOEFL® iBT Tip

TOEFL iBT Tip 5: Both the integrated and independent essays of the TOEFL iBT will be scored based on how well the examinee completes the overall writing task.

○ Point out that the strategy for *Hedging and Avoiding Overstatement* can be useful in the writing section when you want to avoid expressing an opinion that you cannot prove. It is important for students' writing to be succinct, so overstating information should be avoided, particularly in summary writing.

○ In the integrated essay section, examinees will have to make generalizations or form their own opinions about information that they have read and heard. The ability to use hedging strategies will help improve their overall writing skills.

TOEFL® iBT Tip

TOEFL iBT Tip 6: Both the integrated and independent essays of the TOEFL iBT will be scored based on how well the examinee completes the overall writing task. Independent writing tasks require examinees to analyze an idea, present an opinion or perception about a topic, or develop an argument about a controversial issue.

○ Point out that the *Writing a Paragraph of Analysis* strategy will help students improve their coherence and the flow of ideas in their independent essays by taking smaller steps in their essay development.

○ Remind students that working at the paragraph level and demonstrating the ability to support their opinions more concisely will improve their overall essay scores.

○ Direct students' attention to Step E. Go over the directions and have students write their paragraphs.

○ Direct students' attention to Step F. Go over the questions. Have students read and edit their paragraphs, using the questions as a guide.

○ For peer editing, have students exchange paragraphs with a partner, edit, and return to the writer.

○ Go over the directions for Step G. Have students carefully rewrite their paragraphs and hand them in to you.

○ After you have read and returned students' paragraphs, you may want to set aside time for students to read each other's writing or display the paragraphs in the classroom. Have students keep all of their final versions in a notebook or folder so that they can see their progress and improvement over time.

CHAPTER 6 HEROES IN LITERATURE

In this chapter, students will read and write about heroes in literature. In Part 1 of this chapter, students will read a story in which an older man gives advice on traveling to a young man. In Part 2, students will read a transcription of a television interview about heroes in mythology. In Part 3, students will read about a rite of passage of a Native American girl. Part 4 focuses on the mechanics of writing, including parallelism, making a strong argument using *should, ought to,* and *must,* using synonyms; and a review of paraphrasing. In Part 5, students will write a persuasive essay about an issue.

VOCABULARY

blisters	heritage	redemption
bump into	heroine	resurrection
compassionate	look about	revolve around
compelled	match	self-preservation
deed	natural impulse	shrewd
draw close	nature	skirmish
endurance ritual	only way out	trial
endure	paid a visit	undergo
evoked	profited by	unsightly
evolve	put one's foot down	well-fed
fundamental	radiantly healthy	went out of one's way
got aboard	recover	

READING STRATEGIES

Recognizing Euphemisms
Understanding Italics for Foreign Words
Finding the Theme of a Story

CRITICAL THINKING STRATEGIES

Interpreting
Making Connections
Summarizing
Note: The strategy in bold is highlighted in the Student Book.

MECHANICS

Parallelism
Making a Strong Argument: *Should, Ought to,* and *Must*
Using Synonyms
Review: Paraphrasing

WRITING STRATEGIES

Understanding the Organization of an Essay
Writing a Thesis Statement
Writing Topic Sentences in an Essay

TEST-TAKING STRATEGY

Writing Supporting Material in an Essay
Circling the Best Choice

CHAPTER 6 Heroes in Literature

Chapter 6 Opening Photo, page 193

○ Direct students' attention to the photo. Ask them what is happening in the photo.
○ Have students discuss the questions. This can be done in pairs, in small groups, or as a class.
○ Check students' predictions of the chapter topic.

EXPANSION ACTIVITY: Superheroes

○ Put students in pairs or small groups to generate a list of superheroes they know from cartoons, comic books, literature, or movies.
○ Have students list several qualities of each superhero (e.g., Superman: strong, brave, shy, vulnerable to Kryptonite).
○ Ask students to notice any patterns in the traits or qualities.
○ Elicit ideas and write them on the board.

PART ① INTRODUCTION OLD COUNTRY ADVICE TO THE AMERICAN TRAVELER, PAGES 194–199

Before Reading
Thinking Ahead

○ Go over the directions and questions.
○ Have students discuss the questions in small groups.
○ Call on students to share their ideas with the class.

ANSWER KEY
Answers will vary.

🎧 Reading

○ Have students look at the reading.
○ Direct students' attention to the pictures on page 194 and ask questions: *Where is Armenia? Why do you think Saroyan writes about immigrants from Armenia?*

○ Go over the directions and the question.
○ Have students read silently, or have students follow along silently as you play the audio program.

ANSWER KEY
Answers will vary.

Culture Note

○ William Saroyan (1908–1981) wrote novels, plays, and short stories. He won a Pulitzer Prize for Drama in 1939 for *The Time of Your Life.* His novel *The Human Comedy* was made into a movie and won two Academy Awards.

Vocabulary Note

○ In addition to the smoking car and dining car mentioned in the reading, students should also be familiar with other parts of a train such as the engine (first car), caboose (last car), and sleeper (car with beds for overnight travel).

Pronunciation Note

○ In the story, Melik's uncle advises him to say "No speak English." This is an example of pidgin English. Pidgin is defined as simplified speech used when two people speak different languages. Pidgin is a version of English that is not grammatical and often contains words or phrases from someone's native language. Often subjects are left out of "pidgin" but the context, or meaning, is still understood.

EXPANSION ACTIVITY: Oral Reading

○ Point out that there is a lot of quoted speech in this story, but the author does not use quotation marks. It is usually easy to tell what the two characters are saying.

○ Put students into groups of three. Have them look at the reading again and highlight the words Garro says, the words Melik says, and the words of the narrator, each in a different color.

○ Have students read the entire story aloud in their small groups with each member reading a different part.

○ Call on volunteers to read the story aloud to the class.

After Reading

A. Comprehension Check

○ Go over the directions.
○ Put students in pairs to answer the questions.
○ Go over the answer with the class.

ANSWER KEY

1. Garro and Melik; 2. Melik; 3. Don't look at anyone, ignore the ticket takers, tell the young man you don't smoke, ignore the beautiful young woman, eat in the diner, but don't look or speak to the woman, pretend to be deaf, tell the card players you don't speak English, put your money in your shoe or under your pillow; don't sleep; 4. Garro is old, suspicious, easily frustrated/angered. He believes he is wise in the ways of the world and traveling.
5.

Garro's Predictions	Melik's Trip
The two men taking tickets would be impostors.	The men taking tickets were not impostors.
A young man would offer a doped cigarette.	The young man with the doped cigarette did not arrive.
A beautiful girl would approach him and she would be an adventuress.	The beautiful young woman did not sit across from him.
Three middle-aged men would be playing cards.	There were no men playing cards.
	Melik offered another man a cigarette.

He sat at a table with a young lady.

He started a poker game in the smoker.

6. He may have learned not to be afraid, and that traveling can be a fun adventure.

TOEFL® iBT Tip

TOEFL iBT Tip 1: The TOEFL iBT tests the ability to understand key facts and the important information contained within a text. Locating key information in a text and discussing that information will help students improve their overall reading and speaking skills in preparation for the integrated speaking tasks.

○ Point out that the *Comprehension Check* requires students to discuss their answers with other students, which will help them synthesize information and practice their speaking skills for the integrated speaking questions on the test.

○ Students will also have the opportunity to organize ideas and notes in a T–chart, which will help them with many of the reading questions on the test.

B. Vocabulary Check

○ Go over the directions.
○ Have students write the words on the lines.
○ Go over the answers with the class.

ANSWER KEY

1. got aboard; 2. paid him a visit; 3. look about; 4. bump into you; 5. natural impulse; 6. the only way out; 7. went out of his way; 8. profited by

READING STRATEGY: Recognizing Euphemisms

○ Go over the information in the box.
○ Ask questions: *What is a euphemism? Why do we use them?*

C. Recognizing Euphemisms

❍ Go over the directions.
❍ Put students in pairs to guess the meanings of the euphemisms.
❍ Go over the answers with the class.

ANSWER KEY

1. get to know her, start a relationship
2. ignore your feelings; forget what you would do under normal circumstances

D. Making Inferences

❍ Go over the directions.
❍ Have students discuss their ideas with a small group.
❍ Call on students to share their answers with the class.

ANSWER KEY

Garro might have gotten his ideas about travel from his own experiences in another country. Most people don't listen. (I am pleased that *someone* has profited by my experience.)

EXPANSION ACTIVITY: Give Advice

❍ Put students in small groups.
❍ Have students list their own negative experiences with traveling (e.g., *losing checked luggage on a flight*) and then turn that into advice (*Don't ever check your luggage, someone will lose it*).
❍ Collect the lists of advice from each group.
❍ Read a list and have the class guess whose group gave the advice and who in each group is responsible for each piece of advice.
❍ Have the class vote on which pieces of advice they agree with.

E. Discussion

❍ Go over the directions.
❍ Put students in pairs or small groups to discuss the questions.
❍ Call on students to share their ideas with the class.

ANSWER KEY

Answers will vary.

PART ② GENERAL INTEREST READING
THE HERO'S JOURNEY, PAGES 199–206

Before Reading

❍ Direct students' attention to the two photos.
❍ Ask questions: *Who is Luke Skywalker? Who is Han Solo? What was* Star Wars *about?*

Culture Note

❍ *Stars Wars* was the first of movies George Lucas made that tells the story of the conflict between good (the Jedi) and evil (the Empire led by Darth Vader). Although it was the first movie made, it is the fourth episode in the story. In *Star Wars,* Luke discovers he is a Jedi. He and Han Solo do battle with the army of Darth Vader.
❍ The title is *Star Wars: A New Hope* but most people call it *Star Wars* since it is the first movie.

A. Thinking Ahead

❍ Go over the directions and the questions.
❍ Have students discuss the questions in small groups.
❍ Call on students to share their ideas with the class.

ANSWER KEY

Answers will vary.

B. Vocabulary Preparation

❍ Go over the directions.
❍ Have students circle the part of speech and then write their guesses on the lines.
❍ Go over the answers with the class.

ANSWER KEY

1. n, act; 2. v, forced; 3. n, female hero; 4. adj, necessary, important; 5. v, go through, experience; 6. v, develop; 7. n, rising from the dead; 8. n, keeping yourself from harm or death; 9. n, the state of being improved or fixed; 10. adj, sympathetic, caring; 11. v, produced

EXPANSION ACTIVITY: Beanbag Toss

○ Give students five minutes to review the words in Activity B on page 200 of the Student Book.
○ Ask students to close their books. Call on a student, toss a beanbag or ball and say one of the words (e.g. *deed*). Elicit an appropriate completion (e.g. *favor*).
○ Have the student call on a classmate, toss the beanbag or ball, and say a new word.
○ Continue until everyone has had a chance to participate.

C. Choosing the Correct Dictionary Definition

○ Go over the directions.
○ Have students choose the best definitions and then check their answers with a partner.
○ Go over the answers with the class.

ANSWER KEY

1. 1; 2. 3; 3. 2; 4. 2; 5. 1; 6. 2; 7. 1; 8. 2; 9. 3; 10. 1

🎧 Reading

○ Go over the directions and the question.
○ Have students read *The Hero's Journey* silently or follow along silently as you play the audio program.

Culture Notes

○ Joseph Campbell began his lifelong fascination with Native-American culture and myth as a child. He later studied how myths and heroes crossed the boundaries of all cultures. He became famous because of *The Power of Myth*, a popular U.S. television series with Bill Moyers.
○ Bill Moyers was an American television journalist for 30 years. He retired at age 70 in 2004. He established Public Affairs Television as an independent production company and worked in public television for most of his career.

Grammar Note

○ Remind students that this is a transcription of an interview, so it sounds and looks more like speech than more formal writing.
○ You may want to elicit or point out examples:
  Fragments – Because that is what is worth writing about. (Line 2)
  Fillers – well (Line 8)

After Reading

A. Comprehension Check

○ Go over the directions.
○ Put students in pairs to discuss the questions.
○ Go over the answers with the class.

ANSWER KEY

1. A hero is a person who has found or done something beyond the normal range of achievement and experience; someone who has given his or her life to something bigger than him or herself.
2. The hero performs a courageous act in battle or saves a life; or learns to experience the supernormal range of human spiritual life and comes back with a message.
3. He sacrificed his safety for others.

B. Checking Details

○ Go over the directions.
○ Have students discuss the questions and complete the flow chart in small groups.
○ Call on students to share their ideas with the class.

ANSWER KEY

1.

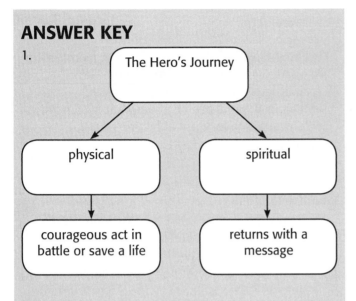

2. that they are worthy of the task
3. as a clown
4. Adolescent shows courage to die to the infantile personality and have a resurrection to a richer or mature condition.

C. Phrases with Prepositions

○ Go over the directions.
○ Have students complete the phrases with prepositions.
○ Have students look back at the reading to check their answers.
○ Go over the answers with the class.

ANSWER KEY

1. off on; 2. up; 3. out of; 4. to; 5. of; 6. from; 7. in/of; 8. up; 9. for; 10. on

CRITICAL THINKING STRATEGY: Interpreting

○ Go over the information in the box.
○ Ask questions: *What do we do when we interpret? Why is this useful?*

D. Interpreting

○ Go over the directions.
○ Have students find examples of the hero's adventure in "Alone on a Hilltop" (Chapter 1, page 29).
○ Elicit examples from the class.

ANSWER KEY

Answers may vary.
adolescent, alone on a journey of sorts, physical discomfort, his purpose is to die to his childhood and become a man, bring back a message

TOEFL® iBT Tip

TOEFL iBT Tip 2: The TOEFL iBT tests the ability to read a passage, listen to a lecture related to that passage, and then write in response to a question based on the two stimuli. This integrated writing skill requires students to think critically about material that they have read, interpret that information and relate it to a lecture, then present ideas in essay format.

○ Point out to students that the critical thinking strategy for *Interpreting* will help them understand what is presented to them in the reading text and in a lecture. It will also help them to make connections between the sources. They should also be able to explain ideas and summarize what the lecturer or author has stated.

E. Avoiding Sexism

○ Go over the directions.
○ Have students rewrite line 19 in two different ways.
○ Call on students to share their ideas with the class.

ANSWER KEY

Answers may vary. Possible answers include:
through which a child is compelled to give up his or her childhood and become an adult—to die, you might say to his or her infantile personality
through which children are compelled to give up their childhoods and become an adults—to die, you might say to their infantile personalities

EXPANSION ACTIVITY: Different Types of Paragraphs

❍ Photocopy and distribute the Black Line Master *Different Types of Paragraphs* on page BLM 12.
❍ Go over the different types of paragraphs.
❍ Have students match the paragraph type to the sample paragraphs. Encourage students to go back and reread *The Hero's Journey* if they need additional context.
❍ Have students discuss their ideas with a partner.
❍ Call on students to share their ideas with the class.
❍ For more advanced students, you could have students write their own paragraph to illustrate one of the other paragraph types.

ANSWER KEY
1. B; 2. F; 3. G; 4. C

EXPANSION ACTIVITY: Paraphrasing

❍ Write these sentences on the board:
   1. *This person then takes off on a series of adventures beyond the ordinary, either to recover what has been lost or to discover some life-giving elixir.*
   2. *That's the basic motif of the universal hero's journey—leaving one condition and finding the source of life to bring you forth into a richer or mature condition.*
   3. *When we quit thinking primarily about ourselves and our own self-preservation, we undergo a truly heroic transformation of consciousness.*
   4. *There would be no hero deed unless there were an achievement.*
❍ Have students paraphrase the sentences after reviewing how to paraphrase on page 79. Remind students to use as many techniques as they can (using synonyms, condensing, expanding, changing the part of speech, and changing sentence structure).
❍ After students paraphrase the sentences, ask: *Is this true to the author's intent? Are the words different enough from the original? Is the grammar O.K.?*

PART ③ ACADEMIC READING
TA-NA-E-KA,
PAGES 207–217

Before Reading

A. Thinking Ahead
❍ Go over the directions.
❍ Have students discuss the questions in small groups.
❍ Call on students to share their ideas with the class.

Culture Notes
❍ *La fiesta de quinceañera* is an occasion celebrated in most Latin American countries. It marks a girl's passage from childhood to becoming a young woman on her 15th birthday. She usually wears a formal white dress. Her friends and family also wear formal clothes. There is usually dancing, music and food.
❍ Some people in the United States participate in a debutante ball. Like the *quinceañera*, it celebrates a young woman's entry into adult society. Usually a group of 18-year-old women "come out" together at a debutante ball. Again, family and friends attend in formal dress.
❍ A *bar mitzvah* is a rite of passage for a 13-year-old male in the Jewish faith. The boy studies the Hebrew language and religious books to prepare for a special religious ceremony. After the ceremony, there is usually a big celebration with friends and family. A *bat mitzvah* is the same rite of passage for a Jewish girl.

ANSWER KEY
Answers will vary.

B. Vocabulary Preparation
❍ Go over the directions.
❍ Have students circle the parts of speech and write their guesses on the lines.
❍ Go over the answers with the class.

ANSWER KEY

1. n, a fight, small battle; 2. v; survive, to live through;
3. v, center around; 4. adj, smart, clever; 5. v, refused;
6. adj, coming near, soon; 7. n, a ritual that involves
difficult activities; 8. n, culture

EXPANSION ACTIVITY: Draw Associations

❍ Model the activity. Draw a picture on the board that illustrates or reminds you of one of the words in Activity B. For example, you might draw Earth revolving around the sun.
❍ Have students think of associations for at least two of the words in Activity B and draw a picture for each.
❍ Put students in pairs to tell their stories.
❍ Call on students to share their stories with the class.

READING STRATEGY: Understanding Italics for Foreign Words

❍ Go over the information in the box.
❍ Ask: *When do we use italics?*

🎧 Reading

❍ Go over the directions before the reading. Read the questions aloud.
❍ Have students read *Ta-Na-E-Ka* silently or play the audio program and have students follow along silently.
❍ Elicit answers to the questions from the class.

ANSWER KEY

Mary is supposed to learn that she is strong enough to survive by herself. She does learn how to survive, but by asking for help from other people.

Culture Note

❍ There is some debate about the author, Mary Whitebird. Some Native Americans say that Mary Whitebird is a pseudonym, and the Kaw tribal headquarters have no record of her. The Kaw tribe feels she is probably Caucasian based on the stories subtext that the boy who "goes native" has a hard time and the girl who follows a more "white" way is

fine. Over 75 percent of calls to tribal headquarters are about this story. The Kaw consider the story an "urban legend" that keeps growing.

After Reading

A. Main Ideas

❍ Go over the directions.
❍ Put students in pairs to discuss the questions.
❍ Call on students to share their ideas with the class.

ANSWER KEY

1. endurance; 2. both do Ta-Na-E-Ka, men and women eat together, women could sit on tribal councils; 3. Yes, because she knows how to exist in a world that wasn't made for Indians.

TOEFL® iBT Tip

TOEFL iBT Tip 3: The TOEFL iBT does not directly test the ability to determine the main idea in a reading. Instead, examinees are required to recognize the minor, less important ideas that do not belong in a summary. They may be required to distinguish between major and minor points of information.

❍ Point out that the activity for *Main Ideas* will help students distinguish between major and minor points in a text on the TOEFL iBT. This activity will also help students prepare for the integrated reading-listening-speaking tasks by encouraging them to think about the main ideas and discuss them with classmates.

B. Review: Making Inferences

❍ Go over the directions.
❍ Put students in small groups to discuss the questions.
❍ Call on students to share their ideas with the class.

ANSWER KEY

Answers may vary.
1. It implies criticism of her people, her culture.
2. She is proud of it, especially the equality of women.
3. Probably not. She is clever and resourceful. She planned ahead in borrowing the money. She has good people skills (as demonstrated in her ability to get along with Ernie). She's honest.

C. Vocabulary Check
○ Go over the directions.
○ Have students write their guesses and then compare answers with a partner.
○ Go over the answers with the class.

ANSWER KEY

Answers will vary.
1. sores, rubbed spots on the skin; 2. ugly; 3. full of food, fat; 4. exceptionally healthy

READING STRATEGY: Finding the Theme of a Story
○ Go over the information in the box.
○ Ask questions: *What is a theme? How can you find an unstated theme?*

D. Finding the Theme
○ Go over the directions.
○ Put students in pairs to discuss the questions.
○ Call on students to share their ideas with the class.

ANSWER KEY

1. Answers may vary. Part of becoming an adult is learning how to survive in the world.
2. Answers may vary.

E. Making Connections
○ Go over the directions.
○ Have students discuss the questions in small groups.
○ Call on students to share their ideas with the class.

ANSWER KEY

Answers will vary.

EXPANSION ACTIVITY: Something About Mary
○ Put students in pairs or small groups to brainstorm a list of qualities that Mary seems to have.
○ Have students write another scene in which Mary is the main character. Explain that they can tell any story they want, but they must be true to Mary's character. You may want to set a time (15 minutes) or length (one page) limit.
○ Put students in pairs to exchange and read stories.
○ Call on volunteers to read their stories to the class.

F. In Your Own Words: Summarizing
○ Go over the directions.
○ Have students write sentences about the topics and the main ideas and then compare sentences with a partner.
○ Call on students to share their ideas with the class.

ANSWER KEY

Answers may vary. Possible answers for the first paragraph include:
1. The paragraph is about how a Native American grandfather maintains harsh traditions that many of his tribe have given up.
2. The author says that the man's granddaughter fears her birthday because of the rite of passage she must go through.

G. Word Journal
○ Go over the directions.
○ Have students write words in their Word Journals.

H. Response Writing
○ Go over the directions.
○ Explain that this is a quick-writing activity and does not have to be perfect. Point out that journal writing can be a warm-up to a more structured writing assignment, helping to generate ideas.

○ Set a time limit of 15 minutes.
○ Put students in pairs to read or talk about their writing.

 Internet Research

○ For additional information on heroes, myths, and rites of passage, see:
  • www.time.com/time/time100/heroes/
  • www.homeofheroes.com/
  • www.pbs.org/opb/thenewheroes/
  • www.ucalgary.ca/~dkbrown/storfolk.html
  • www.pitt.edu/~dash/folktexts.html
  • www.bbc.co.uk/worldservice/africa/features/storyofafrica/6chapter3.shtml
  • anthro.palomar.edu/social/soc_4.htm

PART ④ THE MECHANICS OF WRITING, PAGES 218–223

○ Go over the information about Part 4.

Parallelism

○ Go over the information in the box.
○ Ask comprehension questions: *What is parallelism? How are parallel elements joined? What kind of mistakes do writers often make?*

A. Parallelism

○ Go over the directions.
○ Have students circle the incorrect element and rewrite the sentences using correct elements.
○ Have students compare sentences in pairs.
○ Go over the answers with the class.

ANSWER KEY

1. Many of Saroyan's characters were Californian or (they came) from Armenia.
   Many of Saroyan's characters were Californian or Armenian.
2. Uncle Melik spent most of his trip meeting nice people, playing cards, and (he sang) in a quartet.
   Uncle Melik spent most of his trip meeting nice people, playing cards, and singing in a quartet.

3. Sioux men are not afraid to endure hunger, thirst, and (they are sometimes lonely).
   Sioux men are not afraid to endure hunger, thirst, and loneliness.
4. Mary realized that she didn't have to eat grasshoppers and (she) could eat hamburgers if she wanted to.
   Mary realized that she didn't have to eat grasshoppers and could eat hamburgers if she wanted to.
5. Grandfather demonstrated how to pull off the legs of a grasshopper and (swallowing) it.
   Grandfather demonstrated how to pull off the legs of a grasshopper and swallow it.
6. Mary succeeded due to her intelligence, creativity, and (she was lucky).
   Mary succeeded due to her intelligence, creativity, and luck.

Grammar Note

○ You may want to point out that when we use parallelism we often take out all words that are repeated in parallel elements. For example in number 4, we could write *Mary realized that she didn't have to eat grasshoppers and could eat hamburgers if she wanted to.*

Making a Strong Argument: *Should, Ought to,* and *Must*

○ Go over the information in the box.
○ Ask questions: *What expressions can we use to make a strong argument? How is* must *different from the other two expressions?*

B. Making a Strong Argument

○ Go over the directions.
○ Have students react to the statements by writing responses with *should, ought to,* or *must.*
○ Have students compare sentences with a partner.
○ Call on students to read their sentences to the class.

ANSWER KEY
Answers will vary.

EXPANSION ACTIVITY: Small Group Debates
❍ Put students in groups of four.
❍ Have the groups choose two or three of the statements from Activity B as the basis for their debates. Ask students to rewrite the statements as an argument (e.g., *Animal sacrifice should not be allowed in the religion of Santeria*).
❍ Tell students each group should form two pairs.
❍ Have the pairs take opposite sides of the argument, one listing arguments in favor of the statement, the other opposing.
❍ Challenge students to present their arguments in their groups of four.
❍ Call on volunteers to debate their positions in front of the class.

Using Synonyms
❍ Go over the information in the box.
❍ Ask questions: *When is it helpful to know and use synonyms? What information can you find in a thesaurus? What are some other ways you can use synonyms for paraphrasing?*

C. Using Synonyms
❍ Go over the directions.
❍ Have students answer the questions.
❍ Call on students to share their ideas with the class.

ANSWER KEY
1. a noun; 2. 14; 3. 1; 4. action

TOEFL® iBT Tip

TOEFL iBT Tip 4: Although the TOEFL iBT does not discretely test grammar skills, examinees' essay scores will be determined based on the range of grammar and vocabulary used in their essays.

❍ Point out that the grammar activities in *The Mechanics of Writing* part of this chapter will help them improve their abilities to write essays and use parallelism to make strong arguments.

❍ Show students that using modals can strengthen or soften their argument and that learning synonyms for words will be extremely important when paraphrasing and summarizing in their essays.

Vocabulary Note
❍ *Deed* and *action* could both be used in Activity C. However, you might want to point out to students that because *deed* is already used in the sentence, *action* would be better. Remind students that we try to avoid repeating words in the same sentence, or even in the same paragraph if there is another way to say the same thing equally well.

D. Condensing
❍ Go over the directions.
❍ Have students write the letters on the lines.
❍ Go over the answers with the class.

ANSWER KEY
1. b; 2. a; 3. d; 4. c; 5. e; 6. f

E. Expanding
❍ Go over the directions.
❍ Have students write the letters on the lines.
❍ Go over the answers with the class.

ANSWER KEY
1. e; 2. c; 3. a; 4. b; 5. d

Review: Paraphrasing
❍ Go over the information in the box.
❍ Ask questions: *What is paraphrasing? What should you do when you paraphrase? What are some strategies you can use to paraphrase?*

F. Paraphrasing

○ Go over the directions.
○ Have students paraphrase the sentences.
○ Have students compare their sentences with a partner.
○ Go over the answers with the class.

ANSWER KEY

Answers may vary.

1. Roger and Mary were not allowed to speak to each other during Ta-Na-E-Ka.
2. Grandfather showed Mary and Roger how to eat a grasshopper.
3. For a long time, Mary studied how the Kaws treated women.
4. Berries tasted worse than the grasshoppers.
5. Mrs. Richardson told Mary she was glad to know the money was going to be spent wisely.
6. Roger gave my arm a squeeze.
7. We were trained for Ta-Na-E-Ka by grandfather.

EXPANSION ACTIVITY: Editing Practice

○ Photocopy and distribute the Black Line Master *Editing Practice* on page BLM 13.
○ Have students correct the sentences and then compare ideas with a partner.
○ Go over the answers with the class.

ANSWER KEY

Answers may vary.

1. A hero can either perform a physical act of courage or bring back a spiritual message.
2. In both a *fiesta de quinceañera* and a debutante ball, the young women wear formal dresses, have a party, and invite friends and family.
3. Mary showed her shrewdness by borrowing five dollars, letting herself into the restaurant at night, and making friends with the restaurant owner.
4. Han Solo changes from mercenary to hero when he puts his own life in danger and saves Luke Skywalker.
5. Rites of passage are similar to a hero's journey in that they involve leaving one condition and bringing the person forth into a richer or more mature condition.

PART ⑤ ACADEMIC WRITING, PAGES 223–229

Writing Assignment

○ Go over the information in the box.
○ Have students read the six steps.
○ Direct students' attention to Step A and have students choose one of the two topics.
○ Direct students' attention to Step B. Go over the directions. Have students read and answer the question that corresponds to their chosen topic. Put students in small groups according to their topic to share ideas and take notes. You may want to elicit ideas from the class to answer each question and write the ideas on the board.

WRITING STRATEGY: Understanding the Organization of the Essay

○ Go over the information in the box.
○ Ask questions: *Where do we put the thesis statement? What else goes in the introduction? What are some ways to get the reader's attention? What goes in the body? What should you do in the concluding paragraph?*
○ You may want to read the example essay aloud as students follow silently in their books, or have the students read the essay silently.
○ Read the *Analyzing* directions.
○ Have students answer the questions and then compare answers with a partner.
○ Go over the answers with the class.

ANSWER KEY

1. an anecdote that contains background information
2. The last sentence of the first paragraph. The challenges: hectic pace, lack of community, lure of risky behavior. Noun phrases
3. First body paragraph (or second paragraph of the essay): the first sentence; Third paragraph: the third sentence; Fourth paragraph: the first sentence
4. indentation
5. yes
6. examples
7. restates the thesis

TOEFL® iBT Tip

TOEFL iBT Tip 5: The independent writing task on the TOEFL iBT requires students to think critically about a topic and present their personal preferences or opinions in an organized format.

○ Remind students that the writing strategy for *Understanding the Organization of an Essay* will be important for them to use when writing their essays. They will often be given two ideas and asked to argue for or against one of those ideas, or state a personal preference.

○ The ability to outline and organize an essay in a short period of time will be an invaluable tool to students as they encounter both the independent and integrated writing tasks.

Academic Note

○ You may want to point out that although we usually restate the thesis in the conclusion, the restatement uses the same kinds of strategies as does paraphrasing—it is not simply writing the same sentence again. In fact, stronger conclusions paraphrase the thesis, sometimes refining it slightly to reflect the points made in the essay.

WRITING STRATEGY: Writing a Thesis Statement

○ Go over the information in the box.
○ Ask questions: *What does the thesis statement do? What makes it strong?*

Writing a Thesis Statement

○ Have students write their thesis statements.
○ Put students in pairs to read their thesis statements and get feedback.
○ Call on students to read their thesis statements to the class.

ANSWER KEY

Answers will vary.

WRITING STRATEGY: Writing Topic Sentences in an Essay

○ Go over the information in the box.
○ Ask questions: *What is a topic sentence? What should each topic sentence do?*

Writing Topic Sentences in an Essay

○ Go over the directions.
○ Have students write three topic sentences—one for each body paragraph.

ANSWER KEY

Answers will vary.

TEST-TAKING STRATEGY: Writing Supporting Material in an Essay

○ Go over the information in the box.
○ Ask questions: *What types of evidence can you use as support? What do you need to do if you use ideas from another source?*

❍ Direct students' attention to Step C. Have students organize their information.

❍ Direct students' attention to Step D. Have students write their paragraphs.

❍ Direct students' attention to Step E. Go over the questions. Have students read and edit their paragraphs, using the questions as a guide.

❍ For peer editing, have students exchange paragraphs with a partner, edit, and return to the writer.

EXPANSION ACTIVITY: Presentations

❍ Have students research a myth, hero, or rite of passage.

❍ Instruct students to prepare a one-minute presentation on the topic they researched.

❍ Put students in small groups to give their presentations.

❍ Have volunteers present to the class.

TOEFL® iBT Tip

TOEFL iBT Tip 6: The integrated writing skill on the TOEFL iBT requires students to think critically about material that they have read, interpret that information and relate it to a lecture, then present ideas in essay format.

❍ Remind students that the activities for *Editing* and *Rewriting Your Paragraph* correspond to strategies they will need to use when writing their essays. On the TOEFL iBT, examinees will be able to take notes and summarize ideas in a reading passage or create a brief outline before they write an independent essay.

❍ Students should leave themselves time to read over their work and edit for mistakes, particularly if they choose to type the essay on the computer. Rewriting will give them the opportunity to look at their grammar and punctuation more carefully and refine the organization of the essay.

❍ Go over the directions for Step F. Have students carefully rewrite their paragraphs and hand them in to you.

❍ After you have read and returned students' paragraphs, you may want to set aside time for students to read each other's writing or display the paragraphs in the classroom. Have students keep all of their final versions in a notebook or folder so that they can see their progress and improvement over time.

Unit 3 Vocabulary Workshop

A. Choosing the Correct Dictionary Definition

○ Read the directions.
○ Have students choose the best definition for each sentence.
○ Go over the answers.

ANSWER KEY

1. 3; 2. 4; 3. 2; 4. 1; 5. 2; 6. 1

B. Matching

○ Read the directions.
○ Have students match the definitions to the words.
○ Go over the answers.

ANSWER KEY

1. d; 2. e; 3. b; 4. c; 5. a; 6. f; 7. i; 8. h; 9. j; 10. g

C. Collocations

○ Read the directions.
○ Have students write the correct collocations on the lines.
○ Go over the answers.

ANSWER KEY

1. up; 2. out; 3. back; 4. off; 5. at; 6. on/off; 7. visit;
8. into; 9. natural; 10. of; 11. down; 12. around;
13. from; 14. trial/test; 15. coming

D. Vocabulary Expansion

○ Read the directions.
○ Have students complete the chart with the proper parts of speech.
○ Go over the answers.

ANSWER KEY

	Verbs	Nouns	Adjectives
1.	defer	deference	deferent, deferred
2.	endure	endurance	enduring
3.	profit	profit	profitable
4.	torment	torment	tormented tormenting
5.	diverge	divergence	divergent
6.	prosper	prosperity	prospering prosperous

E. The Academic Word List

○ Read the directions. Remind students the Academic Word List consists of some of the most commonly used words used in English.
○ Have students write the correct words on the lines.
○ Go over the answers.

ANSWER KEY

1. Initially; 2. responses; 3. instructors; 4. formula;
5. contradictory; 6. apparent; 7. focus; 8. participants

UNIT 4

●●●●● ECOLOGY

Unit Opener, page 233

○ Direct students' attention to the photo on page 233. Ask questions: *What do you see? How is this picture related to the unit topic?*
○ Write *ecology* on the board and help students brainstorm words related to endangered species. Ask: *What topics do you think will be in this unit?* Circle the words they suggest.

CHAPTER 7 ENDANGERED SPECIES

In this chapter, students will learn about endangered species, including an endangered way of life for a group of indigenous people. In Part 1 of this chapter, students will read about a group of Indians in Brazil that must be taught to hunt. In Part 2, students will read about the role humans play in the disappearing forests. In Part 3, students will read a research paper detailing ways to save endangered animal species. Part 4 focuses on the mechanics of writing, including understanding ellipses and brackets and a review of source material. Finally, in Part 5, students will write a research paper on a topic related to anthropology, economics, or ecology.

VOCABULARY

biodiversity	game	habitat	sedentary
encroachment	gene pool	indigenous	soil
extinct	greenhouse effect	mammal	wilderness

READING STRATEGIES

Knowing Which New Words to Focus On
Understanding the Passive Voice
Formal Outlining

CRITICAL THINKING STRATEGIES

Thinking Ahead
Making Predictions
Understanding Irony
Outlining
Note: The strategies in bold are highlighted in the Student Book.

MECHANICS

Understanding Punctuation (Ellipses and Brackets)
Review: Using Source Material

WRITING STRATEGIES

Writing a Research Paper
Evaluating Online Sources
Doing Library Research
Writing a Reference List

TEST-TAKING STRATEGY

Finding Errors

CHAPTER 7 Endangered Species

Chapter 7 Opening Photo, page 235

❍ Direct students' attention to the photo. Ask them what is happening in the photo.

❍ Have students discuss the questions. This can be done in pairs, in small groups, or as a class. Define *endangered* (*in danger of disappearing*).

❍ Check students' predictions of the chapter topic.

Culture Note

❍ Pandas are one of the world's most recognized and most endangered animals. Other endangered species include golden lion tamarins, Asian elephants, tigers, cheetahs, clouded leopards, and Micronesian kingfishers. The Smithsonian National Zoological Park website has a photo gallery and information on endangered species.

PART INTRODUCTION
A DUTCH SCIENTIST TEACHES INDIANS TO HUNT, PAGES 236–240

EXPANSION ACTIVITY: Vote with Your Feet

❍ Write *Agree* on one side of the board and *Disagree* on the other.

❍ Explain the activity. As you say a statement, students should move to the word that best expresses their opinion.

❍ Have the students stand or call a group of students to the board.

❍ Read a statement (e.g., *Endangered species should be saved even if it puts people in certain industries out of work*). Remind students to move to express their agreement or disagreement with the statement. Ask students to explain their position. Continue with other statements (and other groups of students). Create your own or use the ones that follow.

❍ *All people should live in a world full of technological advances.*

❍ *Even if certain species of animals, or even groups of people, die out, that's just a consequence of the natural order of living things.*

❍ *We should really try to save all species of plants, not just the ones that are the most profitable to grow.*

Before Reading

CRITICAL THINKING STRATEGY: Thinking Ahead

❍ Thinking ahead is an important critical thinking strategy used throughout the text. By looking at and discussing photos, students can anticipate the content of the reading. Predicting and anticipating content helps students understand new material.

A. Thinking Ahead

❍ Have students look at the photo on page 236. Ask: *Who is this? What kind of life do you think he has?*

❍ Go over the directions and questions. Make sure students know what *game* and *sedentary* mean.

❍ Have students discuss the questions in small groups.

❍ Call on students to share their ideas with the class.

ANSWER KEY

Answers may vary. Possible answers include:

1. One hundred years ago most South American Indians had very few legal rights and were very poor. Since then, some countries have given Indians control over their own land, and their population has begun to increase after centuries of decline. At the same time, their traditional way of life has been threatened as the forests they live in are destroyed.

2. When they couldn't find food, nomadic people moved somewhere else.

3. When nomadic people settle in one place, they may use up the resources of their environment.

Culture Note

❍ The Xavante tribe lives in the Mato Grosso state in Brazil. The tribe is divided into two clans, and marriage is only permitted between the members of different clans. They have a lengthy and complex initiation rite, or rite of passage, for boys. There are fewer than 10,000 members of the tribe today.

🎧 Reading

❍ Have students look at the reading.
❍ Go over the directions and the questions.
❍ Have students read *A Dutch Scientist Teaches Indians to Hunt* silently or have students follow along silently as you play the audio program.

ANSWER KEY

When they became sedentary, the Xavantes forgot their traditional hunting knowledge.
Leeuwenberg is called a "hunting apprentice," but he acts as an advisor to the tribal leaders.

Pronunciation Note

❍ You may want to point out that this reading includes examples of both stressed and unstressed *that*. The word *that* is stressed when it is a subject pronoun (*What is* that?) or a demonstrative (That *student is really smart*.). However, *that* is not stressed when it is used as a relative pronoun (*He is the student that I told you about*.) and introduces an adjective or noun clause. We may also stress *that* when it is followed by a pause.

EXPANSION ACTIVITY: Stressed and Unstressed *that*

❍ Play the audio program or read the passage aloud and have students listen for the word *that*.
❍ Have students underline unstressed *that* and circle the stressed ones.
❍ Go over the answers with the class.

ANSWER KEY

Answers may vary.
All are unstressed except:
The idea is that*, in the future, all Xavantes will be able to combine ancestral techniques with the new knowledge acquired.* (Lines 83–84)
In the second half of the second year, however, the Xavantes began to hunt again in that *area.* (Lines 94–95)

After Reading

A. Comprehension Check

❍ Go over the directions and the questions.
❍ Have students discuss the questions and complete the chart in small groups.
❍ Go over the answers with the class.

ANSWER KEY

1. retrieving hunting techniques; 2. They don't have a concept or words for numbers greater than five.;
3. changing hunting areas when needed;
4.

Traditional Hunting Practices
identify edible fruit migrate to follow game go on family hunting trips fashion bows, arrows, cudgels hunt deer, peccary

How a Sedentary Lifestyle Changed These Practices
family trips less frequent—young people don't learn lost instinct of what and where to hunt more hunting with guns—decrease in game

CRITICAL THINKING STRATEGY: Understanding Irony

❍ Go over the information in the box.
❍ Ask questions: *What is irony? How can we tell when the writer is being ironic?*

B. Understanding Irony
○ Go over the directions and the questions.
○ Have students complete the sentences.
○ Call on students to share their ideas with the class.

ANSWER KEY
Answers may vary.
The irony of *A Dutch Scientist Teaches Indians to Hunt* is that the Xavante Indians need someone from the outside to teach them their own traditions.
This is ironic because the scientist is learning their techniques to teach them back to the Indians.

TOEFL® iBT Tip

TOEFL iBT Tip 1: The TOEFL iBT tests the ability to determine the meaning of words in context. It also requires examinees to understand the purpose of the author, or why the author uses particular words or phrases to illustrate an idea.

○ Point out that the strategy for *Understanding Irony* will help students improve their ability to get the gist and overall understanding of a reading. This is a higher level skill closely linked to inference.

○ This skill will also help students determine the author's purpose; why the author has written the reading in a certain way, or why the author makes a particular statement.

C. In Your Own Words: Summarizing
○ Go over the directions.
○ Have students complete the sentences.
○ Call on students to share their ideas with the class.

ANSWER KEY
Answers will vary.
This reading is about a Dutch scientist who is helping the Xavante Indians keep their hunting traditions.
The author says that Frans Leeuwenberg is learning the Xavante hunting traditions so that he can teach the tribe how to use sustainable hunting techniques.

PART 2 GENERAL INTEREST READING
THE HUMAN FACTOR, PAGES 241–254

Before Reading
A. Thinking Ahead
○ Go over the directions and the questions. Make sure students understand the meanings of *extinct* and *indigenous*.
○ Put students in small groups to discuss the questions.
○ Call on students to share their ideas with the class.

ANSWER KEY
Answers may vary. Possible answers include:
1. *Bio-* means life. Some biomes include grasslands, deserts, tundra, alpine, and savanna. A biome is an environment to which specific forms of life are adapted.
2. People cut down forests for wood or to use the land for farming, construction, or other purposes.
3. Destruction of forests causes increased pollution and loss of plant and animal species. It also threatens the traditional way of life of forest-living people.
4. Dinosaurs died because of climate changes. Climate change created by human pollution may also be the cause of current extinctions. Hunting and the destruction of habitats are other ways humans cause extinctions.
5. A *food chain* is a group of species that eat each other. One example of a food chain is lion-antelope-grass.
6. Indigenous people often live in ways that do not harm their environment. Modern civilizations can control pollution and preserve land as parks.
7. Zoos can preserve endangered species from extinction.
8. Many people think that killing animals for fur is cruel, and some fur comes from illegal hunting of endangered animals.

READING STRATEGY: Knowing Which New Words to Focus On
○ Go over the information in the box.
○ Ask questions: *Do you have to know the meaning of every word you read? How do you know which ones to focus on? When should you look up a word in the dictionary?*

B. Vocabulary Preparation

❍ Go over the directions.
❍ Read the first sentence aloud. Elicit words or phrases that are new to students.
❍ Have students highlight the words they don't know, then decide which ones they can guess, ones they don't need to know, and ones they need to look up.
❍ Elicit examples of each category from the class.

ANSWER KEY

Answers will vary.

🎧 Reading

❍ Go over the directions and the question.
❍ Have students read *The Human Factor* silently or follow along silently as you play the audio program.

ANSWER KEY

Species are becoming extinct because of habitat destruction and pollution. Solutions include the creation of zoos, parks, and gene banks.

Culture Notes

❍ The Chipko movement began spontaneously in the Uttar Pradesh area of the Himalayas. Usually, this kind of activism is by village women, who hug the trees to prevent loggers from cutting them down. It's not clear exactly when the movement began, but it really gained energy in the 1970s.
❍ Edward O. Wilson is a well-known biologist and entomologist (his specialty is ants) who teaches at Harvard. He has written 20 books and has won two Pulitzer Prizes. He has also discovered hundreds of species.
❍ The Cota de Doñana National Park is Spain's largest wildlife reserve. It consists of wetlands and is located on an estuary of the Guadalquivir River. It is home to thousands of birds, 300 species of which are rare. The park is also home to some species of mammals on the verge of extinction (lynx, wild boar).
❍ The Everglades is a national park in southern Florida consisting of sawgrass prairies, mangrove swamps, pine woods, and estuaries. It is home to many species of birds, especially wading birds such as the egret, and animals. It is the only place in the world where alligators and crocodiles live in the same place. For more information, see www.nps.gov/ever/eco/index.htm.
❍ The Sierra Club was founded in 1892, and John Muir, a noted early environmentalist, was its first president. For more than a century, the organization has been involved in preservation of the environment. There are now more than 750,000 members worldwide.
❍ Yellowstone National Park is one of the best-known national parks in the United States. It is located in Idaho, Montana, and Wyoming. It was the first such park in the world, established in 1872. One of the reasons Yellowstone is so attractive to visitors are the geothermal springs, such as Old Faithful, evidence of an active volcano.

After Reading

A. Comprehension Check

❍ Go over the directions.
❍ Put students in small groups to compare main ideas.
❍ Elicit examples from the class.

ANSWER KEY

Answers may vary. Students should note that the world's forests are disappearing due to cutting (for timber, oil prospecting, and growing crops) and pollution, leading to climate change. Many species face extinction due to habitat loss (particularly for specialized habitats) and the introduction of alien species. Efforts have been made to conserve and restore by establishing parks, but more than half of tropical countries have no systematic approach to conservation. Conservation is hampered by social and economic conditions and requires management to be successful. Awareness has grown of the importance of preserving wildlife and plants. As commercial agriculture spreads, traditional crops have been lost. With less plant diversity, our crops are more threatened by disease. Interbreeding can prevent disease and increase yields. National gene banks now exist to preserve genetic diversity of food crops.

READING STRATEGY: Understanding the Passive Voice

○ Go over the information in the box.
○ Ask questions: *When do we use the passive voice? What is the difference in emphasis between passive and active voice?*

B. Understanding the Passive Voice

○ Go over the directions.
○ Put students in pairs to write active voice sentences.
○ Call on students to read their sentences aloud. Ask why the passive voice would be better.

ANSWER KEY

1. People cut much of the rain forest for timber.
2. People clear the land for pastureland for cattle.
3. If people cut the trees down, the trees cease to use carbon dioxide.
4. People may shoot animals such as wolves on sight.
5. In New Zealand, rats from European ships killed flightless birds.
6. Social and economic conditions often hamper conservation.

In all cases, it's more appropriate to focus on the object of the action. In sentences 1–4, the subject is not known, obvious, or not important.

C. Vocabulary Check

○ Go over the directions.
○ Have students match the words and phrases with their definitions.
○ Go over the answers with the class.

ANSWER KEY

1. h; 2. g; 3. b; 4. e; 5. f; 6. c; 7. d; 8. a

EXPANSION ACTIVITY: Describe Your Natural Habitat

○ Model the activity. Tell students about the area you are from using words from Activity C (*There is not a lot of biodiversity where I am from. I grew up in the suburbs of Virginia in the U.S. The most common mammal is the squirrel. The soil is mostly red clay.*

To find a variety of plants and animals, I had to go to the wilderness of the Shenandoah National Forest.).
○ Have students choose four words from Activity C to use in a paragraph describing their native area.
○ Have students write the paragraphs and then share them with a partner.
○ Call on students to read their paragraphs to the class.

D. Collocations

○ Go over the directions.
○ Have students highlight the collocations and then compare ideas with a partner.
○ Call on students to share their ideas with the class.

ANSWER KEY

Answers may vary. Possible answers include:
1. take part in
2. on the brink of extinction
3. known for their intelligence, at the mercy of hunters
4. endangered animals, an educated public

Grammar Note

○ Some grammarians and instructors may distinguish between phrasal verbs (*take part in*) and other types of collocations. In Activity D, it is not important that students make this distinction. The important thing is for students to recognize groups of words that are frequently used in combination.

ANSWER KEY

1. In India, villagers take part in the Chipko movement, which is dedicated to saving Indian forests.
2. There is a decline in species worldwide, and thousands of species are on the brink of extinction.
3. Elephants are known for their intelligence, but they are at the mercy of hunters who kill them for their tusks.
4. Protection of endangered animals requires an educated public and respect for species other than our own.

E. Categorizing

○ Go over the directions.
○ Have students write the more general terms for each group.
○ Call on students to share their ideas with the class.

ANSWER KEY

1. hardwoods; 2. crops grown on cleared tropical forest land; 3. extinct species; 4. recently extinct or near-extinct mammals; 5. species with low rates of reproduction; 6. large species

F. Finding Details

○ Go over the directions.
○ Have students complete the graphic organizers and then compare their answers with a partner.
○ Go over the answers with the class.

ANSWER KEY

1. What are reasons for the clearance of forests?

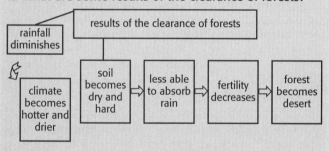

2. What are some results of the clearance of forests?

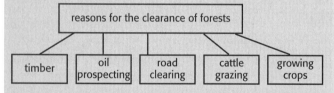

3. What are four causes of the extinction (or near extinction) of animals?

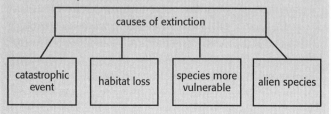

4. What is required in order for conservation sites to be successful?

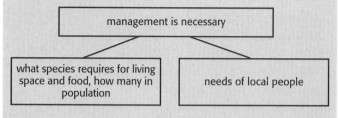

5. How is the interbreeding of crops with wild plants beneficial?

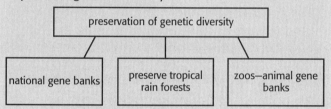

6. In what three ways are attempts being made to preserve genetic diversity?

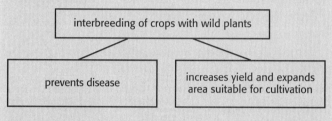

TOEFL® iBT Tip

TOEFL iBT Tip 2: The TOEFL iBT tests the ability to understand key facts and the important information contained within a text. Locating key facts and details in a text will help students improve their overall reading skills.

○ Point out that the reading section of the TOEFL iBT requires examinees to identify information that is included in the passage.

○ The *Finding Details* activity requires students to search for information in the reading based on *wh-* questions (*what*). This is excellent preparation for the factual information questions on the test and can later be applied to questions that require students to select information and organize in schematic tables.

READING STRATEGY: Formal Outlining

○ Go over the information in the box.
○ Ask questions: *How can an outline be helpful? Where do we write the more general topics and ideas?*

G. Formal Outlining

○ Go over the directions.
○ Have students organize the information into an outline.
○ Put students in small groups to compare ideas.
○ Call on students to share their ideas with the class.

ANSWER KEY

Order may vary.

I. Mammals
  A. cats
  B. jaguars
  C. lions
  D. tigers
  E. deer
  F. whales
  G. pandas
II. Birds
  A. eagles
  B. peacocks
  C. pigeons
III. Fish
  A. sharks
  B. tuna

H. Taking Notes

○ Go over the directions.
○ Have students complete the outline and then compare outlines with a partner.
○ Call on students to share their ideas with the class. Consider reproducing the outline on the board.

ANSWER KEY

I. Disappearing Forests
  A. Facts about forests
    1. disappearing faster than any other biome
    2. a third of total tree cover lost since agriculture began
    3. home to more species than any other biome

  B. Tropical rain forests
    1. support at least 50% of world's species
    2. are cut or cleared for
      a. timber
      b. oil prospecting
      c. road clearing
      d. cattle grazing
      e. growing crops
    3. by 1990s—less than $1/2$ of the Earth's original rain forests remained
  C. Forests outside the tropics
    1. are being cleared for
      a. fuel
      b. mining operations
    2. temperate forests are Earth's largest land-based source of carbon
    3. Problem: cut trees can't use carbon dioxide, so CO_2 increases, contributing to the greenhouse effect
  D. Pollution
    1. Europe and North America: pollution is bigger problem than clearing
    2. China: 90% of forests have died from pollutants
  E. Results of the clearing of forests
    1. rainfall diminishes
    2. soil becomes hard and dry
    3. climate becomes hotter and drier
    4. soil less able to absorb rain
    5. fertility decreases
    6. forest becomes desert
II. Under threat of extinction: causes
  A. catastrophic event
  B. habitat loss
    1. clearance of land
    2. water extraction to support development
      a. wetlands drying out
      b. bird species affected
  C. species vulnerable to extinction
    1. specialized habitat
    2. specialized diet
    3. low rates of production
    4. targets of hunters
    5. unusual behavior
  D. other
    1. alien species
    2. humans (tourists) disturbing endangered animals

EXPANSION ACTIVITY: Facts and Opinions

❍ Photocopy and distribute the Black Line Master *Facts vs. Opinions* on page BLM 14.
❍ Elicit ways we can distinguish between fact and opinions. For example, facts are often historical or numerical pieces of information that can be confirmed. Opinions often are indicated by modals, adjectives (especially superlatives), and expressions (*I think*).
❍ Have students look through the reading to find at least three examples of each.
❍ Have students compare ideas with a partner.
❍ Call on students to share their ideas with the class.

ANSWER KEY
Answers may vary.

FACTS	OPINIONS
Tropical rain forests once covered 12 percent of the land of the planet.	This rate of extinction carries with it some terrible consequences.
Millions of hectares of trees in 21 countries are dead or dying.	Habitat loss is one of the most important causes of extinction.
The same damage is occurring in China, where 90 percent of Sichuan province's forests have died.	The needs of local people must also be considered.
Dinosaurs, saber-toothed tigers, and the dodo bird are famous examples of animals that have become extinct.	In southern Africa, most protected areas are those that contain large numbers of mammals, while other areas— equally valuable—are ignored.
Between 20,000 and 30,000 species become extinct every year.	

PART ❸ ACADEMIC READING
THE EDGE OF EXTINCTION, PAGES 255–260

Before Reading
A. Thinking Ahead
❍ Go over the directions and the questions.
❍ Have students discuss the questions in small groups.
❍ Call on students to share their ideas with the class.

ANSWER KEY
Answers will vary.

B. Vocabulary Preparation
❍ Go over the directions.
❍ Have students highlight new vocabulary, then decide which words to look up.
❍ Have students compare ideas in small groups.
❍ Elicit examples of important new vocabulary from the class.

ANSWER KEY
Answers may vary.

🎧 Reading
❍ Go over the directions before the reading. Read the question aloud.
❍ Have students read *The Edge of Extinction* silently or play the audio program and have students follow along silently.
❍ Elicit answers to the question from the class.

ANSWER KEY

The writer advocates studying animals and their habitats, supporting captive breeding programs, and preserving habitats for endangered species.

Culture Note

○ Earthwatch Institute is an international organization that concerns itself with the planet's future. The Institute was founded in 1971 and offers over 4,000 volunteers a year the chance to do research around the world. Volunteers collect data in rain forest ecology, wildlife conservation, marine science, and archaeology. The organization raises $15 million a year in its efforts to save the Earth. Although their headquarters are in Massachusetts in the United States, there are other offices in England, Australia, and Japan.

Pronunciation Notes: Prominence

○ Point out that in each thought group there will usually be one prominent, or stressed, word. Often when words are defined in the sentence, the word being defined will be stressed as well as a key word in the definition. Sometimes there can be more than one prominent word.

○ Demonstrate this with a sentence from the reading: *Clearly, it is possible for human beings to destroy animal life on a vast scale.* Ask students to predict which words might receive greater stress or prominence (e.g., *clearly, possible, beings, destroy, vast*).

EXPANSION ACTIVITY: Prominence in Explanations

○ Have students highlight or underline all the sentences in the reading that explain terms, organizations, or people. Have students mark the thought groups with slashes and then circle words they expect will be more prominent.

○ Call on students to share their ideas with the class.

○ Replay the audio program or read the research paper aloud to have students check their answers.

After Reading

A. Analysis: Essay Format

○ Go over the directions.

○ Put students in pairs to compare highlighted information and then discuss the questions.

ANSWER KEY

1. Thesis statement: Now is the time for humans to reverse this trend by focusing on research, breeding programs for endangered species, and safe habitats for animals in the wild, as a number of organizations are attempting to do in different but overlapping ways (last sentence in first paragraph). Three parts: 1. focusing on research; 2. breeding programs; 3. safe habitats

2. Opener: first sentence

3. Any action taken to save endangered species must be based on solid research.
   Human encroachment into what used to be wilderness makes natural habitats increasingly dangerous places for wildlife, necessitating captive breeding programs to save species from extinction. Safe, natural habitats are crucial to species' ultimate survival.

4. Yes.

5. the thesis

B. Comprehension Check

○ Go over the directions.

○ Brainstorm ideas for different types of graphic organizers (*T-chart, Venn diagram, cause and effect chain, flow chart, cluster diagram*) and write them on the board.

○ Have students create graphic organizers for the three body paragraphs.

○ Put students in small groups to compare graphic organizers.

○ Call on students to share their ideas with the class.

ANSWER KEY

Answers will vary.

C. In Your Own Words: Summarizing

○ Go over the directions.

○ Have students complete the sentences.

○ Call on students to read their sentences to the class.

CHAPTER 7 • Endangered Species • **105**

ANSWER KEY

Answers may vary.

First body paragraph:

The section is about research. The writer says that the research provided, often by volunteers, informs both scientists and the public.

Second body paragraph:

The section is about the need for captive breeding programs. The writer says that captive breeding programs, such as the one begun by Gerald Durrell at a zoo in England, can save endangered species.

Third body paragraph:

The section is about safe habitats. The writer says that safe, natural environments are necessary if species are to survive.

ANSWER KEY

maintaining animal gene banks, breeding in captivity, preserving habitats

TOEFL® iBT Tip

TOEFL iBT Tip 4: The TOEFL iBT tests the ability to understand key facts and the important information contained within a text. Locating key words and ideas in a text will help students build vocabulary and improve their reading skills.

❍ Point out that the *Making Connections* activity focuses on making connections between ideas and will prepare students for integrated questions on a test.

❍ Students will benefit from locating ideas in the text and then sharing their opinions or thoughts about those ideas. This can also help them to synthesize information.

TOEFL® iBT Tip

TOEFL iBT Tip 3: The TOEFL iBT writing section requires examinees to summarize major points and important details from sources. This is more evident in integrated tasks, but this skill can also be applied to independent writing tasks.

❍ Point out to students that several activities in this chapter (vocabulary, scanning, main idea, details, and inference) will help them to interpret what they hear and read and then write about the topic *in their own words*. Summarizing should be clear and succinct, without further explanation.

CRITICAL THINKING STRATEGY: Making Connections

❍ Making connections is an important critical thinking strategy. By connecting new information to something we know or have read, we are better able to understand, synthesize, and remember.

D. Making Connections

❍ Go over the directions.
❍ Put students in small groups to discuss the question.
❍ Call on students to share their ideas with the class.

 EXPANSION ACTIVITY: Endangered Species

❍ Write these words on the board: *mammal, fish, bird, reptile, amphibian.*
❍ Have students do research on the Internet to find four examples of endangered species in each group. You may want to assign students different areas in the world to narrow their research.
❍ Put students in small groups to compare examples.

E. Word Journal

❍ Go over the directions.
❍ Have students write words in their Word Journals.

F. Taking a Survey

○ Go over the directions.
○ Have each student interview two other students. If you do this in class, have students stand and ask two classmates the questions and record the answers. As an out-of-class assignment, have students interview two other students. Encourage students to interview people who know about different countries.
○ Call on students to share what they found out with the class.

ANSWER KEY

Answers will vary.

G. Response Writing

○ Go over the directions.
○ Explain that this is a quick-writing activity and does not have to be perfect. Point out that journal writing can be a warm-up to a more structured writing assignment, helping to generate ideas.
○ Set a time limit of 15 minutes.
○ Put students in pairs to read or talk about their writing.

Internet Research

○ For additional information on conservation, see:
  • www.wcs.org/
  • www.nature.org/
  • www.iucn.org/
  • www.panda.org/
  • www.nature.nps.gov/globalconservation/index.cfm
  • www.earthwatch.org/site/pp.asp?c=8nJELMNkG iF&b=1322375

EXPANSION ACTIVITY: Presentations on Endangered Species

○ Put students in pairs or small groups.
○ Have students research an endangered species. You may want to provide these guidelines: description of species, description of habitat, analysis of threats, possible solutions.
○ Have students prepare a three to five minute presentation on their topic.
○ Have students present to the class.

PART ④ THE MECHANICS OF WRITING, PAGES 261–263

○ Go over the information about Part 4.

Understanding Punctuation: Ellipses and Brackets

○ Go over the information in the box.
○ Ask comprehension questions: *When do we use ellipses? How can we indicate that material has been added?*

A. Understanding Punctuation: Ellipses and Brackets

○ Go over the directions.
○ Have students highlight the examples of ellipses and brackets.
○ Go over the answers with the class.

ANSWER KEY

Ellipses:
species are . . . disappearing . . . a thousand times faster (Line 7)
is to help save a generation of endangered turtles, . . . the real value (Line 23)
which closely resemble their natural homes . . . in the wild (Line 36)
that's more than 30 years old . . . funded (Line 43)
from it's 2.5 million members . . . [is] saving (Line 44)
Brackets:
three [species] per hour (Line 6)
from it's 2.5 million members . . . [is] saving (Line 44)
[and] protecting oceans (Line 45)

Review: Using Source Material

○ Go over the information in the box.
○ Ask questions: *What do you have to do if you copy material? What should you do when you paraphrase someone else's ideas? What do you need to be careful about when you weave in quotations?*

B. Using Source Material

❍ Go over the directions.
❍ Read the source paragraph aloud or have students read it silently.
❍ Have students read the paragraphs by Students A and B.
❍ Put students in pairs to discuss the questions.
❍ Call on students to share their ideas with the class.

ANSWER KEY

1. Student A
2. The ideas are too much like the source; the wording only changed slightly. The writer did not cite the source. There are grammatical mistakes.
3. Student B
4. The student used quotes correctly, cited the source immediately, paraphrased where possible, and was grammatically correct.
5. ellipses used for deletions; brackets for additions

C. Using Source Material

❍ Go over the directions.
❍ Have students write paragraphs for each box.
❍ Put students in small groups to discuss the questions.
❍ Call on students to share their ideas with the class.

ANSWER KEY

Answers will vary.

EXPANSION ACTIVITY: Editing Practice

❍ Photocopy and distribute the Black Line Master *Editing Practice* on page BLM 15.
❍ Have students correct the references and then compare ideas with a partner.
❍ Go over the answers with the class. Have students compare their corrections with page 259 of the Student Book.

ANSWER KEY

See Student Book, p. 259.

TOEFL® iBT Tip

TOEFL iBT Tip 5: Although the TOEFL iBT does not discretely test grammar skills, examinees' essay scores will be determined based on the range of grammar and vocabulary used in their essays.

❍ Point out that the grammar activities in *The Mechanics of Writing* part of this chapter will help them improve the organization and coherence of their essays. It will also benefit students to work with conditional forms in preparation for cause and effect or persuasive/argumentative essays that they may write on the test.

PART ⑤ ACADEMIC WRITING, PAGES 264–269

Writing Assignment

❍ Go over the information about the assignment in the box.
❍ Ask questions: *How long will your research paper be? How many sources do you need?*

WRITING STRATEGY: Writing a Research Paper

❍ Go over the information in the box.
❍ Ask: *What is a research paper? What are criteria? What's the difference between an essay and a research paper? What is another word for a list of references? What is a style sheet or a style manual? What do they tell you?*

❍ Direct students' attention to Step A. Have students choose a topic. Encourage students to select a topic they find interesting after discussing the choices in small groups.

WRITING STRATEGY: Evaluating Online Sources

○ Go over the information in the box.
○ Ask comprehension questions: *What are some possible problems with online research? What are some ways you can make sure the information on a website is reliable? What is a source log and why should you keep one on your computer?*

○ Direct students' attention to Step B. Ask: *What types of information should you record on your source log?* Have students create a template for their source logs on the computer.

WRITING STRATEGY: Doing Library Research

○ Go over the information in the box.
○ Ask comprehension questions: *When will you use books as source material? How can you search for a book? What are periodicals? How can you find articles on your topic? What is an abstract? Where can you find very old periodicals?*

○ Direct students' attention to the source log in Step C. Ask questions: *What information should you record? What questions surprise you?* Go over the directions for Step C. Have students begin researching their topics. Remind students to record their source information on a source log for their books and periodicals.
○ Direct students' attention to Step D. Go over the directions and the techniques. Have students read their sources using one of the techniques.

WRITING STRATEGY: Writing a Reference List

○ If you have a particular style you want students to use (e.g., one required by your school), you should bring the information and present it to the students.
○ Go over the information in the box.
○ Ask comprehension questions: *Where can you find a complete list of rules for writing a reference list? What do you usually put at the top? How are sources usually listed? What are some differences between how books, periodicals, and websites are listed?*

TOEFL® iBT Tip

TOEFL iBT Tip 6: The independent writing task on the TOEFL iBT requires students to think critically about a topic and present their ideas in an organized format.

○ Tell students that the *Writing Strategies* in this chapter will help them to improve their overall research methodologies and the process of writing a research paper. Although they will not have to go through these processes for the TOEFL iBT, these strategies will help students formalize their essays and understand how they are developed.

○ Remind students that paraphrasing, summarizing, and knowing when to use quotes will be invaluable to them in their academic writing as well as on the TOEFL iBT. They should also devote time to correcting their essays and using the correct punctuation, which will help improve their overall scores.

○ Direct students' attention to Step E. Go over the directions. Have students create their own reference lists.
○ Direct students' attention to Step F. Go over the directions. Put students in groups of four to exchange and edit lists. Remind students to exchange with each of the other members in the group. Have students rewrite their lists.
○ Collect the lists and provide feedback.

CHAPTER 8 HUMAN ECOLOGY

In this chapter, students will learn about human ecology. In Part 1, students will read about nine steps people can take to achieve a healthier environment. In Part 2, students will read part of a chapter about pesticides. In Part 3, students will read a research paper on the health problems caused by the disposal of old or obsolete computers. Part 4 focuses on the mechanics of writing, including reducing adjective clauses to participial phrases, using participial phrases at the beginning and end of a sentence, using internal citations, varying citation forms, citing sources that cite sources, and learning to include long quotes. In Part 5, students will write the research paper they planned in Chapter 7.

VOCABULARY

aquifers	exterminators	mortality	solvents
diminish	fumigate	obsolete	swell
discarded	halve (halving)	residues	toxicity
drastic	innovative	resource-intensive	
emission	lethal	respiratory	

READING STRATEGY

Organizing Ideas

CRITICAL THINKING STRATEGIES

Thinking Ahead
Making Connections
Seeing Both Sides of an Argument Part 1
Note: The strategy in bold is highlighted in the Student
  Book.

MECHANICS

Reducing Adjective Clauses to Participial Phrases
Using Participial Phrases at the End of a Sentence
Using Participial Phrases at the Beginning of a Sentence
Using Internal Citations
Varying Citation Forms
Citing Sources that Cite Sources
Including Long Quotes

WRITING STRATEGIES

Planning an Essay by Using a Formal Outline
Writing Introductions–Writing Conclusions

TEST-TAKING STRATEGIES

Practicing Fill-in-the-Blank Questions
Finding Errors

Chapter 8 Opening Photo, page 271

○ Direct students' attention to the photo. Ask them what is happening in the photo.
○ Have students discuss the questions. This can be done in pairs, in small groups, or as a class. Define *human ecology* (*the interaction between people and their environment*).
○ Check students' predictions of the chapter topic.

PART ❶ INTRODUCTION
SIMPLE SOLUTIONS, PAGES 272–276

EXPANSION ACTIVITY: Category Sort

○ Explain the activity. Tell students that they will stand and you will ask questions. The students should walk around and ask their classmates questions and then stand with people who have the same or similar answers to the question.
○ Ask: *What is the most important thing you do to help the environment?* Remind students to move around and talk to each other so that they can group themselves according to response. When students are grouped, ask each group what they represent (e.g., *contribute to an organization, ride bike to school*).
○ Ask questions related to the topics in the chapter. Create your own or use the ones below.
What is the thing you do that causes the most damage to the environment?
What environmental problem are you most concerned about?
How likely are you to eat all-organic food?

Before Reading

EXPANSION ACTIVITY: Writing Prompt

○ Have students choose one of the photos and write about it for five minutes. Tell students they can describe what they see, tell a story, or discuss their feelings or ideas about the photo.

○ Put students in pairs to talk about their writing.
○ Call on volunteers to share what they wrote with the class.

Thinking Ahead

○ Have students look at the photos on page 272.
○ Go over the directions and questions.
○ Have students discuss the questions in small groups.
○ Call on students to share their ideas with the class.

ANSWER KEY

Answers may vary. Possible answers include:
1. Feedlot beef production is wasteful of water, grain, and soil. Rush hour causes air pollution. Agricultural pesticides cause air and water pollution. Recycling computers releases many toxic chemicals into the environment.
2. Most of the pictures show activities involving toxic chemicals. All these can directly harm human health. Beef production is destructive to the environment, which harms health indirectly.
3. Answers will vary.

Reading

○ Go over the directions and the question.
○ Have students read silently, or have students follow along silently as you play the audio program.
○ Ask students the question and elicit answers.

ANSWER KEY

any or all of the nine steps in the reading

Culture Note

○ Every April, the United States celebrates Earth Day. Ideas the Earth Day supporters promote are vacuum and dust your home often to help purify the air, choose organic clothing, use water purification systems, burn soy candles, and plant more trees.

EXPANSION ACTIVITY: Ranking
- ❍ Photocopy and distribute the Black Line Master *Ranking: Nine Steps to a Healthier Environment* on page BLM 16.
- ❍ Have students rank the nine steps in order of most likely to implement to least likely to implement.
- ❍ Have students compare rankings with a partner.
- ❍ Call on students to tell the class what they would be most likely to try and least likely to try.

ANSWER KEY
Answers will vary.

After Reading

A. Comprehension Check
- ❍ Go over the directions.
- ❍ Put students in small groups to discuss the questions.
- ❍ Go over the answers with the class.

ANSWER KEY
1. Wealthy countries use the most resources and make the most pollution.
2. Steps 1, 4, 5, 6, 8
3. Step 7 (Steps 2, 4, and 8 save water.)

B. Vocabulary Check
- ❍ Go over the directions.
- ❍ Have students write the words on the lines.
- ❍ Have students check their answers with a partner.
- ❍ Go over the answers with the class.

ANSWER KEY
1. respiratory; 2. innovative; 3. drastic; 4. emission;
5. resource-intensive; 6. halving; 7. diminishing;
8. swell

TOEFL® iBT Tip

TOEFL iBT Tip 1: The TOEFL iBT tests the ability to determine the meaning of words in context.

- ❍ Point out that the *Vocabulary Check* activity will help students improve their vocabulary for the TOEFL iBT. By identifying words that are used as synonyms or explanations of other words and understanding their meanings, students will be able to apply this information toward further understanding the concepts presented in the text.

- ❍ This skill will also help them in paraphrasing and summarizing when they need to use definitions or synonyms for words found in the text.

C. Taking a Survey
- ❍ Go over the directions.
- ❍ Have students stand and walk around the room to complete the chart.
- ❍ Call on students to share what they learned with the class.

ANSWER KEY
Answers will vary.

D. Extension
- ❍ Go over the directions.
- ❍ Put students in small groups to discuss what people in other countries could do.
- ❍ Call on students to share their ideas with the class.

ANSWER KEY
Answers will vary.

EXPANSION ACTIVITY: Ad Campaigns

○ Put students in pairs or small groups.
○ Have students choose one of the nine steps from the reading on pages 273–274 of the Student Book for which they will develop an ad campaign. Explain that students can create a print ad, a public service radio ad, or a television ad to encourage people to adopt the step.
○ Have students present their ideas to the class.
○ Vote on the best ad.

PART ② GENERAL INTEREST READING
ARE PESTICIDES SAFE?, PAGES 277–285

Before Reading
A. Thinking Ahead
○ Go over the directions and the questions.
○ Have students discuss the questions in small groups.
○ Call on students to share their ideas with the class.

ANSWER KEY
Answers may vary. Possible answers include:
1. Answers will vary.
2. It is likely that some pesticides can cause cancer in humans. Some pesticides may also be neurotoxic to (that is, harm the nervous systems of) young children.
3. It is very difficult to avoid pesticides which are present throughout the environment.

B. Vocabulary Preparation
○ Go over the directions.
○ Have students identify the words they don't know, then decide which ones they can guess, which words they don't need to know, and which ones they need to look up.
○ Elicit examples of each category from the class.

ANSWER KEY
Answers will vary.

EXPANSION ACTIVITY: Original Sentences

○ Have students choose five new words from Activity B and write each in an original sentence.
○ Have volunteers write sentences on the board, omitting the new vocabulary words and substituting blanks.
○ Have students complete the sentences.

Reading

○ Go over the directions and the questions.
○ Have students read *Are Pesticides Safe?* as a homework or lab assignment.

ANSWER KEY
We encounter pesticides almost everywhere: in food, water, air, homes, workplaces, fabrics, household cleaners, insect repellents, flea collars, paint, and carpeting.
Dangers of pesticides include poisoning, internal bleeding, respiratory failure, and cancers.

EXPANSION ACTIVITY: Updating

○ Point out that scientific information changes all the time, especially statistics.
○ Put students in small groups.
○ Assign each group one of the organizations mentioned in the reading (EPA, NRDC, NTP, NCI, or NAS). Have students individually look for updated information from the organization's website.
○ Have students compare information in their original small groups.
○ Regroup students so that each member of the new group represents a different organization. Have students share what they found out.

Academic Notes

○ Explain that certain types of readings often use sidebars—boxes placed to the side of the main text—to highlight information related to the main content of the reading.

○ Point out the sidebar in this reading. Elicit ideas as to why this material is boxed.

Pronunciation Note

○ You may want to point out that appositive constructions (the phrases and clauses that follow and modify a noun or noun phrase) usually have a certain intonation pattern. This pattern starts low, rises a little in the middle, then falls again. This reading includes examples of appositive constructions. See the following Expansion Activity that includes practice to reinforce this concept.

EXPANSION ACTIVITY: Appositive Constructions

○ Direct students' attention to Lines 13–18 in the reading *Are Pesticides Safe?* Elicit the appositive construction.

○ Have students underline appositive constructions in the reading.

○ Play the audio program or read the passage aloud and have students confirm the intonation pattern.

ANSWER KEY

Lines 67–69: a California physician who has treated many migrant farm workers with pesticide-related illnesses and who is now head of San Francisco's Pesticide Education Center; Lines 78–79: a fumigant banned in 1983; Line 80: one of the scientists; Line 81: another banned chemical; Lines 82–83: a place to store drinking water; Lines 88–90: a Natural Resources Defense Council [NRDC] scientist; Line 103: mainly pesticides; Lines 104–105: a coalition of environmental, business, and governmental groups; Line 107: heaven's gentle dew; Line 118: the lucky ones; Lines 121–122: a common herbicide; Lines 143–144: chairman of the Academy of Pediatrics

environmental hazards committee; Line 153: alachlor; Lines 185–186: the years it was in common use; Lines 208–209: one of Berton Roeuche's always-fascinating "Annals of Medicine"

After Reading

A. Comprehension Check

○ Go over the directions.

○ Put students in pairs to discuss the questions.

○ Call on students to share their ideas with the class.

ANSWER KEY

Refer to the Answer Key for the Reading questions on page 113 of the Teacher's Edition.

EXPANSION ACTIVITY: Scanning

○ Have students write three questions that can be answered by scanning. *According to the National Academy of Sciences (NAS), how many Americans will develop cancer because of pesticide residues on produce? (20,000)*

○ Put students in pairs to exchange and answer questions.

○ Call on students to give examples of questions and answers.

B. Vocabulary Check

○ Go over the directions.

○ Have students match the new words with their definitions.

○ Go over the answers with the class.

ANSWER KEY

1. f; 2. g; 3. b; 4. c; 5. e; 6. a; 7. d

C. Collocations

○ Go over the directions.

○ Put students in small groups to discuss and highlight the collocations.

○ Go over the answers with the class.

ANSWER KEY

1. For a man who wanted to (take a break) after burglarizing (an empty house) that was being fumigated, crime did not pay.
2. Neighbors found him (writhing in pain) naked (on the front lawn) of the San Fernando, California, home, having (torn off his clothes) in an (attempt to) (rid himself) of their pesticide contamination.
3. Obviously, pesticides are not (something to fool) (around with).

READING STRATEGY: Organizing Ideas

○ Go over the information in the box.
○ Ask questions: *What are some ways to organize information? What can graphic organizers show?*

D. Organizing Ideas

○ Go over the directions.
○ Brainstorm ideas for different types of graphic organizers (*T-chart, Venn diagram, cause and effect chain, flow chart, cluster diagram*) and write them on the board.
○ Elicit ideas for what each type of chart can show (e.g., *Venn diagram—compare and contrast*).
○ Have students create graphic organizers for the reading.
○ Put students in pairs or small groups to compare graphic organizers.

ANSWER KEY

Answers will vary.

CRITICAL THINKING STRATEGY: Seeing Both Sides of an Argument

○ Go over the information in the box.
○ Ask questions: *Why is it important to be able to see both sides of an argument? How can you practice this strategy?*

E. Seeing Both Sides of an Argument

○ Go over the directions.
○ Put students in small groups to develop arguments in favor of pesticides.
○ Call on students to share their ideas with the class.

TOEFL® iBT Tip

TOEFL iBT Tip 2: The integrated writing skill on the TOEFL iBT requires students to think critically about material that they have read, interpret that information and relate it to a lecture, then present ideas in essay format.

○ Point out that the *Seeing Two Sides of an Argument* activity corresponds to a strategy they will need to use when writing both integrated and independent essays. They may be presented with two ideas and asked to argue for or against one of those ideas, or state a personal preference about an issue. They may also be required to listen to part of a lecture or conversation and read a related text, then analyze both sides of an issue.

EXPANSION ACTIVITY: Party Small Talk

○ Explain the activity. Students will take on the roles of certain characters, three of whom are presented in Activity E (the farmer, the fumigator, the scientist). They will stand and mill around the room as if they were at an informal party for people with different points of view on pesticides.
○ Assign everyone a role. It is O.K. if the roles are duplicated. Create your own or use the ones below (in addition to the three in the book).
  A mother whose child has cancer
  A former worker in a pesticide factory who has respiratory problems
  A supermarket owner who wants to provide low-cost fruits and vegetables to his inner-city customers
  The principal of a school who is concerned about both student health and school costs
○ Have students stand and walk around the room to talk about the pros and cons of pesticide use.
○ After 15 minutes, call on students to share what they learned with the class.

F. Making Connections

❍ Go over the directions.
❍ Have students discuss the question in small groups.
❍ Call on students to share their ideas with the class.

PART ③ ACADEMIC READING
THE EFFECTS OF E-WASTE, PAGES 285–291

Before Reading

A. Thinking Ahead

❍ Direct students' attention to the photo and ask: *What do you think about what you see in this photo?*
❍ Go over the directions and the questions.
❍ Have students discuss the questions in small groups.
❍ Call on students to share their ideas with the class.

ANSWER KEY

Answers may vary. Possible answers include:
1. As well as plastic, glass, and silicon, computers contain metals such as lead, mercury, cadmium, and copper.
2. Heavy metals are toxic if ingested, and the flame retardants used on computers may be harmful to women and children. Some kinds of plastic release toxic chemicals when they are burned.
3. Most discarded computers are sent to be recycled in developing countries.
4. Answers will vary.

B. Vocabulary Preparation

❍ Go over the directions.
❍ Have students highlight new vocabulary and decide which words to look up.
❍ Put students in small groups to compare highlighted words.
❍ Call on students to share their ideas with the class. You may want to assign words to different students to look up and report the definitions to the class.

ANSWER KEY

Answers will vary.

EXPANSION ACTIVITY: Class Flash Cards

❍ Assign new vocabulary from Activity B to students to look up. You may want to include new vocabulary from other parts of this chapter or even other chapters.
❍ Give each student an index card to write his or her word on.
❍ Have students look up their words and write the definition(s) on the back of the index card.
❍ Collect the cards. Go over the definitions.
❍ Put the cards in an index card box and keep it as a resource in the classroom. Students can use the flash cards to prepare for chapter tests.

∩ Reading

❍ Go over the directions before the reading. Read the question aloud.
❍ Have students read *E-Waste* silently or play the audio program and have students follow along silently.
❍ Elicit answers to the question from the class.

ANSWER KEY

Three dangerous chemicals found in computers are polybrominated diphenyl ethers (PBDEs), Polyvinyl chloride (PVC), and heavy metals (such as lead and mercury).

Pronunciation Note

❍ This reading contains several compound nouns. In a compound noun, such as *law enforcement*, the first word usually receives more stress.

EXPANSION ACTIVITY: Identify Compound Nouns

❍ Have students reread the passage and underline compound nouns.
❍ Put students in pairs to compare ideas.
❍ Call on students to share their ideas with the class.
❍ Play the audio program or read the passage aloud to confirm stress.

ANSWER KEY

Law enforcement, healthcare, e-waste contamination, workforce, computer monitors, health effects, flame retardants, computer screens, household objects, fire retardants, breast milk, behavior problems, human body, heart disease

After Reading

A. Main Ideas

○ Go over the directions and the questions.
○ Put students in pairs or small groups to discuss the answers to the questions.
○ Call on students to share their ideas with the class.

ANSWER KEY

Heavy metals—health effects such as cancer, birth defects, hormone disruption, neurological damage
Flame retardants—affect breast milk, causes learning, memory, and behavioral problems in lab animals
PVCs—dioxin is carcinogenic, also leads to reproductive and developmental problems and increased heart disease and diabetes

B. Analysis: Essay Format

○ Go over the directions.
○ Put students in small groups to discuss the main ideas and answer the questions.
○ Go over the answers with the class.

ANSWER KEY

1. thesis statement—last sentence of the first paragraph—personal computers contain lead and many other heavy metals . . . Three parallel parts: heavy metals, flame retardants, PVCs
2. opener—first paragraph
3. first sentences of the three body paragraphs
4. yes
5. the introduction and thesis

C. Checking Details

○ Go over the directions.
○ Have students create graphic organizers for each of the body paragraphs and then compare ideas in small groups.
○ Call on students to share their ideas with the class.

D. In Your Own Words: Summarizing

○ Go over the directions.
○ Have students complete the sentences to summarize one of the body paragraphs.
○ Call on students to share their ideas with the class.

ANSWER KEY

Body Paragraph 1: This paragraph is about the harmful effects of lead. The author says that the improper disposal of lead causes environmental and health problems including cancer, birth defects, hormone disruptions, and neurological damage.
Body Paragraph 2: This paragraph is about the effects of flame retardants. The author says that PBDEs are in many household objects and can be found in the breast milk of mothers, causing learning, memory, and behavior problems in women and children.
Body Paragraph 3: This paragraph is about the plastic, PVC. The writer says that PVC is the main source of dioxin, a substance that causes cancer.

E. Making Connections

○ Go over the directions.
○ Have students discuss their ideas in small groups.
○ Call on students to share their ideas with the class.

F. Word Journal

○ Go over the directions.
○ Have students write words in their Word Journals.

G. Response Writing

○ Go over the directions.
○ Explain that this is a quick-writing activity and does not have to be perfect. Point out that journal writing can be a warm-up to a more structured writing assignment, helping to generate ideas.
○ Set a time limit of 15 minutes.
○ Put students in pairs to read or talk about their writing.

TOEFL® iBT Tip

TOEFL iBT Tip 3: The TOEFL iBT requires examinees to synthesize information from spoken and written texts and respond in a speaking task or a writing task. Response writing is a good way to help students express themselves openly in preparation for these types of tasks.

○ Point out that being able to read and explain or interpret a text will be helpful in building up to the integrated writing and speaking tasks. The *Response Writing* activity will help students get their ideas down on paper to be able to construct an opinion about a specific topic. It will help them to activate the vocabulary that they already have in mind for a particular topic and practice incorporating new vocabulary words in their responses.

 Internet Research

○ For additional information on ecology and the environment, see:
- www.ewaste.ch/
- www.svtc.org/cleancc/pubs/sayno.htm
- www.ciwmb.ca.gov/Electronics/WhatisEwaste/
- www.pesticides.gov.uk/
- www.epa.gov/pesticides/
- www.infochangeindia.org/toxictours13.jsp
- es.epa.gov/techinfo/facts/nc/nc-fs6.html

PART THE MECHANICS OF WRITING, PAGES 292–299

○ Go over the information about Part 4.

Reducing Adjective Clauses to Participial Phrases

○ Go over the information in the box.
○ Ask comprehension questions: *Why do we sometimes use participial phrases? What participle do we use if the clause is in the passive? In the active?*

A. Reducing Adjective Clauses to Participial Phrases

○ Go over the directions and the examples.
○ Have students rewrite the sentences using participial phrases.
○ Have students compare sentences in pairs.
○ Go over the answers with the class.

ANSWER KEY

1. A woman in India, having been exposed to dioxin, was diagnosed with heart disease.
2. The discarded computers polluting the drinking water had been sent from the United States.
3. The CEO, notified of the dangers of offshore computer recycling, decided to take more responsibility for discarding of his company's product.
4. Gallons of sewage flowing directly into the river last Friday contaminated New Jersey beaches.
5. The 50-year-old woman from Utah, growing up near a nuclear test site, always wondered if she would someday develop cancer.
6. According to Lawson, average Americans, surrounded by deadly pesticides, are continually risking their health.
7. The school sent a note home to parents complaining about the use of toxic cleaners in the classrooms.
8. I knew that the product was dangerous because I read the list of ingredients appearing on the packaging.

Using Participial Phrases at the End of a Sentence

○ Go over the information in the box.
○ Ask questions: *Why would you put a participial phrase at the end of the sentence? Does it go before or after the noun it modifies?*

B. Sentence Combining

○ Go over the directions.
○ Have students combine each pair of sentences using the second clause as a participial phrase.
○ Have students compare sentences with a partner.
○ Call on students to read their sentences to the class.

ANSWER KEY

1. This is the woman from Utah diagnosed with heart disease.
2. The floors of many houses are covered with dust containing pesticides.
3. Dust with pesticides makes floors dangerous to babies crawling across them.
4. Tim watched the plane spraying pesticides on the crops.
5. Sarah worried about the farm workers affected by the fumes.

Using Participial Phrases at the Beginning of a Sentence

○ Go over the information in the box.
○ Ask questions: *What does a participial phrase at the beginning of a sentence refer to? What does such a participial phrase indicate?*

C. Analysis

○ Go over the directions.
○ Put students in pairs to discuss the questions as they apply to each sentence.
○ Go over the answers with the class.

ANSWER KEY

1. past, passive, cause; 2. past, passive, cause; 3. present, active, less important; 4. past, passive, cause; 5. present, active, cause

EXPANSION ACTIVITY: Find Examples

○ Bring in examples of readings from textbooks, magazine articles, online articles, and newspapers, or have students bring in examples as an out-of-class assignment.
○ Have students find as many examples as they can of participial phrases.
○ Put students in pairs to compare their findings.
○ Call on students to share examples with the class.

D. Sentence Combining

○ Go over the directions.
○ Have students combine the sentences and then compare answers with a partner.
○ Go over the answers with the class.

ANSWER KEY

Answers may vary. Possible answers include:
1. Containing pesticides, pressure-treated wood can make carpenters sick.
2. Living in areas with high herbicide use, these people are 60 percent more likely to die of leukemia.
3. Concerned about how the media would present her company's policies, the CEO called a press conference about recycling practices.
4. Not agreeing with Lawson's ideas, I went to the library to find an article on the other side of the issue.
5. Angered about an article on offshore recycling, the CEO changed her company's recycling policies.

TOEFL® iBT Tip

TOEFL iBT Tip 4: Although the TOEFL iBT does not discretely test grammar skills, examinees' essay scores will be determined based on the range of grammar and vocabulary used in their essays.

○ Point out that the grammar activities in *The Mechanics of Writing* part of this chapter will help them improve their abilities to write essays by using adjective clauses and participial phrases to modify nouns in their sentences. This will help them write in a more sophisticated style. Their essays may be given higher scores based on their use of correct grammar, punctuation, and sophisticated language.

Using Internal Citations/General Guidelines/Variations

○ Go over the information in the box.
○ Ask questions: *What is an internal citation? What are some ways we can write an internal citation?*

E. Using Internal Citations
○ Go over the directions and the examples.
○ Have students work in pairs to look through the research paper and find examples.
○ Call on students to share their ideas with the class.

ANSWER KEY
1. none; 2. Birnbaum and Staskal (2004), Lunder and Sharp (2003), (Lunder & Sharp, 2003, p. 5); 3. (Puckett et al., 2002, p. 2); 4. the Premier Safety Institute (2005), (Agency for Toxic Substances and Disease Registry [ATSDR], 1992, pp. 7–8), (Silicon Valley Toxics Coalition, n.d., ¶36), (U.S. Department of Health and Human Services, 2003); 5. "milk from two study participants . . . " (Lines 42–44)

Varying Citation Forms
○ Go over the information in the box.
○ Ask questions: *Why should you vary your citation formats? What are some different things you may want to emphasize?*

Citing Sources that Cite Sources
○ Go over the information in the box.
○ Ask questions: *What expression should you use when citing a source that is citing another source? Do you need to include both sources in your reference list?*

Including Long Quotes
○ Go over the information in the box.
○ Ask questions: *What is a block quote? How do we format a block quote?*
○ Ask students to find the block quote, the source, and the page number.

F. Varying Citation Formats
○ Go over the directions.
○ Have students look back at the three research papers and find examples of the different citation forms.
○ Elicit examples.

G. Citing Sources Internally
○ Go over the directions.
○ Have students practice summarizing, paraphrasing, quoting, and citing sources internally. You may want to give students specific assignments on each skill (e.g., write a summary of the paragraph, paraphrase two sentences, use a quote in a paraphrase, use an internal citation), or you may want students to write a summary only half the length of the original paragraph that uses all strategies.
○ Put students in pairs to exchange and read summaries.
○ Call on students to read their summaries to the class.

EXPANSION ACTIVITY: Editing Practice
○ Photocopy and distribute the Black Line Master Editing Practice on page BLM 17.
○ Have students correct the sentences and then compare ideas with a partner.
○ Go over the answers with the class.

ANSWER KEY
1. ~~Exposing~~ ^Exposed^ to their pets' flea collars, many children developed cancer.
2. Kansas farmers ~~used~~ ^using^ the weed killer 2, 4-D had a higher-than-average risk of contracting malignant lymphoma.
3. ~~Contained~~ ^Containing^ fungicide, human shampoos may also be somewhat hazardous to your health.
4. Replacing my standard bulbs with energy-efficient CFLs ^,^ I saved money on my electric bills.
5. Animals ~~catching~~ ^caught^ accidentally as a result of wasteful fishing techniques are known as *bycatch*.
6. The company was reluctant to hire fired from his last job the CEO.

PART ⑤ ACADEMIC WRITING, PAGES 299–302

Writing Assignment
- ❍ Go over the information in the box.
- ❍ Direct students' attention to Step A and have students write a thesis statement and three topic sentences. You may want to have students discuss their ideas in pairs.
- ❍ Direct students' attention to Step B. Go over the directions and the bulleted steps. Have students take notes on their evidence, following the guidelines.

WRITING STRATEGY: Planning an Essay by Using a Formal Outline
- ❍ Go over the information in the box.
- ❍ Ask questions: *How can an outline help you? What does the introduction include? How many body paragraphs are there? How many examples or key points support each body paragraph? What do you think should go in the conclusion?*

- ❍ Go over the directions for Step C. Have students create outlines for their essays.

TOEFL® iBT Tip

TOEFL iBT Tip 5: The independent and integrated writing tasks on the TOEFL iBT require students to think critically about a topic and present their opinions in an organized format.

- ❍ Remind students that the strategy for writing a *Formal Outline* will help them to put their ideas down on paper in a succinct and organized way. Though they will not have a lot of time to write essays on the TOEFL iBT, one way they can benefit from outlining is when they are taking notes on lectures or while reading a text.

- ❍ As students prepare to write their essay for the TOEFL iBT, they should make sure that they include an introduction with an opener and thesis statement, body paragraphs, and a strong conclusion. The outlining strategy and an activity based on this strategy will provide students with the practice they need to write an essay under timed conditions.

WRITING STRATEGY: Writing Introductions/Writing Conclusions
- ❍ Go over the information in the box.
- ❍ Ask comprehension questions: *Why is the graphic for the introduction an inverted pyramid? What does it show? How should the introduction begin? How should it end? Why does the conclusion have the opposite structure? What does a good conclusion do?*

TOEFL® iBT Tip

TOEFL iBT Tip 6: Both the integrated and independent essays of the TOEFL iBT will be scored based on how well the examinee completes the overall writing task.

○ Point out that the strategies for *Writing Introductions* and *Writing Conclusions* in this chapter will help students improve their coherence and the flow of ideas in their essays by taking smaller steps in their essay development. The "process writing" approach will help students organize their thoughts and take meaningful steps toward developing their essays.

○ Remind students that constructing an appropriate introduction to an essay will help in the organization and development of ideas in the essay. The reiteration of their topic and the ideas that they express in the conclusion by rewording the thesis statement will also strengthen their TOEFL iBT essay and improve their overall score.

EXPANSION ACTIVITY: Presentations
○ Have students research a topic related to the content of the chapter such as a specific conservation strategy or pollutant.
○ Instruct students to prepare a five-minute presentation on the topic they researched.
○ Put students in small groups to give their presentations.
○ Have volunteers present to the class.

○ Direct students' attention to Step D. Have students write their introductions and conclusions. Remind students to use an attention-getting opener. Walk around the room to monitor the activity and provide help as needed. Put students in pairs to exchange and evaluate paragraphs.
○ Direct students' attention to Step E. Have students write their first drafts.
○ Direct students' attention to Step F. Go over the questions. Have students read and edit their paragraphs, using the questions as a guide.
○ For peer editing, have students exchange paragraphs with a partner, edit, and return to the writer.
○ Go over the directions for Step G. Have students carefully rewrite their paragraphs and hand them in to you.
○ After you have read and returned students' research papers, you may want to set aside time for students to read each other's writing or display the papers in the classroom. Have students keep all of their final versions in a notebook or folder so that they can see their progress and improvement over time.

Unit 4 Vocabulary Workshop

A. Analyzing Word Choice
❍ Read the directions.
❍ Have students choose better words for the sentences.
❍ Go over the answers.

ANSWER KEY
Answers may vary.

1. Ecologists are ~~making a study of~~ ^studying^ giant turtles in Malaysia.

2. Avery ~~got~~ ^caught^ malaria when he was living in the tropics.

3. There are ~~some~~ ^15^ endangered animal species in ~~my country~~ ^China^ .

4. "Hunters return to the village and tell stories about the day's hunt," she ~~told~~ ^said^ .

5. Paula ~~got~~ ^received^ her doctorate in 1996.

6. ~~A lot~~ ^Thousands of^ animals are killed by poachers.

7. Three ~~things~~ ^aspects^ of this problem are important to consider.

8. People internationally ~~got~~ ^became^ concerned about the endangered aye-aye of Madagascar.

9. The Belize Zoo spends ~~a lot of~~ ^extensive^ time on educating children about the importance of rare species in their homeland.

10. Due to global warming, the situation in the Arctic is ~~really bad~~ ^drastic^ for polar bears.

11. ~~Many evidences indicate~~ ^A great deal of evidence indicates^ that the number of gorillas in the wild is ~~going down a lot~~ ^decreasing drastically^ .

12. Jack placed three ~~things~~ ^objects^ on the table.

13. Several recent ~~researches~~ ^studies^ explore the relationship between farmers and wildlife.

B. Choosing Words with the Correct Connotation
❍ Read the directions.
❍ Have students write the correct words on the lines.
❍ Go over the answers.

ANSWER KEY
1. livestock; 2. beast; 3. game; 4. terrain;
5. surroundings; 6. vicinity; 7. subsist; 8. thrive;
9. live; 10. fertile; 11. rich; 12. affluent

C. Miscellaneous Problematic Words
❍ Read the directions.
❍ Have students determine if each sentence is correct or incorrect.
❍ Ask students to correct the incorrectly used words.
❍ Go over the answers.

ANSWER KEY
1. x, hard; 2. x; economic; 3. OK; 4. x, on the other hand; 5. x, Even if; 6. OK; 7. x, on the contrary; 8. OK;
9. x, effect; 10. OK

Editing Practice

Directions: In each sentence, find and correct the error in the adjective clause, coordinating conjunction, or adverbial conjunction.

1. A vision quest is a solitary journey who an adolescent takes in order to become a man or a

woman and receive an adult name.

2. In Siberia, a shaman goes into a trance as part of a healing ritual in which fulfills a

psychological need.

3. American baseball players practice certain rituals, but they will do better in a game.

4. A christening is a ritual which a baby often receives a name and is presented to God and the

community in.

5. During the 1960s, many young people felt rebellious towards those in authority. However,

they grew their hair long in defiance of society's rules.

What Type of Essay Do I Write?

Directions: Read the definitions of different types of essay questions. Then read the essay questions below. What type of paragraph(s) does the teacher expect? Choose from the types in the box.

Analysis: Examine the basic parts of something to discover meanings and relationships.
Cause and Effect: List the causes and/or effects of an action.
Comparison/Contrast: Discuss the ways in which two or more things are similar and different.
Definition: Give the meaning of a word or term.
Description: Give details about how something looks, works.
Facts with explanation: State facts and give reasons for them.
Illustration (Example): Make a statement and provide one or more examples to support it.
Process: Say the sequence of steps.
Summary: Tell the main ideas.

_____ **1.** Define the term *vision quest.*

_____ **2.** What are examples of colors with symbolic meaning?

_____ **3.** Describe the throne of King Tutankhamen.

_____ **4.** Analyze the symbolism of food in Indian culture.

_____ **5.** Compare and contrast a traditional Mexican house with a contemporary one.

_____ **6.** Summarize the significance of sports as a metaphor in politics.

_____ **7.** Explain the steps in a Navajo healing ceremony.

_____ **8.** Give reasons for the importance of the number eight in Chinese culture.

_____ **9.** How is a Navajo sand painting similar to or different from a Buddhist mandala?

_____ **10.** What does *feng shui* mean?

_____ **11.** Why does a California legislator want a change in the law?

_____ **12.** Analyze the importance of hair length as political expression.

Name: _____ **Date:** _____

Comparing Humans and Chimpanzees

Directions: Complete the Venn diagram to compare humans and chimpanzees. Write at least three things in each section of the diagram (either from the readings or from your own research).

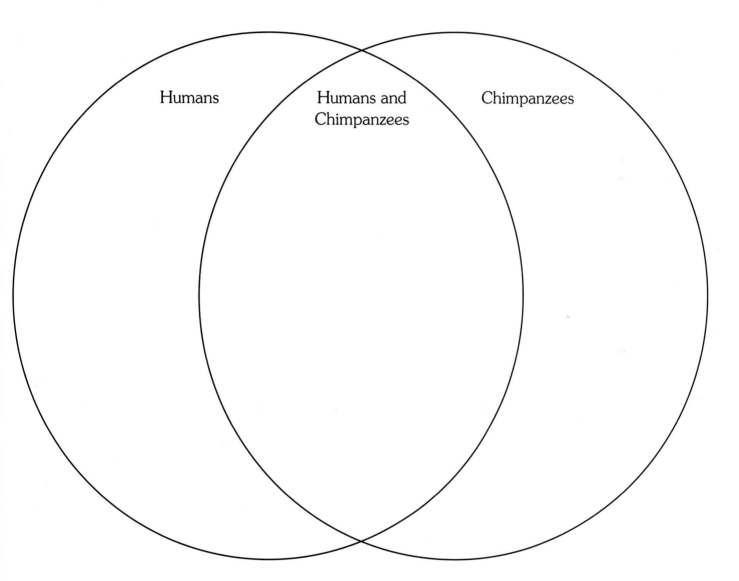

Humans

Humans and
Chimpanzees

Chimpanzees

Activity for Stressed Words

Directions: Read the paragraph below. Guess which content words (nouns, verbs, adjectives, or adverbs) have been removed and write them on the lines. Compare ideas with a partner.

Chimpanzees have a lot in common with _____. Like

_____, chimps can use _____. For example, they use

twigs to get _____ to eat. _____ also

_____ leaves as "_____" to soak up

_____ to drink. Chimps don't _____, but they do use

other communication systems. They make _____ expressions and

_____ movements to communicate. They also can be

_____ to use Ameslan.

Editing Practice

Directions: In each sentence, find and correct the errors in adverbial or subordinating conjunctions.

1. Sumatran orangutans have fine hair. While Kalimantan orangutans have coarser hair.

2. Some primates show artistic ability, like Nonja. In contrast, some other animals such as elephants seem to like to paint and draw.

3. Humans share food, when monkeys fend for themselves.

4. While humans can speak the vocal tract of apes doesn't permit them to use language in the same way.

5. Washoe, the chimp, learned to use American Sign Language. Similar, Koko the gorilla acquired a vocabulary of 2,000 signs in Ameslan.

6. Although winter lasted nine months, people had fewer problems preserving food in this subarctic environment.

Name: _____ **Date:** _____

Graphic Organizer for *A Bank for the Down and Out*

Directions: Complete the graphic organizer below to take notes on the reading *A Bank for the Down and Out* on pages 95–96. This organizer shows the process, or series of events, that the Grameen Bank encourages.

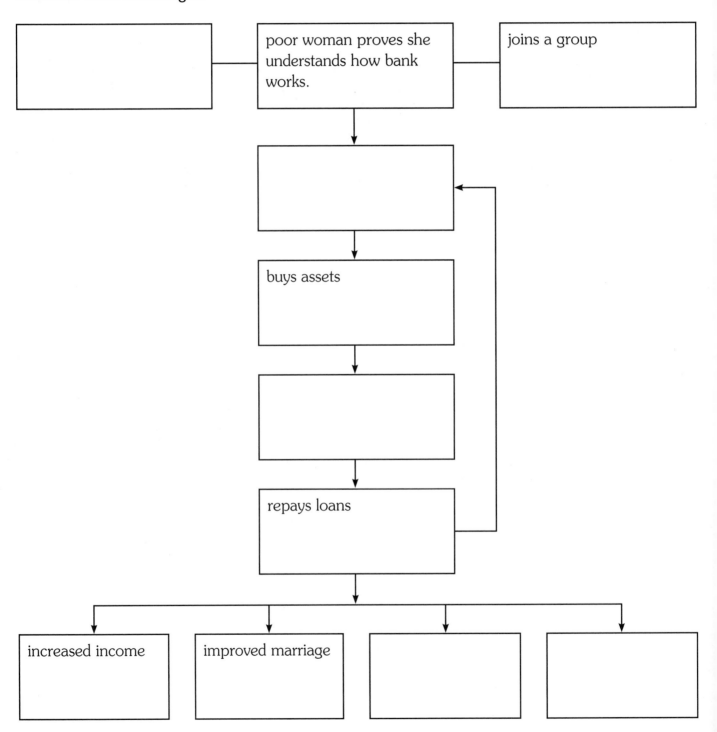

poor woman proves she understands how bank works.

joins a group

buys assets

repays loans

increased income

improved marriage

Editing Practice

Directions: In the paragraphs, find and correct the errors in reporting verbs and punctuation.

According to Jolis Mohammud Yunus is a visionary, his dream "the total eradication of poverty from the world. Yunus is attempting to do this through micro-credit, the lending of very small amounts of money to the destitute. Jolis mentions that this idea is both terribly simple and, in the field of development and aid, completely revolutionary. In order to receive the loan, the borrower must join a group, which Jolis says that "provides a borrower with self-discipline and courage."

A typical borrower from his bank would be a Bangladeshi woman, who has never touched money before. Yunus lends her money and doesn't regret it. She uses the loan to buy an asset that can immediately start paying income such as cotton to weave or raw materials for bangles to sell or a cow she can milk. She repays the loan in tiny installments until she becomes self-sufficient. Then if she wants she can take out a new, larger loan. Either way, she is no longer poor.

Comparing Information from Text and Illustrations

Directions: Look back at the reading *International Trade* on pages 136–141. Complete the graphic organizer.

Topic	Information in Text	Information in Illustrations
U.S. imports from other countries		
U.S. exports to other countries		
Oil producing countries		
Absolute advantage		
Comparative advantage		

Editing Practice

Directions: In each sentence, find and correct the errors in the present unreal conditional, conditionals with *without*, or transition of cause and effect.

1. If there are no trade barriers, more domestic workers would be displaced.

2. If the company researched the language and culture it would know that the product name was inappropriate.

3. Without I didn't have a driver's license, I couldn't drive.

4. The United States is in better shape economically if it didn't have to import so much oil.

5. Call centers in India and other countries will be more accepted by American customers if their employees spoke English with a less-pronounced accent.

6. Customer-service centers would be less effective without they had more bilingual workers.

7. Due to we import so much from Japan, we have a trade imbalance.

8. "Sucks" in American slang has a negative connotation, therefore the Electrolux ad campaign was not successful.

Predicting Content

Rhyme is when the stressed vowel sound and the consonants after them sound the same in two or more words.

End rhymes can fall into a repeating pattern called a rhyme scheme.

Rhythm is the order of stressed and unstressed syllables.

Imagery helps us to see, hear, feel, taste, and smell the world.

Figurative language includes similes and metaphors.

A poem often has several stanzas.

A poem with a closed form follows traditional rules of rhythm, rhyme, number of syllables, and number of lines.

Open form poems have no formal groupings.

The title of a poem is a kind of introduction.

The theme is the meaning of the poem.

A narrative poem tells a story.

A lyric poem expresses personal thoughts and emotions.

Editing Practice

Directions: In the sentences, find and correct the errors.

1. Robert Frost says in his poem. That taking the road less traveled "has made all the difference."

2. The speaker in "Deferred" believes that he can study French now that his job has changed, however he may be fooling himself.

3. Billy Collins does not seem to share the attitude of the history teacher, he seems to be less naïve.

4. In "Marrying," Charles Webb compares. Marriage to buying a hat.

5. Many people thought Richard Cory had all he could want out of life he didn't.

6. "The History Teacher" uses humor to make a point. As in the line about the Boer War.

7. Langston Hughes was an important poet of the 20th century, he was African American but his themes are universal.

8. All the poets in this chapter are male, many important poets are women.

Different Types of Paragraphs

Directions: Read the information about the purposes of different types of paragraphs. Match the paragraph type to each paragraph from *The Hero's Journey.*

    A. **Cause and Effect:** presents one or more causes and one or more effects
    B. **Definition:** defines or explains a key term
    C. **Illustration (Example):** provides an example in support of an assertion
    D. **Process:** explains how something happens, step by step
    E. **Narrative:** tells a story, usually with a beginning, middle and end
    F. **Classification:** divides material into classes or groups
    G. **Comparison/Contrast:** discusses the similarities and/or differences between two things

1.   Even in popular novels, the main character is a hero or heroine who has found or done something beyond the normal range of achievement and experience. A hero is someone who has given his or her life to something bigger than him or herself. _____

2.   There are two types of deed. One is the physical deed, in which the hero performs a courageous act in battle or saves a life. The other kind is the spiritual deed, in which the hero learns to experience the supernormal range of human spiritual life and then comes back with a message. _____

3.   But the structure and something of the spiritual sense of this adventure can be seen already anticipated in the puberty or initiation rituals of early tribal societies, through which a child is compelled to give up its childhood and become an adult—to die, you might say, to its infantile personality and psyche and come back as a responsible adult. This is a fundamental psychological transformation that everyone has to undergo. We are in childhood in a condition of dependency under someone's protection and supervision for some 14 to 21 years—and if you're going for your Ph.D., this may continue to perhaps 35. You are in no way a self-responsible, free agent, but an obedient dependent, expecting and receiving punishments and rewards. To evolve out of this position of psychological immaturity to the courage of self-responsibility and assurance requires a death and a resurrection. That's the basic motif of the universal hero's journey—leaving one condition and finding the source of life to bring you forth into a richer or mature condition. _____

4.   Yes, there Solo has done the hero act of sacrificing himself for another . . . It depends on what system of ideas you want to apply. Solo was a very practical guy, at least as he thought of himself, a materialist. But he was a compassionate human being at the same time and didn't know it. The adventure evoked a quality of his character that he hadn't known he possessed.

_____

Editing Practice

Directions: Rewrite the sentences below using parallelism.

1. A hero can either perform a physical act of courage or bringing back a spiritual message.

_____

_____

2. In both a *fiesta de quinceañera* and a debutante ball, the young women wear a formal dress, have a party, and friends and family.

_____

_____

3. Mary showed her shrewdness by borrowing five dollars, letting herself into the restaurant at night, and made friends with the restaurant owner.

_____

_____

4. Han Solo changes from mercenary to hero when he puts his own life in danger and Luke Skywalker is safe.

_____

_____

5. Rites of passage are similar to a hero's journey in that they involve leaving one condition and bring the person forth into a richer or more mature condition.

_____

_____

Name: _____ **Date:** _____

FACTS vs. OPINIONS

Directions: Write examples of facts from *The Human Factor* on pages 243–247 in the left column. Write opinions in the right column.

FACTS	OPINIONS
Tropical rain forests once covered 12 percent of the land of the planet.	This rate of extinction carries with it some terrible consequences.

Editing Practice

Directions: Look at the general guidelines for writing a reference list on pages 268–269. Make corrections in the list below.

References

Durrell, G. Died. [Electronic version]. (1995, February 13). *Time, 145,* 23.

Durrell Wildlife Conservation Trust. (n.d.) Jersey Zoo: A very special place. Retrieved March 13,2005 from http://www.durrellwildlife.org/index.cfm?a=6

Historic land save in Mexico [Electronic version]. (Winter 2005). *American forests, 110,* 23.

Linden, E. (1990, April 2). Challenges for earth patriots: Stalking dwarf hamsters in Siberia [Electronic version] *Time, 135,* 70.

Morgan, Stephen. (1995). *Ecology and the environment.* New York: Oxford University Press.

The Nature Conservancy. (2005). How we work: Our methods, tools, and techniques. Retrieved March 13, 2005 from http://nature.org/aboutus/howwework/.

Perney, L., and Emanoil, P. (1998, September–October). Where the wild things are: 25 ways to get close to nature this winter [Electronic version]. *Audubon, 100,* 82.

Speciation and biodiversity: Interview with Edward O. Wilson. (2002, February). Retrieved June 24, 2005 from www.actionbioscience.org/biodiversity/wilson.html

Ranking: *Nine Steps to a Healthier Environment*

Directions: Complete the chart below to rank the nine steps and give reasons for the rankings. Then compare your rankings with a partner.

Rank (1 is most likely to implement)	Step	Reason for ranking (e.g., convenience, impact, ease, expense)
1		
2		
3		
4		
5		
6		
7		
8		
9		

Editing Practice

Directions: In the sentences, find and correct the errors.

1. Exposing to their pets' flea collars, many children developed cancer.

2. Kansas farmers used the weed killer 2, 4-D had a higher-than-average risk of contracting malignant lymphoma.

3. Contained fungicide, human shampoos may also be somewhat hazardous to your health.

4. Replacing my standard bulbs with energy-efficient CFLs I saved money on my electric bills.

5. Animals catching accidentally as a result of wasteful fishing techniques are known as *bycatch*.

6. The company was reluctant to hire fired from his last job, the CEO.

Name: _____ **Date:** _____ **Score:** _____

○ Reading

Directions: Read the information below. Fill in the correct answer for each of the questions that follow.

Halloween: An American Ritual of Rebellion

Brazil is famous for Carnival, a festival celebrated the four days before Ash Wednesday (the first day of Lent—a 40-day period of fasting before the Christian Easter holiday). Carnival occurs in a limited way in the United States. The city of New Orleans in Louisiana is famous for its carnival celebration. France and Italy also have carnival. Nowhere, however, do people invest as much in carnival—in money, costumes, time, and labor—as they do in Rio de Janeiro. There on the Saturday and Sunday before Ash Wednesday, several samba schools take to the streets to compete in costumes, rhythmic dancing, chanting, and singing.

The United States lacks any national celebration that is exactly like carnival, but it does have Halloween. This holiday occurs on October 31, and it is similar in some ways to carnival. Even if Americans don't dance in the streets on Halloween, children do go out ringing doorbells and demanding "trick or treat." American children do things they don't normally do on ordinary nights; for example, they wear costumes, just as Brazilians do.

Halloween and carnival are similar in that they are times of culturally permitted *inversion*. In the United States, Halloween is the only nationally celebrated occasion that dramatically inverts the normal relationship between children and adults. Halloween is a night of disguises and reversals. Normally, children are at home or in school, taking part in supervised activities. Children are domesticated and diurnal (daytime). Halloween permits them to become—once a year—nocturnal (nighttime) invaders of public space. In addition, *they can be bad*. Halloween's symbolism is potent. Children love to dress themselves as evil creatures or characters, and they enjoy the special privileges of naughtiness . . . By allowing the "tricks," adults do not have to give a "treat" and the power is reversed.

Halloween is like the "rituals of rebellion" that anthropologists have described in African societies. Such rituals are times when normal power relations are inverted. The powerless turn on the powerful, expressing resentments they suppress (keep from thinking about) during the rest of the year. Children can command adults to obey them and punish the adults if they don't. Halloween behavior inverts the scoldings adults inflict on kids. For adults, Halloween is a minor occasion, not even a holiday. For children, however, it's a favorite time, a special night. Kids know what rituals of rebellion are all about.

Source: *Anthropology: The Exploration of Human Diversity* (Kottak)

1. What is the main idea of this reading?

    Ⓐ Halloween is the American Carnival.

    Ⓑ Halloween is an American ritual of reversal and rebellion.

    Ⓒ Brazil is famous for *Carnaval.*

    Ⓓ Carnival occurs in a limited way in the United States.

2. How is Halloween like Carnival?

    Ⓐ Both holidays permit reversals of usual roles and behaviors.

    Ⓑ Both take place in October.

    Ⓒ Both are celebrated throughout the United States.

    Ⓓ Both involve dancing and singing.

3. What is one way that Halloween is celebrated?

    Ⓐ Children sing and dance in the streets at night.

    Ⓑ People wear costumes.

    Ⓒ Parents play tricks on their children.

    Ⓓ People eat a lot before Lent.

4. What is inverted at Halloween?

    Ⓐ parents and children relationships   Ⓒ rich and poor

    Ⓑ good and bad   Ⓓ both A and B

5. What American city celebrates a carnival?

    Ⓐ Rio de Janeiro   Ⓒ Italy

    Ⓑ Mardi Gras   Ⓓ New Orleans

◯ Strategy: Guessing the Meaning from Context

Directions: Refer to the reading. Match the words on the left and definitions on the right.

_____ **6.** nocturnal   a. behavior that is not good

_____ **7.** inversion   b. reversal

_____ **8.** suppress   c. active during the night

_____ **9.** domesticated   d. keep from thinking about

_____ **10.** naughtiness   e. trained, able to stay in a house

○ Vocabulary

Directions: Fill in the blanks with words from the box.

amulet	castes	craze	stamina	trance
artificial	clutter	monotheism	symbol	urged

11. Our instructor _____ us to study for the exam next week.

12. Tony wears a(n) _____ around his neck, to keep bad energy away.

13. For hundreds of years, people in India have been divided into _____, or different classes of society.

14. _____ is the belief in a single God.

15. _____ plants are just as pretty as real ones.

16. iPods and other MP3 players were a big _____ in 2006.

17. The eagle is a _____ of the United States, representing strength and freedom.

18. My desk is covered with _____. I can't even see the surface.

19. People who are in a _____ don't seem to hear or see what is happening around them.

20. If you have _____, you can continue an activity for a long time.

○ Mechanics

Directions: Circle the correct word in parentheses to complete the sentences.

21. An Obi is a leader for (which/whom) people have a great deal of respect.

22. A ritual is an activity (which/who) follows certain rules or patterns of behavior.

23. Most of the year, children are active during the day, (but/for) on Halloween, they are allowed to roam the streets at night.

24. I want to study English in New York, (therefore/so) I applied to several schools there.

25. Most of the world's major religions are monotheistic. (That is/For example), Muslim, Christian, and Jewish followers all worship a single deity.

26. To understand a culture, you should learn about how the society is structured and what customs the people observe. (However/Furthermore), you should try to learn about their religious beliefs.

27. Native American boys and sometimes girls often go off on a difficult journey alone. (As a result/In contrast), they are considered adults upon their return.

28. I get really sick when I fly. (So/Even so), I fly several times a month.

29. Length of hair can indicate rebellion to authority; (for instance/in short), young men in the 1960s often had long hair.

30. A shaman is someone to (who/whom) people often go for healing rituals.

○ Editing

Directions: Find and correct the error in each sentence.

31. A rite of passage is a ritual in which marks the transition from one stage of life to another.

32. Baseball players are very ritualistic; however, they often follow the same patterns of behavior before every game.

33. An amulet is a charm, that you might wear to protect yourself from evil spirits.

34. There are many things that people don't understand, for they use religion to fill the gaps in their understanding.

35. Cultural anthropology which is the study of people in groups, can tell us a lot about others and about ourselves.

Name: _____ **Date:** _____ **Score:** _____

Reading

Directions: Read the information below. Fill in the correct answer for each of the questions that follow.

Primate Society

Most primates spend their lives in social groups, although some species of monkeys live most of their lives alone. The social groups are of different types: female with children, one male-one female, polyandrous, polygynous (or polygamous), multi-male/multi-female, and fission-fusion. Orangutans represent the social unit made up of a single female and her offspring. Adult male orangutans join females to mate but then return to living mostly on their own. Monogamous social units (one male-one female and their children) are typical of gibbons and indris primates, and, of course, humans. Polyandrous groups exist in human society in isolated areas in Nepal, India, Tibet, and Sri Lanka, but are rare among other primates. Some small New World monkeys such as marmosets and tamarins are polyandrous, meaning that one female may live and mate with more than one male. Gorillas usually live in groups consisting of one male and several females, known as polygynous or polygamous groups. In such social groups, there is often dimorphism, or extreme differences between the male and female of the species. Male gorillas are much larger than their female counterparts. Baboons and macaques usually live in very large multi-male/multi-female groups. This is probably to provide better protection for the smaller primates from predators. In these large groups, there is usually a dominance hierarchy, with one male and one female more dominant than the others. Such large groups often display aggression to define their territories, making loud calls to chase away other primates. Chimpanzees live in what animal behaviorists call a fission-fusion society. Fission means to divide or break apart; fusion is to join or come together. Chimps join a troop of other chimps, but many females may leave to join other troops to mate and reproduce. Groups may break up and re-form to forage, hunt, or sleep together. Because of these looser, more fluid connections, chimpanzees display more complicated social behavior.

1. What is the main idea of this reading?
   - (A) Primates live in small groups.
   - (B) Other primates are like humans in terms of social organization.
   - (C) Different species of primates live in different types of social groups.
   - (D) Primates communicate with each other.

2. Which group is most like humans in its social organization?
   - (A) orangutans   (B) gibbons   (C) baboons   (D) chimpanzees

3. What kind of social organization do gorillas have?
   - Ⓐ polyandrous   Ⓑ polygynous   Ⓒ monogamous   Ⓓ fission-fusion
4. What is the social structure of chimpanzees?
   - Ⓐ polyandrous   Ⓑ polygynous   Ⓒ monogamous   Ⓓ fission-fusion
5. Why do baboons live in large groups?
   - Ⓐ to protect themselves   Ⓒ to show aggression
   - Ⓑ to mate   Ⓓ to gather food

○ Strategy: Understanding Pronoun References

Directions: Circle the referent for the bolded pronoun.

6. Baboons usually live in very large social groups. **They** sometimes change groups or break off into smaller groups for periods of time.

7. The fission-fusion social structure is unique to chimpanzees. Unlike other monkeys, **they** divide and re-form groups frequently.

8. Polyandry is a social structure characterized by one female in a unit with several males. **It** is the opposite of a polygamous social structure.

9. The primary unit for orangutans is a mother with her children, while adult males live more solitary lives. **This** is the smallest unit that represents a primate social structure.

10. This reading described social organization of primates. **It** focused on classification.

○ Vocabulary

Directions: Fill in the blanks with words from the box.

descend	endangered	omnivorous	prey	terrestrial
dominate	exogamy	orangutan	seclusion	twigs

11. Chimpanzees use tools such as _____ to catch termites for food.

12. Certain primates live on the ground and so are _____.

13. Other primates, which live primarily in the trees, _____ from the canopy to get food.

14. _____ is the practice of marrying outside the group.

15. Humans, like some primates, are _____, which means they eat both animals and plants.

16. Some species of plants and animals are _____ and may soon be extinct.

17. Male gorillas are often much larger than females. Therefore, they can easily

_____ the smaller gorillas.

18. Animals that are _____ are hunted by other animals.

19. A type of primate that lives in Indonesia is the _____.

20. In some rites of passage, adolescents go off in _____ for several days, returning to the group after their time alone.

○ Mechanics

Directions: Use a word or phrase from the box to complete the sentences. More than one answer may be correct, but use each word only once. You will not use all the words.

although	by the time	since	whenever
as soon as	if	unless	whereas
because	in case	until	while

21. You cannot get a new job _____ you fill out the application.

22. Gibbons live in small family groups, led by one male and one female,

_____ baboons often live in groups of a hundred or more.

23. _____ a boy in the Jewish religion turns 13, he can participate in a special ceremony known as a *bar mitzvah*.

24. Laura cries _____ she hears that song.

25. We know that some other primates can understand both grammar and vocabulary

_____ they can use American Sign Language in creative ways.

26. _____ macaques can learn from both males and females, they learn much more quickly from the male leader of the group.

27. In some species of primates, the young males stay with their family group

_____ they become adolescents, and then they go off on their own.

28. You might want to take an umbrella _____ it rains later.

29. Joe will go to the store _____ his roommates wash dishes.

30. _____ I finish my homework, it will be dark outside.

○ Editing

Directions: Find and correct the error in each sentence.

31. For most primates, the male and female are similar, however, male gorillas are much larger

than females.

32. While humans are usually monogamous male gorillas live and mate with more than one

female.

33. In some early societies, men were hunters. Whereas women were the foragers.

34. Humans usually leave their nuclear families when they get married. Similar, chimpanzees

often join a new group to mate and reproduce.

35. Marmosets live in polyandrous groupings (one female with several males). In contrast,

some isolated groups of people in Tibet have units consisting of one woman with more than

one man.

Name: _____ **Date:** _____ **Score:** _____

Reading

Directions: Read the information below. Fill in the correct answer for each of the questions that follow.

Doing a World of Good

Bill Gates is not the only successful entrepreneur trying to help the world, although he may operate on a much larger scale. Gates and his wife Melinda were two of *Time's* People of the Year in 2005 for their philanthropic work, especially in their attempts to eradicate disease and help children in Africa. Now other entrepreneurs are getting into the act. Nearly half of the business schools in the United States offer courses that deal with non-profit content, compared with only 10 a couple of decades ago. Many business students leave graduate school and head directly to work for non-profit agencies, applying business smarts to address social problems. Others use for-profit ventures to finance projects that help address those social problems.

Priya Haji, 35, Siddharth Sanghvi, 30, and David Guendelman, 28, started World of Good, which sells scarves, bags, and jewelry, in 2005. This for-profit company makes grants to its non-profit sister company "that is committed to building a stronger Fair Trade crafts movement in the United States, to promoting clear and transparent international standards for Fair Trade crafts, and to investing in economic and social development projects in craft-producer communities" (according to World of Good's mission statement). World of Good's products are made in developing countries around the world. The company is committed to paying fair wages, providing safe and healthy working conditions, and encouraging good environmental practices. They also provide financial and technical assistance to the people who make the crafts. Their business plan won the Global Social Venture Competition, awarded for high economic and social returns.

Even large companies are taking a look at how to do more good while making a profit. Coffee companies, including Starbucks to some extent, offer "fair trade" coffee, guaranteeing a fair living wage is paid to the growers. The successful grocery chain Whole Foods is a Fortune 500 company committed to practices such as not selling overfished seafood, giving to charity, and helping growers in developing countries.

1. What is the main idea of this reading?
- Ⓐ Bill Gates is a great businessman.
- Ⓑ A World of Good is a gift company that sells crafts from developing countries.
- Ⓒ Fair trade is supported by many businesses.
- Ⓓ Many businesses and entrepreneurs are taking more of an interest in trying to solve social problems.

2. What is fair trade?

   Ⓐ the practice of paying a fair living wage to producers

   Ⓑ getting a reasonable price for a product

   Ⓒ using producers in developing countries

   Ⓓ providing goods or services in return for a product

3. Why did the entrepreneurs who founded World of Good get an award?

   Ⓐ for their philanthropic work on AIDS

   Ⓑ for helping children in Africa

   Ⓒ for a business plan that made money and helped solve social problems

   Ⓓ for helping growers in developing countries

4. How are business schools changing?

   Ⓐ They offer more awards for doing good work.

   Ⓑ They offer courses that deal with non-profit organizations.

   Ⓒ They offer more scholarships.

   Ⓓ They teach about social problems and solutions.

5. Which company sells jewelry?

   Ⓐ A World of Good

   Ⓑ Starbucks

   Ⓒ Whole Foods

   Ⓓ Microsoft

○ Strategy: Finding the Meaning of Words with Multiple Definitions

Directions: Refer to the dictionary definitions for the word *fair.* Write the number of the definition next to the sentence.

fair *adj.* 1. reasonable, what people would normally accept as right; 2. equal; 3. average, in the middle; 4. light in color; 5. sunny; 6. beautiful

6. They're predicting fair weather for tomorrow. _____

7. The World of Good company pays a fair price for its goods. _____

8. The movie was only fair. I'm not sure I'd recommend it. _____

9. Julia has fair hair and skin. _____

10. Our inheritances were not fair. My brother got all the money, and I only got the car. _____

◯ Vocabulary

Directions: Fill in the blanks with words and phrases from the box.

| assets | capital | destitute | frugality | incentive |
| brink | default | fluctuations | hinder | launched |

11. Many Americans have never known what it's like to be truly _____ because they experience relative wealth.

12. Poverty and disease can _____ a developing nation's progress.

13. To start your own business, you're going to need a certain amount of

_____ .

14. I heard they're going out of business. They will have to sell their _____ to pay off their debts.

15. Bill and Melinda Gates _____ their charitable foundation in 2000.

16. John is known for his _____—he doesn't spend money on anything.

17. The _____ in gasoline prices make it very difficult to plan the monthly expenses.

18. Our instructor is giving us a(n) _____ to participate in the discussion group. We get 10 extra credit points.

19. If you _____ on your loan, it means that you don't pay it back.

20. Many very poor countries are on the _____ of disaster. One year of drought and they could face starvation.

◯ Mechanics

Directions: Cross out the word that is not similar to the other two in the set.

21. stress   emphasize   mention

22. argue   deny   assert

23. point out   suggest   propose

24. speculate   explain   wonder

25. indicate   point out   warn

26. question   ask   determine

27. discuss   quote   explain

28. paraphrase   generalize   specify

29. recommend   acknowledge   admit

30. write   note   conclude

○ Editing

Directions: Read the sentences. Fill in the problem.

31. As Clayton says that, "Religious beliefs may also stand in the way of economic development."
   - (A) no citation
   - (B) inappropriate verb
   - (C) incorrect use of *as*
   - (D) punctuation

32. Corruption at any level of government is an obstacle to economic development.
   - (A) no citation
   - (B) inappropriate verb
   - (C) incorrect use of *as*
   - (D) punctuation

33. Clayton speculates that trade barriers need to be reduced or eliminated.
   - (A) no citation
   - (B) inappropriate verb
   - (C) incorrect use of *as*
   - (D) punctuation

34. Clayton warns that there are some success stories.
   - (A) no citation
   - (B) inappropriate verb
   - (C) incorrect use of *as*
   - (D) punctuation

35. As Clayton stated "Governments in developing countries need to invest more in education."
   - (A) no citation
   - (B) inappropriate verb
   - (C) incorrect use of *as*
   - (D) punctuation

Name: _____ **Date:** _____ **Score:** _____

Reading

Directions: Read the information below. Fill in the correct answer for each of the questions that follow.

The Trade Deficit

The United States has a trade deficit (imbalance). What do numbers about trade deficits really mean and how does a trade imbalance affect the economy?

The Problem of a Trade Deficit

(1) A large, long-lasting trade imbalance reduces the value of a country's currency on the foreign exchange markets. Devalued currency causes a chain reaction that affects output and employment in that country's industries. The large deficit in the United States' balance of payments in the 1980s, for example, flooded the foreign exchange markets with dollars. An increase in the supply of dollars causes the dollar to lose some of its value on the foreign currency markets.

(2) When the dollar gets weaker, American consumers have to pay more for imports, and foreigners pay less for American exports. As imports fall and exports rise, unemployment results in the industries in the United States that depend on imports. In time, however, the dollar will get strong again and the process reverses. The resulting shift (change) in employment between export and import industries is one of the biggest problems with a trade deficit.

International Value of the Dollar

(3) Since floating rates became the standard in 1971, the Federal Reserve System has kept a statistic called the trade-weighted value of the dollar. This index shows the strength of the dollar against a group of foreign currencies.

(4) When the dollar reached its strongest level in 1985, foreign goods became less expensive, and American exports became more costly for the rest of the world. As a result, imports rose, exports fell, and the United States suffered a record trade deficit of $163 billion in 1986.

(5) As the deficits continued, the value of the dollar fell, making imports more expensive and U.S. exports more attractive to the rest of the world. By 1991, the overall deficit in the balance of payments had fallen to just under $4 billion. The trade deficit will continue to rise and fall as the value of the dollar continues to change.

Source: *Economics: Principles and Practices* (Clayton)

1. What is NOT covered in this reading?

    (A) tariffs   (B) trade deficits   (C) value of the dollar   (D) effect on employment

2. What is another word for *deficit*?

    (A) currency   (B) shortfall   (C) shift   (D) increase

3. What is the relationship between a U.S. trade deficit and employment?

    (A) As the U.S. deficit increases, unemployment decreases.

    (B) When unemployment increases, the deficit increases.

    (C) Unemployment rises when the trade deficit increases.

    (D) Employment rises when the U.S. imports more.

4. What is an advantage of a weak dollar?

    (A) U.S. exports are relatively cheaper.

    (B) U.S. imports are cheaper.

    (C) The value of foreign currency is less.

    (D) Employment goes down.

5. What happened between 1986 and 1991?

    (A) The trade deficit increased.

    (B) The value of the dollar increased.

    (C) The value of the dollar decreased.

    (D) Floating rates became standard.

○ Strategy: Summarizing Your Reading

Directions: Write the number of the paragraph next to each summary sentence.

6. A statistic maintained by the Federal Reserve System shows the value of the dollar against other currencies. _____

7. The rate of unemployment varies with the value of the dollar. _____

8. A trade deficit reduces the value of the dollar. _____

9. As deficits increase and the value of the dollar decreases, U.S. exports rise, causing the deficit to drop and the dollar to increase in value. _____

10. When the dollar was very strong, U.S. goods were relatively more expensive so other countries bought less, leading to a trade deficit. _____

○ Vocabulary

Directions: Fill in the correct answer.

11. A _____ is a little song that conveys a message about a product.
  Ⓐ slogan   Ⓑ logo   Ⓒ jingle

12. A tariff designed to raise money is known as a _____ tariff.
  Ⓐ revenue   Ⓑ protective   Ⓒ quota

13. A _____ is a design that represents a company, brand, or product.
  Ⓐ slogan   Ⓑ logo   Ⓒ jingle

14. A tariff that is high enough to protect less efficient industries is a _____ tariff.
  Ⓐ revenue   Ⓑ protective   Ⓒ quota

15. A _____ is a saying that encourages consumers to remember the product.
  Ⓐ slogan   Ⓑ logo   Ⓒ jingle

16. Limits place on the quantities of a product that can be imported are _____.
  Ⓐ revenues   Ⓑ protections   Ⓒ quotas

17. Another word for segment is _____.
  Ⓐ recruit   Ⓑ sector   Ⓒ attribute

18. If you can speak many languages, you are _____.
  Ⓐ multilingual   Ⓑ diverse   Ⓒ potential

19. If you want to keep your employees, you need to focus on _____.
  Ⓐ recruiting   Ⓑ retention   Ⓒ protection

20. If you favor trade barriers that protect domestic industries, you are a _____.
  Ⓐ technical support professional   Ⓑ free trader   Ⓒ protectionist

○ Mechanics

Directions: Complete the sentences with the correct form of the verb in parentheses to create present unreal conditionals.

21. If I _____ (not/have) a car, I couldn't take this class.

22. We would have higher rates of inflation if the Federal Reserve _____ (not/set) interest rates.

23. If you didn't live here, you _____ (not/be) able to go to this school.

24. Dylan _____ (do) better in this class if he studied more.

25. Remembering a product would be easier if the company _____ (have) a better slogan.

26. Without effective ad campaigns, many companies _____ (not/sell) their products.

27. I _____ (pass) any course without a lot of studying.

28. If I _____ (be) you, I would talk to the teacher right away.

29. Mary _____ (go) to college if her parents gave her some financial help.

30. I _____ (not/lose) weight without a lot of exercise.

○ Editing

Directions: Find and correct the error in each sentence.

31. Because of trade deficits result in fewer exports, unemployment in certain industries

increases.

32. If the value of the dollar stayed high, exports probably fell.

33. Without you have any money, you couldn't pay your bills.

34. Snehal can work at a call center in India if he could speak English better.

35. If we didn't have a global market, we will have higher prices.

Name: _____ **Date:** _____ **Score:** _____

○ Reading

Directions: Read the poem below. Fill in the blanks with information from the poem.

Who Will Teach Me?
By Nancy Wood

Who will teach me now that my fathers
Have gone with the buffalo?
Who will tell of times I wish I knew?
Who will direct my journey
So that I will come out right?
The years are clouds which
Cover my ancestors.
Let them sleep.
I shall find my way alone.

Source: "Who Will Teach Me?" (Wood)

1. According to the speaker, what two things are gone? _____

2. Who are the "fathers" the speaker describes? _____

3. In the poem, what is the speaker's "journey"? _____

4. Who is the author of the poem? _____

5. What does the speaker decide to do at the end of the poem? _____

○ Strategy: Analyzing Poems

Directions: Fill in the correct answer.

6. The "clouds" in the poem are an example of _____.

    Ⓐ closed form   Ⓑ a metaphor   Ⓒ rhyme   Ⓓ a simile

7. This poem _____.

    Ⓐ has a closed form

    Ⓑ has an open form

    Ⓒ is a quatrain

    Ⓓ has stanzas

8. Which of the following does the poem have?

    Ⓐ rhyme

    Ⓑ predictable rhythm

    Ⓒ a theme

    Ⓓ similes

9. What is the theme?

    Ⓐ a story about ancestors

    Ⓑ how the buffalo have disappeared

    Ⓒ how the speaker will find his/her way in life

    Ⓓ how history is passed down

10. What is most necessary to understanding this poem?

    Ⓐ the title

    Ⓑ the rhyming pattern

    Ⓒ the closed form

    Ⓓ the theme

⭘ Vocabulary

Directions: Fill in the blanks with words from the box.

analyze	clear-cut	diverged	outbreak	surface
bewildered	defer	layers	pattern	torment

11. The road _____, and I had to decide which direction to go.

12. One similarity between science and poetry is the need to find _____, or levels, of meaning.

13. To _____ poetry, you must look at sound, form, language, and meaning.

14. If you _____ something, you put it off until a later time.

15. Many health professionals fear a(n) _____ of a disease that they are not prepared to treat.

16. When I was growing up, my brother used to _____ me, making me miserable.

17. The teacher was so _____ by the students' answers on the test, she had to give another test.

18. Regular, repeated ordering is a _____ often studied in math classes.

19. There is really no _____ answer to that question. Several responses are possible.

20. The top or outside layer is also called the _____.

○ Mechanics

Directions: Complete the sentences with a word from the list. Use each word only once.

appears	indicate	might	represent	symbolize
associated	may	must	symbolic	symbols

21. An eagle may _____ freedom and independence.

22. A need for alcohol could _____ sadness or desperation.

23. A dove is _____ of peace.

24. Flags are _____ of different nations.

25. Black is _____ with mourning in the United States.

26. John _____ be angry. There's no other explanation for what he did.

27. The road _____ represent choices we make in life.

28. It _____ that the speaker feels lost and without direction.

29. The color red can _____ anger.

30. White _____ represent purity.

○ Editing

Directions: Identify each item as a run-on (R), comma splice (CS), fragment (F), or good sentence (O.K.). Then correct the errors.

_____ **31.** Nancy Wood has written poetry about the Pueblo Indians, she writes often about their interconnectedness to the land.

_____ **32.** Some of her writing for young adult readers.

_____ **33.** Wood lives in Santa Fe, New Mexico she is a photographer as well as a writer.

_____ **34.** The landscape and the legends of the Native Americans inspire her writing.

_____ **35.** Other writers using Native American themes (Louise Erdrich, James Welch, Michael Dorris).

Name: _____ **Date:** _____ **Score:** _____

Reading

Directions: Read the information below. Fill in the correct answer for each of the questions that follow.

Who Is Your Hero?

Myhero.com is a not-for-profit website that allows people to post online information about their own heroes online as part of an educational project. The website also includes teacher resources and lesson plans. Hero profiles include:

The Dalai Lama is an apostle for peace, urging people of all religions to live in harmony and try to understand one another. He received the Nobel Peace Prize in 1989. For centuries, the Dalai Lama was the title given to the spiritual and political leader of the kingdom of Tibet, the reincarnation of the great spiritual teacher of the 14th century, Bodhisattva. The current Dalai Lama lives a simple life in exile, continuing to speak on behalf of the people of Tibet. He was driven from Tibet for speaking out against the Chinese oppression of his homeland. He is an example of nonviolence and compassion.

Aminta Sow Fall is a novelist from Senegal who was recently profiled on the website as a hero for her sympathetic treatment of those in or on the brink of poverty. Her characters have dreams but also take control of their lives.

Raoul Wallenberg was a well-to-do businessman from Sweden during World War II. On a visit to Palestine, he heard stories from Jews who had escaped from Nazi Germany. In 1944, as first secretary of the Swedish legation in Budapest Hungary, he distributed Schutz passes, which declared the bearer of the pass to be under protection of the Swedish government and not to be harmed. He may have helped save 15,000 people in this way. He later opened Swedish safe houses to offer refuge to Jews. Wallenberg also intervened when the Nazis tried to massacre the Jews in Budapest just before the end of the war. He was arrested by the Russians and believed to have died in captivity.

Judith Blair is a single mother with two sons, who used to play college basketball and competed in other sports. When she learned that a friend of her son's was going to die if he didn't receive a kidney transplant, she offered to donate one of her own. Although she was already in good health, Blair decided to get her kidney in top shape. She trained for the Senior Olympics and won gold, silver, and bronze medals. Then she gave away her kidney.

1. Why are the people in the reading heroes?

    Ⓐ for their physical courage　　Ⓒ for their sacrifices

    Ⓑ for the spiritual message　　　Ⓓ for all of the above
       they bring

2. Which hero is a spiritual leader?

    Ⓐ the Dalai Lama　　　　　Ⓒ Raoul Wallenberg

    Ⓑ Amita Sow Fall　　　　　Ⓓ Judith Blair

3. Who was imprisoned?

    Ⓐ the Dalai Lama　　　　　Ⓒ Raoul Wallenberg

    Ⓑ Amita Sow Fall　　　　　Ⓓ Judith Blair

4. Why might Fall be considered a hero?

    Ⓐ She is a spiritual leader.　　Ⓒ She saved the lives of others.

    Ⓑ She gave away a kidney.　　Ⓓ She brings a message of hope to the poor.

5. What is the purpose of the website?

    Ⓐ to educate people about heroes

    Ⓑ to encourage people to be heroes

    Ⓒ to show the role of heroes in literature

    Ⓓ to provide financial rewards to heroes

○ Strategy: Recognizing Euphemisms

Directions: Fill in the correct meaning for each euphemism.

6. Amy's <u>not the sharpest knife in the drawer</u>, but she studies very hard.

    Ⓐ Amy is not going to hurt anyone.　　Ⓒ Amy is lazy.

    Ⓑ Amy is not very intelligent.　　　　Ⓓ Amy works in a kitchen.

7. Peter's company has <u>made</u> him <u>redundant</u>. Now he has to look for work.

    Ⓐ given him a raise　　　　Ⓒ given him time off

    Ⓑ fired him　　　　　　　Ⓓ required him to repeat his work

8. My neighbor <u>passed away</u> last week after a long illness.

    Ⓐ moved　　　　　　　　Ⓒ died

    Ⓑ graduated　　　　　　　Ⓓ drove faster

9. <u>I'm not ready for a relationship.</u>

    Ⓐ I'm too young.　　　　　Ⓒ I don't like you that much.

    Ⓑ I need to get some counseling.　　Ⓓ I'm lonely.

10. Sasha's looking for the <u>restroom</u>.

    Ⓐ the toilet   Ⓒ a place to rest

    Ⓑ a bath   Ⓓ a snack

◯ **Vocabulary**

Directions: Fill in the blanks with words and phrases from the box.

compassionate compelled	heritage redemption	self-preservation shrewd	skirmishes undergo	unsightly well-fed

11. Paula is a great nurse because she is so _____. Her patients really know that she cares.

12. I can't go to work—I've got this _____ rash on my face!

13. Most religions support the idea of _____, that people can turn their lives around.

14. Maya's straight black hair is part of her Native American _____.

15. I've got a great instinct for _____. I run away at the first sign of danger.

16. The two armies had a few _____ before the war really broke out.

17. Rob's business is going very well because he made a couple of very _____ decisions.

18. Hannah's cancer may have come back. She's going to have to _____ more tests.

19. The dog was nearly starving before he got to the animal shelter, but now he's looking

_____.

20. You can be _____ to testify in a trial. The court can require you to tell what you know.

⭕ Mechanics

Directions: Identify the type of element in each parallel structure.

21. I've always enjoyed swimming, golfing, and playing tennis.
    - Ⓐ noun
    - Ⓑ gerund
    - Ⓒ adjective
    - Ⓓ verb phrase

22. Most heroes are brave, strong, and willing to do something difficult.
    - Ⓐ noun
    - Ⓑ gerund
    - Ⓒ adjective
    - Ⓓ verb phrase

23. Melik had a good trip because he didn't ignore the young ladies on the train, avoid card games, or follow Garro's other suggestions.
    - Ⓐ noun
    - Ⓑ gerund
    - Ⓒ adjective
    - Ⓓ verb phrase

24. Mary knew how to plan ahead, to think creatively, and to act on her ideas.
    - Ⓐ verb phrase
    - Ⓑ gerund
    - Ⓒ infinitive
    - Ⓓ prepositional phrase

25. Sometimes I find my keys on the kitchen table, in the bathroom, or even at the bottom of my purse.
    - Ⓐ verb phrase
    - Ⓑ gerund
    - Ⓒ infinitive
    - Ⓓ prepositional phrase

26. Joseph Campbell said that a hero is someone who has performed a courageous act or had a spiritual experience.
    - Ⓐ verb phrase
    - Ⓑ gerund
    - Ⓒ infinitive
    - Ⓓ prepositional phrase

27. Roger's experience was different from Mary's in that he stayed outside, he ate very little, and he followed grandfather's directions.
    - Ⓐ verb phrase
    - Ⓑ gerund
    - Ⓒ infinitive
    - Ⓓ clause

28. My class starts next week, but I don't know the time, the classroom, or the name of the teacher.
    - Ⓐ verb phrase
    - Ⓑ noun phrase
    - Ⓒ infinitive
    - Ⓓ clause

29. Some of the best stories involve heroes, a journey, and a conflict between good and evil.
    - Ⓐ verb phrase
    - Ⓑ noun phrase
    - Ⓒ infinitive
    - Ⓓ clause

30. A strong plot, good characters, and effective description make for a good story.

- Ⓐ noun phrase
- Ⓒ adjective
- Ⓑ gerund
- Ⓓ verb phrase

○ Editing

Directions: Find and correct the errors in parallelism.

31. In *Star Wars,* Darth Vader represents power, evil, and he made bad choices.

32. Superman can see through buildings, flying, and leap tall buildings in a single bound.

33. A boy prepares for his *bar mitzvah* by practicing Hebrew, reading religious books, and he needs to learn about his religion.

34. Rites of passage sometimes involve leaving the group, wear special clothes, and doing something difficult.

35. Heroes may fight their battles on a real battlefield, out in the world, or fight them in their own hearts.

Name: _____ **Date:** _____ **Score:** _____

⚪ Reading

Directions: Read the information below. Fill in the correct answer for each of the questions that follow.

The Ideas of Edward O. Wilson

Edward O. Wilson is an American entomologist and biologist known for his work in ecology, sociobiology, and evolution. He became interested in science because of his early fascination with insects. A childhood accident injured an eye and impaired his vision, so he studied things he could look at up close. Wilson first fell in love with flies and butterflies as a child, but then became interested in ants. He discovered that ants communicated with each other through chemical signals. He began to see similarities between ants and other species such as lions and primates.

In an interview on National Public Radio, Wilson said insects are very valuable for our understanding of the natural world and for our own quality of life. For instance, a decline in the insect population would first of all mean a loss of the pollinators, the insects that help plants to reproduce. If we lose our pollinators, plants would start to die off. Without certain critical insects that live in the soil, our soil wouldn't be rejuvenated. Most living things would begin to die. Humanity would probably survive, but humans would have a severely restricted diet, and the human population would be very much reduced.

Not all insects are good, however, according to Wilson. The *anopheles* mosquito has caused a lot of problems for humanity, and no obvious benefit. The *anopheles* mosquito spreads disease, particularly in Africa. When it appeared in South America, the public health organizations there did not allow the mosquito to gain a foothold. By eliminating the mosquito, South American countries were able to prevent disease.

1. What is the main idea of this reading?

    Ⓐ Edward O. Wilson studies insects because of a childhood accident.

    Ⓑ Not all insects are good, although many are.

    Ⓒ Wilson believes that insects for the most part are beneficial to the world and our understanding of it.

    Ⓓ A decline in the insect population would mean the decline of humanity.

2. What do you think an entomologist is?

    Ⓐ someone who studies plants   Ⓒ someone who studies primates

    Ⓑ someone who studies insects   Ⓓ someone who studies mosquitoes

3. What are pollinators?

    Ⓐ insects that help plants reproduce   Ⓒ plants that use pollen to grow

    Ⓑ insects that improve the soil   Ⓓ people who study pollen

4. How do ants communicate?

    Ⓐ through body language   Ⓒ through sounds

    Ⓑ through American Sign Language   Ⓓ through chemicals

5. What is an example of an insect that is not beneficial to humanity?

    Ⓐ ant   Ⓒ butterfly

    Ⓑ bee   Ⓓ mosquito

◯ Strategy: Formal Outlining

Directions: Use the reading to complete the outline.

I. Background on Wilson

    A. areas of work: **(6)** _____

    B. first reason for studying insects: **(7)** _____

    C. discovery about ants: **(8)** _____

II. Results of the loss of insects

    A. loss of pollinators leads to loss of **(9)** _____

    B. loss of soil insects means soil wouldn't **(10)** _____

    C. impact on other life, including humanity

III. The *anopheles* mosquito

    A. not beneficial, causes disease

    B. response of South America: Public health didn't let mosquito survive

◯ Vocabulary

Directions: Fill in the blanks with words and phrases from the box.

biodiversity	gene pool	habitat	mammal	soil
encroachment	greenhouse effect	indigenous	sedentary	wilderness
game				

11. _____ is another word for dirt or earth.

12. Land that hasn't been developed at all is _____.

13. Kudzu, the vine, comes from Asia. It is not _____ to the United States.

14. Animals that we hunt and eat are known as _____.

15. Air pollution contributes to the _____ which in turn contributes to an increase in the temperature of Earth's atmosphere.

16. The variety of Earth's species and ecosystems is called _____.

17. An animal that gives birth to live young and produces milk is a _____.

18. Some rain forests are dying because of the _____ of people and development into what was once undisturbed forest.

19. I could probably lose weight if I had a more active and less _____ lifestyle.

20. The local environment in which a plant or animal lives is known as its

_____.

○ Mechanics

Directions: Read the excerpt from *Ecology and the Environment*. Then read the student paragraph on the next page. Find and correct 10 errors.

> Dinosaurs, saber-toothed tigers, and dodo birds are famous examples of animals that have become extinct. In the case of the dinosaurs, it seems likely that a catastrophic event (probably a meteorite strike) altered the global climate enough to lead to their disappearance. More recent extinctions and near-extinctions—such as the blue whale, tiger, panda, and North American bison—have been the direct result of human activity. Between 20,000 and 30,000 species become extinct every year, a figure quoted by the American biologist Edward O. Wilson of Harvard University, based on his most conservative estimates. This rate of extinctions carries with it some terrible consequences. Each plant that becomes extinct, for example, may take with it as many as 30 insects and animals that depend on it for food.
>
> **Source:** *Ecology and the Environment* (Morgan)

Dodo birds, dinosaurs, and saber-toothed tigers are famous examples of animals that have become extinct. It seems likely that "a meteor strike or other catastrophic event" caused the disappearance of the dinosaurs because of a global climate change. Human activity caused the recent extinctions of the blue whale, tiger, and panda. It is estimated that between 20,000 and 40,000 species become extinct every year according to Edward O. Wilson. "This rate of extinctions [causes] terrible consequences," for example, as each plant becomes extinct, so might as many as 30 insects and animals.

○ Editing

Directions: In each sentence, find and correct the error in the passive voice.

31. Much of wilderness has been developing by real estate companies.

32. People have been exploited natural resources for decades.

33. *Ecology and Environment* was wrote by Morgan.

34. The hunting practices of the Xavantes Indians studied by Frans Leeuenberg.

35. Hundreds of research projects have been funding by Earthwatch.

Name: _____ Date: _____ Score: _____

Reading

Directions: Read the information below. Fill in the correct answer for each of the questions that follow.

Biotech: Seeds of Discontent

Taste Test

In Europe, many farmers understand the benefits of biotechnology, the study of biology in genetic engineering. Some consumers do too. Last year, Britain's Zeneca Group PLC quietly introduced one of the first gene-altered foods into the European market—a paste made from tomatoes modified to create a thicker texture. Labeled as a product of biotechnology, the paste also was priced 10 percent below its natural counterparts and was an instant success. It was a "test of our hypothesis that Europeans are not necessarily anti-biotech," says Nigel Paul, Zeneca's external regulatory affairs director.

Few anti-biotechnology protesters are influenced by such examples, however. They have lobbied relentlessly for Europewide rules that would place labels on all foods produced from genetically modified soybeans and corn, but seed companies complain that their requirements are vague. Potentially, anything exposed to genetically modified crops—including milk—could be labeled. That alarms U.S. government officials. "Strict adherence to labeling requirements would do damage to our trade," warns Timothy J. Galvin, associate administrator of the Agriculture Department's Foreign Agricultural Service. U.S. shipments of corn to Europe exceed $200 million a year.

Ultimately, food fights won't get Europe very far. "Our genes are incorporated into about 1.9 million acres around the world—covering an area larger than Switzerland and the Netherlands combined," says Tom McDermott, Monsanto's European public affairs head. "Can Europe at this point really resist?" That's a question many concerned consumers are asking—on both sides of the Atlantic.

The Pros and Cons of Gene-Altered Foods

The good news
- Genetically modified seeds promise higher yields, lower pesticide costs to farmers, and crops that tolerate droughts or salty soil.
- Gene-altered foods may offer retailers and consumers lower-cost products that taste good and are easy to transport.
- To date, there have been no clear-cut health or safety problems from genetically modified crops.

The bad news
- Some scientists fear that pesticide-resistant genes engineered into seed crops could leak to other plants.
- Over time, pests will almost certainly build up resistance to anti-pest toxins in gene-altered plants.
- Adding genes to plants may cause unexpected results. In Mississippi, some gene-altered cotton plants have dropped their bolls (the seed-bearing part) early.

Source: "Biotech: Seeds of Discontent" (Flynn)

1. What was one of the first gene-altered foods to be introduced in Europe?
   - (A) tomato paste
   - (B) beef
   - (C) milk
   - (D) soybeans

2. What were its advantages?
   - (A) size and price
   - (B) taste and packaging
   - (C) texture and price
   - (D) higher yields and better taste

3. What is the U.S. Department of Agriculture worried about?
   - (A) gene-altered foods
   - (B) labeling requirements in Europe
   - (C) the cost of shipping corn to Europe
   - (D) marketing in Europe

4. Who works for Monsanto?
   - (A) Nigel Paul
   - (B) Zeneca PLC
   - (C) Timothy J. Galvin
   - (D) Tom McDermott

5. What is a disadvantage of gene-altered foods?
   - (A) increased resistance by pests
   - (B) crops that tolerate salty soil
   - (C) predictable results
   - (D) clear-cut safety problems

○ Strategy: Organizing Ideas

Directions: Complete the graphic organizer with information from the reading.

	Idea	Support (quote, example, detail)
6.	Some consumers understand the benefits of biotech.	
7.		Protesters have lobbied for labels on genetically-modified foods.
8.		U.S. shipments of corn to Europe exceed $200 million a year.

9.	Food fights won't get Europe very far.	
10.		Gene-altered cotton plants have dropped their bolls.

○ Vocabulary

Directions: Fill in the blanks with words from the box.

diminishes	emissions	innovative	mortality	solvents
drastic	fumigate	lethal	respiratory	toxicity

11. _____ refers to how poisonous or dangerous to your health something is.

12. If you _____ your house, you will get rid of all the pests.

13. The company tried everything they already knew before they came up with a truly

_____ solution.

14. The government regulates how much pollution can be produced by car

_____.

15. The boy consumed a potentially _____ amount of the medication, so he was rushed to the emergency room.

16. Many _____ used in manufacturing are hazardous to your health.

17. We can't afford to be cautious in addressing some environmental issues. Sometimes really

_____ changes are needed.

18. Some diseases are very deadly, so the _____ rate, or rate at which people die, is very high.

19. Air pollution can cause _____ problems.

20. As species become extinct, biodiversity _____.

○ Mechanics

Directions: Change the adjective clauses to participial phrases.

21. I gave the message to the woman who was taking notes.

_____

_____

22. The woman, who was surprised by the information, made a phone call.

_____

_____

23. The company that advertised online made more money last year.

_____

_____

24. We might still be able to save some species that are becoming extinct.

_____

_____

25. Chemicals that are used as flame retardants can cause cancer.

_____

_____

26. The CEO didn't get the report that was sent last week.

_____

_____

27. The steps that were taken to save energy resulted in a cost savings as well.

_____

_____

28. Now I drive a car that combines energy sources.

_____

_____

29. The manufacturing process that was considered hazardous was stopped temporarily.

_____

_____

30. We found hundreds of computers that were discarded last year.

_____

_____

○ Editing

Directions: Find and correct the errors.

31. Walking to the store, a car crashed right in front of me.

32. The customer filed a complaint angered by the poor service.

33. Containing a cancer-causing chemical, the company took the cereal off the market.

34. Deciding to move to the United States, I couldn't find work in my native country.

35. Found no one at home, the florists left the flowers on the doorstep.

Chapter 1

Reading
1. B; 2. A; 3. B; 4. D; 5. D

Strategy
6. c; 7. b; 8. d; 9. e; 10. a

Vocabulary
11. urged; 12. amulet; 13. castes; 14. monotheism; 15. artificial; 16. craze; 17. symbol; 18. clutter; 19. trance; 20. stamina

Mechanics
21. whom; 22. which; 23. but; 24. so; 25. For example; 26. Furthermore; 27. As a result; 28. Even so; 29. for instance; 30. whom

Editing

31. A rite of passage is a ritual ~~in~~ which marks the transition from one stage of life to another.

32. Baseball players are very ritualistic; ~~however~~ ^therefore^ , they often follow the same patterns of behavior before every game.

33. An amulet is a charm/ that you might wear to protect yourself from evil spirits.

34. There are many things that people don't understand, ~~for~~ ^so^ they use religion to fill the gaps in their understanding.

35. Cultural anthropology ^,^ which is the study of people in groups, can tell us a lot about others and about ourselves.

Chapter 2

Reading
1. C; 2. B; 3. B; 4. D; 5. A

Strategy
6. (Baboons) usually live in very large social groups. They sometimes change groups or break off into smaller groups for periods of time.

7. The fission-fusion social structure is unique to (chimpanzees). Unlike other monkeys, they divide and reform groups frequently.

8. (Polyandry) is a social structure characterized by one female in a unit with several males. It is the opposite of a polygamous social structure.

9. (The primary unit) for orangutans is a mother with her children, while adult males live more solitary lives. This is the smallest unit that represents a primate social structure.

10. (This reading) described social organization of primates. It focused on classification.

Vocabulary
11. twigs; 12. terrestrial; 13. descend; 14. exogamy; 15. omnivorous; 16. endangered; 17. dominate; 18. prey; 19. orangutan; 20. seclusion;

Mechanics
21. unless; 22. whereas/while/although; 23. as soon as; 24. whenever; 25. because/since; 26. although/whereas/while; 27. until; 28. in case; 29. while; 30. by the time

Editing

31. For most primates, the male and female are similar/ ^;^ however, male gorillas are much larger than females.

32. While humans are usually monogamous ^,^ male gorillas live and mate with more than one female.

33. In some early societies, men were
hunters/_∧ ^lc w^ Whereas women were the
foragers.

34. Humans leave their nuclear families when
they get married. Similar_∧^ly^, chimpanzees
often join a new group to mate and
reproduce.

35. Marmosets live in polyandrous groupings
(one female with several males). _∧^In a similar way^ ~~In
contrast~~, some isolated groups of people
in Tibet have units consisting of one
woman with more than one man.

Chapter 3

Reading
1. D; 2. A; 3. C; 4. B; 5. A

Strategy
6. 5; 7. 1; 8. 3; 9. 4; 10. 2

Vocabulary
11. destitute; 12. hinder; 13. capital; 14. assets;
15. launched; 16. frugality; 17. fluctuations;
18. incentive; 19. default; 20. brink

Mechanics
21. mention; 22. deny; 23. point out; 24. explain;
25. warn; 26. determine; 27. quote; 28. specify;
29. recommend; 30. conclude

Editing
31. C; 32. A; 33. B; 34. B; 35. D

Chapter 4

Reading
1. A; 2. B; 3. C; 4. A; 5. C

Strategy
6. 3; 7. 2; 8. 1; 9. 5; 10. 4

Vocabulary
11. C; 12. A; 13. B; 14. B; 15. A; 16. C; 17. B;
18. A; 19. B; 20. C

Mechanics
21. didn't have; 22. didn't set; 23. wouldn't be;
24. would/could do; 25. had; 26. wouldn't/couldn't
sell; 27. wouldn't/ couldn't pass; 28. were;
29. would/could go; 30. wouldn't/couldn't lose

Editing
31. Because ~~of~~ trade deficits result in fewer
exports, unemployment in certain
industries increases.

32. If the value of the dollar stayed high,
exports probably ~~fell~~ _∧^would fall^ .

33. Without ~~you have~~ any money, you
couldn't pay your bills.

34. Snehal ~~can~~ _∧^could^ work at a call center in
India if he could speak English better.

35. If we didn't have a global market, we
~~will~~ _∧^would^ have higher prices.

Chapter 5

Reading
1. buffalo/fathers; 2. ancestors; 3. her life; 4. Nancy Wood; 5. find her way

Strategy
6. B; 7. B; 8. C; 9. C; 10. D

Vocabulary
11. diverge; 12. layers; 13. analyze; 14. defer; 15. outbreak; 16. torment; 17. bewildered; 18. pattern; 19. clear-cut; 20. surface

Mechanics
21. symbolize/represent; 22. indicate; 23. symbolic; 24. symbols; 25. associated; 26. must; 27. may/might; 28. appears; 29. symbolize/represent; 30. may/might

Editing

 CS 31. Nancy Wood has written poetry about the Pueblo Indians/∧; ∧*She* ~~she~~ writes often about their interconnectedness to the land.

  F 32. Some of her writing ∧*is* for young adult readers.

  R 33. Wood lives in Santa Fe, New Mexico∧ ∧*She* ~~she~~ is a photographer as well as a writer.

 OK 34. The landscape and the legends of the Native Americans inspire her writing.

  F 35. Other writers using Native Americans themes ∧*include* /Louise Erdrich, James Welch, Michael Dorris/.

Chapter 6

Reading
1. D; 2. A; 3. C; 4. D; 5. A

Strategy
6. B; 7. B; 8. C; 9. C; 10. A

Vocabulary
11. compassionate; 12. unsightly; 13. redemption; 14. heritage; 15. self-preservation; 16. skirmishes; 17. shrewd; 18. undergo; 19. well-fed; 20. compelled

Mechanics
21. B; 22. C; 23. D; 24. C; 25. D; 26. A; 27. D; 28. B; 29. B; 30. A

Editing

31. Darth Vader from *Star Wars* represents power, evil, and ~~he made~~ bad choices.

32. Superman can see through buildings, fly~~ing~~, and leap tall buildings in a single bound.

33. A boy prepares for his bar mitzvah by practicing Hebrew, reading religious books, and ~~he needs to learn~~ ∧*learning* about his religion.

34. Rites of passage sometimes involve leaving the group, wear∧*ing* special clothes, and doing something difficult.

35. Heroes and heroines may fight their battles on a real battlefield, out in the world, or ~~fight them~~ in their own hearts.

Chapter 7

Reading
1. C; 2. B; 3. A; 4. D; 5. D

Strategy
6. ecology, sociobiology, evolution; 7. childhood injury; 8. may use chemicals to communicate; 9. plants; 10. rejuvenate

Vocabulary
11. soil; 12. wilderness; 13. indigenous; 14. game; 15. greenhouse effect; 16. biodiversity; 17. mammal; 18. encroachment; 19. sedentary; 20. habitat

Mechanics
Dodo birds, dinosaurs, and saber-toothed tigers [21. exact words just rearranged, [22. citation needed in first sentence] are famous examples of animals that have become extinct [23. exact words need quotes]. It seems likely that [24. this needs quotes] "a meteor strike or other catastrophic event" [25. this shouldn't have quotes] caused the disappearance of the dinosaurs because of a global climate change. Human activity caused the recent extinctions of the blue whale, tiger, and panda [26. incorrect, these animals are near extinction]. It is estimated that between 20,000 and 40,000 [27. incorrect figure] species become extinct every year according to Edward O. Wilson [28. missing complete citation information]. "This rate of extinctions [29. need ellipses] [causes] terrible consequences," for example, as each plant becomes extinct, so might as many as 30 insects and animals. [30. missing source information]

Editing
31. Much of wilderness has been developing~~ing~~ ^{ed}∧ by real estate companies.

32. ↖ ~~People~~ have been exploited (natural resources) for decades.

33. *Ecology and Environment* was ~~wrote~~^{written}∧ by Morgan.

34. The hunting practices of the Xavantes Indians ^{were}∧ studied by Frans Leeuenberg.

35. Hundreds of research projects have been fund~~ing~~^{ed}∧ by Earthwatch.

Chapter 8

Reading
1. A; 2. C; 3. B; 4. D; 5. A

Strategy

	Idea	Support (quote, example, detail)
6.	Some consumers understand the benefits of biotech.	Tomato paste was an instant success.
7.	Few protesters are influenced by such examples.	Protesters have lobbied for labels on genetically-modified foods.
8.	Labeling requirements (e.g., on corn) alarm U.S. government officials.	U.S. shipments of corn to Europe exceed $200 million a year.
9.	Food fights won't get Europe very far.	Genes incorporated into 1.9 million acres (McDermott)
10.	Adding genes may cause unexpected results.	Gene-altered cotton plants have dropped their bolls.

Vocabulary
11. toxicity; 12. fumigate; 13. innovative; 14. emissions; 15. lethal; 16. solvents; 17. drastic; 18. mortality; 19. respiratory; 20. diminishes

Mechanics
21. I gave the message to the woman taking notes.
22. The woman, surprised by the information, made a phone call.
23. The company advertising online made more money last year.
24. We might still be able to save some species from becoming extinct.

25. Chemicals used as flame retardants can cause cancer.
26. The CEO didn't get the report sent last week.
27. The steps taken to save energy resulted in a cost savings as well.
28. Now I drive a car combining energy sources.
29. The manufacturing process considered hazardous was stopped temporarily.
30. We found hundreds of computers discarded last year.

Editing

31. **While I was** ∧ /lc w/ Walking to the store, a car crashed right in front of me.

32. /lc t/ ∧ The customer filed a complaint uc A ∧ (angered by the poor service,).

33. /lc c/ ∧ Containing a cancer-causing chemical / (the company took the cereal) off the market.

34. ~~Deciding to move to the United States, I couldn't find work in my native country.~~
    Rewrite: Not finding work in my native country, I decided to move to the United States.

35. **Finding** ∧ ~~Found~~ no one at home, the florists left the flowers on the doorstep.

Credits

p. T1: "Halloween: An American Ritual of Rebellion" adapted from *Anthropology: The Exploration of Human Diversity.* Copyright 1997 by McGraw-Hill. Reprinted with permission of the McGraw-Hill Companies.
p. T13: "Financing and Trade Deficits" adapted from *Economics: Principles and Practices.* Copyright 1995 by Glencoe/McGraw-Hill. Reprinted with permission of the McGraw-Hill Companies. p. T17: "Who Will Teach Me" from *Many Winters.* Copyright Nancy Wood 1971. All rights reserved. p. T28: From "The Human Factor" by Sally Morgan, *Ecology and the Environment,* 1995, pp. 136–143. p. T30–31: "Biotech: Seeds of Discontent" adapted from *Business Week,* February 2, 1998, Volume 3563, page 62. Copyright 1998 by the McGraw-Hill Companies. Reprinted with permission of *Business Week.*